DIANA

Unlawful Killing

"There are 'forces' at work in this country about
which we have no knowledge."
- Queen Elizabeth II

Enjoy the read, best regards.

Simon .

Published by

Hakon Books

Text Copyright © Simon Tomlin 2013

Diana: Unlawful Killing

ISBN **978-1502564573**

TABLE OF CONTENTS

PROLOGUE

The name of Princess Diana, like her picture, 'tells a thousand' words. The face of Helen of Troy was said to have 'launched a thousand ships'. But in Diana's case, her face kept afloat a thousand publications from newspapers, fashion magazines and a multiple selection of books covering her life and death from every possible angle.

This book concentrates entirely on the last few days of her life, leading up to the terrible crash in the Alma Tunnel in Paris. This is an investigation of the events leading up to Diana's death and assesses the alleged role of British, French and American Intelligence agents in her death. Too many books have been published, claiming to be the definitive story of how Princess Diana was killed, only for readers to find one or two chapters, scantily covering the issue.

Mindful of the serious let downs of other authors in this field, I have spared no blushes, as no investigative journalist should, and I have directly named interested parties and in many cases, where available, published their photographs. Too many authors have pulled their punches but I have not.

As one might expect, I am not in the business of covering up or suppressing unpleasant truths and facts which must be heard if the truth of Diana's death and the cause of it, is ever to be known. And Lady Di's story had everything....

A high speed car chase through the streets of Paris, the world's most romantic city, with an exotic Egyptian lover, son of a billionaire, allegedly pursued by sinister forces, culminating in a tragic road traffic 'accident' which robbed the world of the People's Princess and that special brand of inimitable magic she oozed into the lives of millions of people.

But millions of people do not accept the 'great accident theory' and believe that Diana and Dodi were murdered on the orders of the British Secret Intelligence Service (MI6) to eliminate the considerable threat she posed to the House of Windsor.

Other people say that Diana was killed because she was expecting the baby of a Muslim and a mixed-race Muslim sibling to the heirs to the British throne was unacceptable to the Royal Family. Prince Philip described Dodi Fayed as an "oily little bed hopper" and the Al Fayed family were despised by the British Establishment he had embarrassed so often.

I

Diana's anti-landmines campaign is also said to be the reason she was murdered to prevent arms dealers losing out on vast fortunes, amassed from the misery caused by landmines. Plots and schemes abound but is there any evidence to support the allegations?

Conspiracy theorists speculate wildly, as they always do, that the Spencer family was in search of the Holy Grail and Diana was close to finding it and had to be killed to prevent her from becoming the most powerful person on earth. This is utter nonsense and serves no purpose other than distraction from the facts.

Others have come up with various murder plots, alleging that the seatbelts in the Mercedes S280 were tampered with to ensure the occupants were killed when the car crashed but bodyguard Trevor Rees-Jones survived! Some say it was MI5 who killed her, others say it was MI6 and the French DST. But what is the truth?

And then there is the allegation that VX nerve gas was planted on Henri Paul by a mysterious lover working for French Intelligence. When the car entered the Alma Tunnel, the VX nerve gas, hidden in a pin on Henri Paul's lapel, was detonated by remote control, causing him to lose consciousness....

And equally interesting theories are circulated by the French and British authorities, desperate to bring the entire matter to an end. Their story is that Diana was killed as part of a series of random events which caused a terrible accident.

Certainly, there has been extensive suppression of the truth by the French and British authorities. Witnesses who saw the events immediately before and after the crash have been ignored and in the case of Eric Petel, threatened by French police to "forget" what he saw. By definition, accidents do not need to be covered up, so why ignore witnesses to the crash and threaten those who refuse to conform to the great accident theory?

In this web of intrigue and real and imagined conspiracies, lies flourish like wheat sheaves in the August sunshine, waiting to be cut down. This book uncovers the main culprits behind the lying game and their reasons for attempting to mislead millions of people desperate for the truth.

The various 'theories' are tested and examined to see if they hold water, and the majority simply do not! But there are disturbing elements in the lying game that caused me to conduct this investigation to attempt to get at the truth or at the very least take the whole process one step closer to the truth. There is abundant evidence now available to prove that Princess Diana was under surveillance by American Intelligence and the surveillance product was shared with MI6 and the French DST. The question is why was Diana under surveillance in the first place?

Evidence has also been uncovered to prove that French photo agencies were having their communications intercepted in the hours leading up to the fatal crash. If intelligence agents were not involved in Diana's death, why were the photo agencies having their communications intercepted? Just 24 hours after the crash two photographers who received photos of the crash were raided in London, by mysterious 'burglars'. Who were these burglars and what were they looking for?

The questions are replete with intrigue but answers can be found if one knows where to look. The Paget Investigation of Lord Stevens concluded with the French 'investigation' that the crash was an accident but there is a whole lot more to this murky business than a simple accident. Indeed, most of the conspiracy theories are disproved with ease but there are occurrences for which there is hard evidence and they cannot be dismissed.

This book covers the last days of Diana's inimitable life and death through to dispatches from the Royal Courts of Justice in London, between December 2006 and August 2007 at the Inquest into her death. This is not a book for the faint-hearted, don't read it alone, this is the lying game and it is one of truly shocking historic proportions in the foremost 'unlawful killing' of the last century.

Chapter 1

'Tell Me Yes'

The much vaunted romance between Princess Diana and the Oscar winning playboy and film producer Dodi Fayed began in earnest, aboard his father's yacht Jonikal, moored in the harbour at Cannes in the south of France, a haven for the super-rich and tax exiles.

Mohamed Al Fayed had mentioned his opulent St Tropez villa to Diana in a conversation the two friends had at a charity dinner in the winter of 1996 and suggested she could holiday there. The princess later mentioned that she needed a haven for a summer break with her two sons and the suggestion soon became a firm invitation. Diana was not immune to gate crashing into her friends lives.

Diana, Dodi and Mohamed Al Fayed aboard the yacht Jonikal

Three weeks before the Al Fayed family left for their summer holiday, Diana telephoned the tycoon and complained that she was lonely. She needed a summer break with her boys the princes and Al Fayed offered the use of his villa and yacht for their leisure. Security would also be supplied by Al Fayed's permanent security team comprised of former elite soldiers and senior police officers. He had the best money could hire.

When Al Fayed's Gulfstream IV private jet, adorned in its distinctive green and gold Harrod's livery took off from Gatwick

Airport carrying the Al Fayed family to Nice Airport in France, Diana, Prince William and Prince Harry were aboard with them. This development caused Prince Philip much chagrin and he had already ordered MI6 (Secret Intelligence Service) to draw up a dossier on the Al Fayed family. Prince Philip renowned for his caustic wit, later described Dodi as an "oily bed hopper".

The Windsors were furious. Diana was clearly rubbing the Royal noses in the trough again by deporting to holiday with the Al Fayed's. For years Mohamed Al Fayed had been denied a British passport and the British citizenship he prized and felt he deserved. There was serious talk among Buckingham Palace courtiers that Harrods should be stripped of the Royal Crest and the furore grew stronger as Al Fayed's private jet soared into the sky for hotter climes. At home too, matters were warming up considerably behind the scenes....

Ever the consummate media manipulator, Diana knew exactly what she was doing when she picked the Al Fayed's as her holiday hosts and the Harrod's tycoon as her new protector. The cash for questions scandals in Parliament had left Al Fayed a 'marked man'. He embarrassed the British Establishment by showing up their Parliament as being weak, venal and corrupt and it is. The Tories under Prime Minister John Major detested him and had long been bent on revenge, on pulling him down a peg or two.

By accepting Diana as the inimitable holiday guest, Al Fayed had succeeded to unite both the Royal Family and Parliament against him. Hence the MI6 dossier was ordered to prepare a damning offensive in the public domain against Al Fayed and his colossal business interests. Diana knew only too well that her former in-laws would be outraged at her flagrantly flying the Al Fayed flag in their face. She had raised her standard, and like Charles I raising his Standard in Nottingham at the outbreak of the English Civil War, Diana later found herself completely out of her depth.

From the moment Diana stepped aboard Al Fayed's private jet, intense media speculation gripped the globe and raced across the international news wires. There was a family history between Diana and Al Fayed. In 1986, Al Fayed revived the Harrods polo competition at the Guards Club in Windsor Great Park where his rejuvenated team, championed by his beloved son Dodi, went on to squarely beat Prince Charles's team.

Al Fayed had also been a trusted friend of Diana's father and had acted as a surrogate father to her since the earl's death.

Diana's once hated stepmother, whom she nicknamed 'acid Raine', was a director of Harrods. The bitterness Diana felt for Raine Spencer from childhood blossomed into a warm adult friendship and the forlorn princess rated her advice highly, often counting on her stepmother in times of crisis and there were many.

It seemed lost on most observers that Diana actually enjoyed the raucous and earthy sense of humour for which Al Fayed was famous, perhaps notorious. And Al Fayed had long entertained the idea that one day Diana would marry his 41-year-old son Dodi. Al Fayed was convinced that Dodi and Diana would form a tryst that would be the romance of the century and of course, stick two fingers up to the Royal Family!

Dodi, occasional film producer, who revelled in fast cars and beautiful women, soon boarded a private jet from Paris racing south to confront what Al Fayed saw as a destined meeting with Diana. With plush apartments in Los Angeles, New York, London, Paris and the United Arab Emirates and a dream mansion in Malibu, the playboy son of the Harrods tycoon was a dream catch. His allowance from his father at the time was set at £7.5 million a year, or $300,000 a week.

Dodi's mother was Samira Khashoggi, sister of Middle Eastern arms dealer and rumoured billionaire Adnan Khashoggi. The playboy son of Al Fayed was obsessed with beautiful and exciting women. Among his lovers were rated Princess Stephanie of Monaco, Brooke Shields, Tina Sinatra and Patsy Kensit. He also had a penchant for stunning fashion models and as he set off to meet Diana, he was dating a gorgeous Californian model, Kelly Fisher, left behind to brood at his opulent Paris apartment.

Dodi left behind his friends to celebrate Bastille Day without him. He had answered his father's urgent summons and the promise of altogether more exciting company to play with in Cannes – the promise was irresistible. As his private jet left Le Bourget airport on 14 July 1996, he could have no idea that he was indeed racing to a meeting with destiny and certain immolation, if only as a footnote in the history books.

Al Fayed would take his holiday party on his £20 million yacht, the Jonikal, to Cannes, and rendezvous there with Dodi to celebrate the town's perennial Bastille Day fireworks. Dodi's yacht, the Cujo, a converted motor torpedo boat, was moored along the coast and he managed to reach Cannes harbour just minutes before the Jonikal, obviously wanting to impress his father and the errant princess.

Dodi immediately transferred to his father's larger and rather more impressive yacht, leaving the bewildered Kelly Fisher on board the Cujo. Fisher would later claim that Dodi proposed marriage to her and bought her an engagement ring but no one has seen this ring. From the moment Dodi met Diana, it was clear that Fisher was history.

Dodi abandoned the Cujo the next day and moved into his father's villa. Fisher was to see very little of him during the following week, as he spent the whole time wining and dining Diana, keen to impress not just the princess but also his father. Friends remember that from the moment they met, Diana and Dodi only had eyes for each other.

The day after he joined her, Diana's close friend and world-famous fashion designer Gianni Versace was murdered, and Dodi provided a much needed shoulder to cry on. They very quickly discovered a mutual liking which became something considerably deeper as the days wore on. Diana loved his "laid back" approach to life. One of his friends said: "He strolled through life. There was nothing pushy or aggressive about his approach to women." And Diana, the world wary über-celebrity, warmed to his pleasant manner and affectionate touch.

Dodi was rich, polite and genuinely affectionate and Diana compared him favourably to the previous men in her life. The Daily Mirror quoted a friend, who the princess had confided in: "I trust him. I think he can provide absolutely everything I need." Diana was smitten and Dodi was bitten too.

And for Diana there was the undeniable pleasure of irritating the despised British Establishment by completely embracing Mohamed Al Fayed. But the princess had little idea just how deeply enraged the Royal Family were, at what they saw as her 'antics' with the Fayeds. The legion of flunkies and courtiers who surround the royals were livid, plotting and scheming behind the scenes. Prince Philip had ordered MI6 to draw up a damning dossier on the Fayeds. A counter-attack was in the offing and it would come soon.

During her holiday, Diana was shockingly candid with her hosts about the very real fears she had for her safety, and of the secrets she had locked away as insurance against assassination. No one knew at the time of the existence of the letter she had penned in October 1996 and which was later revealed by her former butler Paul Burrell. The letter read: -

'I am sitting here at my desk today in October [1996] longing for someone to hug me and encourage me to keep strong and hold my head high. This particular phase in my life is the most dangerous. My **husband** *is planning an accident in my car, brake failure and serious head injury in order to make the path clear for Charles to marry [Camilla Shand].*

'I have been battered, bruised and abused mentally by a system for 15 years now, but I feel no resentment, I carry no hatred. I am weary of the battles, but I will never surrender. I am strong inside and maybe that is a problem for my enemies.

'Thank you Charles, for putting me through such hell and for giving me the opportunity to learn from the cruel things you have done to me. I have gone forward fast and have cried more than anyone will ever know. The anguish nearly killed me, but my inner strength has never let me down, and my guides have taken such good care of me up there. Aren't I fortunate to have had their wings to protect me.'

That the princess would eagerly confide in the man who had personally destroyed the careers of Neil Hamilton and Jonathan Aitken and humiliated the Conservative government, left the palace courtiers aghast and anxious. Diana was becoming too much of a very real threat to the stability of the monarchy and the Queen's aides and courtiers were determined on a course of action to eliminate the threat she posed.

Mohamed Al Fayed later revealed what she had confided in them. "This was not play-acting. She was genuinely concerned that there were powerful people at court who meant to harm her. Who were determined to arrange her death and make it look an accident. She was very upset, and in tears, when she told us, and sobbed that she lived in the constant fear that the nightmare world of paid assassins was all set to engulf her. She even warned Dodi that she strongly believed anyone who became too close to her would also find himself in danger. Dodi tried to brush it off with a light remark but she told him to treat the threat seriously. "People who get close to me are in mortal danger," she warned."

But most of Diana's time with the Fayeds was light-hearted and happy, as one would expect on a holiday. She told Al Fayed and his Finnish wife Heini that she was having the best holiday of her life. It would be hell going back to England and having to hand over the two princes to their father to join the Royal Family at Balmoral. "She didn't know that after that she was destined never to see them again," Al Fayed said.

On the day of Camilla's birthday party, Diana made quite sure which photographs would swamp the front pages of the British press. They were of herself in a purple swimsuit, looking absolutely stunning, playing with her boys and Dodi's arm around her waist. Mohamed Al Fayed in matching purple trunks provided the light entertainment. The royals were disgusted and both Charles and Camilla were deeply angry that they had again been upstaged by Diana. The press, naturally, loved it.

CHEST WISHES ON YOUR BIRTHDAY, CAMILLA

Other pictures showed the loving couple cavorting on the boat and in the sea, and no one at the time could remember any set of pictures that had caught Diana in a happier mood. One could not imagine anything more different from the pictures taken of her during her loveless fifteen-year marriage to Prince Charles. For someone who had been 'starved of love' for so long, her future looked rose-tinted and the princess was determined to enjoy the sweet scent of it.

During one bizarre incident, she sailed quite close to the launch carrying the British royal press corps – the crème de la scum as they are known – and told them, "You are going to get a big surprise at the next thing I do."

Diana told close friends that Dodi showered her with love and expensive gifts. "He's so wonderful she confided. "He doesn't need to give me expensive things. I'd willing give myself to him for nothing." Probably for the first time in her life, Diana was being treated like a princess instead of a baby-carrier to the heirs to the throne.

The two young princes were certainly impressed by their mother's paramour. They approved of Dodi's visits to a local fun fair and his booking a local disco exclusively for them and the Fayed family. They appreciated the fact that Dodi presumed the princes would stay up to participate in the revelry and enjoy it and they did.

Diana should have returned to London on 18 July but stayed on a couple of extra days because she was so happy. Back in England, looking tanned and relaxed, not recognisable from the pale, tearful figure of the previous year, Diana told her step-mother Raine Spencer, "It was the best family holiday I've ever had." Raine Spencer said: "She told me she had met someone special. Someone who liked her for who, rather than what, she was."

After Diana left on 20 July, Dodi rejoined Kelly Fisher on the Cujo and two days later he flew with the bemused American model back to Paris, where she soon discovered her days of flying by private jet were over. Dodi dumped her promptly and with little fuss but allowed her to keep the engagement ring.

The next day Fisher was given a first-class one-way ticket back to Los Angeles. She threw a press conference, bad-mouthing Dodi and warning Princess Diana against trusting her playboy ex-boyfriend, thus earning herself a footnote in British royal history, that of the discarded bit-part. Fisher was treated badly but was soon ignored by the press.

Dodi flew to London to rendezvous with Diana, who had also returned there after attending Versace's funeral in Milan. It was bizarre, perhaps chilling so, that six weeks later Diana would be killed dressed from head to toe in clothes crafted for her by the late Gianni Versace .

As soon as she was back, Dodi invited the princess on their first real date, a secret tryst in Paris. Unbeknown to them both, the CIA were bugging their calls and relaying the 'product' to MI6. The royals in turn, through the Queen's private secretary Sir

Robert Fellowes, were updated regularly as to the couple's activities and intentions.

Sunday Express, 4th February 2007, page 39:

Ministers are refusing to explain secret wire taps on Princess Diana's telephone in the days before she died.

Foreign Secretary Margaret Beckett has refused to comment on why Diana's calls were bugged by the American secret service in the run-up to the Paris car crash which killed her and her lover, Dodi Fayed, on August 31, 1997.

Norman Baker MP has led calls for greater clarification from the Government as to why the CIA had Diana and her contacts under round-the-clock surveillance.

Asked to explain the bugging in Parliament, Mrs Beckett replied: "It is the long-standing policy of the Government not to comment on intelligence matters." MP Norman Baker is leading the demands for more information: "Margaret Beckett's response is totally unsatisfactory," he said. "We need to know whether the Americans were doing this just for themselves, which would be outrageous, or were being asked to do it by the British Government, which would also be outrageous.

"There's been sufficient evidence of interception of the conversations of members of the Royal Family over the years to justify an explanation. In a mature democracy, we are entitled to find out what's going on in our name." The surveillance arm of the US security service admitted compiling a 1,054-page dossier on Diana, after coming under pressure from Dodi's father, Mohamed Al Fayed.

And the ever-faithful butler Paul 'Diana's rock' Burrell further clarified the fact that Diana was under constant surveillance by British intelligence, in his acclaimed book A Royal Duty. He wrote: -

Pages 319/320: -

She also shared with me her concern that she was constantly monitored. It is naïve of anyone to think that the princess, from the moment she married Prince Charles, would not have had her telephone calls bugged, or that the associations she made were not checked. It is a matter of routine that members of government and the Royal Family are monitored.

If there was one thing about life at KP that the princess loathed it was the inescapable feeling of constantly being listened to or watched. It was one of the reasons why she shed her police protection. She didn't trust the police as tools of the state. In fact, she had a deep-seated suspicion about anything and everything to do with the State.

Even another member of the Royal Family warned the princess: "You need to be discreet – even in your own home – because 'they' are listening all the time."

Before my trial at the Old Bailey in 2002, I witnessed, with my legal team, documented evidence that even my telephone lines, during the course of the police inquiry, had been 'intercepted' without my knowledge and at least twenty telephone numbers had been monitored.

Diana was being monitored by the global ECHELON system. ECHELON is a term associated with a global network of computers that automatically search through millions of intercepted messages for pre-programmed keywords or fax, telex and e-mail addresses. Every word of every message in the frequencies and channels selected at a station is automatically searched.

The processors in the network are known as the ECHELON Dictionaries. ECHELON connects all these computers and allows the individual stations to function as distributed elements in an integrated system. An ECHELON station's Dictionary contains not only its parent agency's chosen keywords, but also lists for each of the other four agencies in the UKUSA system, NSA, GCHQ, DSD, GCSB and CSE.

That evening, under electronic and covert surveillance by the CIA and MI6, aware of their every move, the Harrods helicopter whisked them to Paris where they had dinner before retiring to the most lavish and regal suite at the Ritz Hotel (owned by Mohamed Al Fayed) – the £6,000 a night Imperial Suite. Destiny was beginning to take a most devastating fledging shape.

Chapter 2

The Royal Crest

Back in London, after their brief trip to Paris, Diana spent virtually every free moment with Dodi at his apartment in London's Park Lane or together at Kensington Palace, which rankled the royals greatly. Prince Philip was enraged that the "oily little bed-hopper" was shacked up with Diana, their constant thorn, in a royal palace. The royals went apoplectic.

When photographed arriving at Dodi's apartment, Diana walked in without a care who saw her. She seemed to be telling the world that her romance was for real and that she had nothing to hide. Dodi had their meals ferried in on silver trays from the nearby Harry's Bar. Just months before Diana was accustomed to smuggling her lover, Dr Hasnat Khan, into KP hidden in a blanket in the back of her car driven by her butler Paul Burrell. But things had changed and for the better and she could at last be open about her relationship with the Harrod's heir.

When she was informed by a courtier that Prince Charles was expressing 'concern' about the effect the new man in her life might be causing on their sons, Diana said his worries were 'laughable' in view of his own undisguised affection for a woman other than their mother. What was good for the goose, was good for the gander and Charles did not like it one bit.

The suave heir to Al Fayed's vast fortune would make Diana an ideal husband, announced blonde Sky News presenter Tania Bryer, who had dated Dodi in the past. "He is warm and gentle. Not an aggressive macho sort. I can see why he appeals to Diana," she warbled, paid to incite such juicy gossip 24/7. "He is absolutely charming and one of the most genuine people you could meet."

Diana seemed to have come to the same conclusion. She was not concerned about this latest insight of her private life, and assured friends: "I am in good hands!" A confidante of the princess was quoted as saying, "Her friends are in no doubt that the princess is in love. It is the real thing."

There was real sexual chemistry between them, said one journalist when shown intimate photographs of the couple taken aboard the Jonikal. "They are oblivious to everyone and everything around them!" The Queen's courtiers were equally eager to assure their press contacts that the "whole thing is an act", to annoy the Royal Family.

In 2005, Piers Morgan, former editor of the Daily Mirror wrote in *The Insider*, 'Lots of pictures of her [Diana's] boys, the young heirs, the men who will perhaps kill off, or secure, the very future of the monarchy'. And yet Morgan despite his friendship with Mark Bolland, an aide to Prince Charles, was convinced that Diana and Dodi were for real.

One of the photographs to which he was referring - of the bikini-clad princess kissing Dodi on the deck of the Jonikal – was splashed across the front page of the Daily Mirror. Piers Morgan had bought it on a one-day-exclusive basis from an Italian paparazzi photographer who had staked out the yacht. The following day the picture was bought by other national newspapers and given similar premier treatment.

It made the photographer more than £1 million – a sheer indication of the incredible interest in their romance at the time. Publication of grainy photographs did not cause the princess's smile to wane in the slightest. In fact she asked the photographers why the pictures were so "grainy". She was revelling in it. Of interests also, the princess was not complaining that her privacy was being invaded.

There was a palpable sense of relief that their relationship was right out there in the open and that the world's press were fixated on them. Diana was dictating the pace of events, as she loved, and the royals hated every minute of being overshadowed again. Diana was rubbing it in and she knew it and so did the royals. The British Establishment had reached zero tolerance with Diana and her risqué relationship with the son of their arch-enemy Al Fayed.

For one so deeply concerned that she was a target for assassination, Diana was doing everything she could think of to invite that eventuality. A covert relationship was one thing but flaunting it so openly was another and yet it was lost on the royals that Diana was the world's foremost celebrity and the colossal interest of the press in her every move was inevitable and indeed highly profitable for the press barons.

The counter-attack on the Al Fayeds and Diana in the public domain was imminent. The royals were waiting on MI6 to complete the dossier before leaking it to the press through their courtiers. The battle-lines were drawn irrevocably and there was no turning back. The royals and Charles in particular greatly feared what Diana might leak to Al Fayed. It was common knowledge in royal circles that Diana kept a 'treasure trove' of highly damaging secrets at KP and their revelation could bring down the monarchy.

And the slightest thought of marriage between the princess and the son of Mohamed Al Fayed sent shudders of revulsion through the ranks of Buckingham Palace courtiers. They were not impressed by the remark of Dodi's friend, who said: "With him, Diana can have everything the royal family gave her, without the annoyance of the royal family." The conflict grew wider and more serious albeit behind the scenes for the most part.

On 8 August, Diana was snapped leaving Dodi's apartment adjacent the Dorchester Hotel at one in the morning. Just hours later she flew to Bosnia to further her anti-landmines campaign. She had become more than a troublesome thorn in the Royal Family's side, she was also considered to be a menace by the majority of the world's arms industry. Her visit to Bosnia was a direct threat to their billons and escalation of the campaign to ban the use of Landmines.

Diana on the anti-landmines crusade in war-ravaged Angola. The British Establishment, toadying to the Americans and international arms dealers, labelled the determined Diana a "loose cannon".

Diana, radiant and forever smiling in the face of adversity, had focused the world's attention on the landmines issue. In Bosnia, she was greeted by over sixty photographers. She highlighted the very real human misery caused by the deployment of landmines. For three days she talked to surviving victims of random mines. People who had lost limbs and suffered hideous debilitating injuries, were embraced by Diana and she made them feel special with her special brand of magic.

One newspaper described Diana as a "Mother Teresa with a crown" and experienced opinion-shapers were astonished that this not very eloquent woman had become the most influential personality in the world. At the Pentagon and among some of America's wealthiest arms dealers, the realisation dawned that Diana had become their most potent and vitriolic opponent, threatening their vast power base. Former British Foreign Secretary Lord Howe, had dubbed Diana as a "loose cannon" and at any time she could blow up in their faces.

The moneyed elite of the Western world needed to eliminate the Diana threat. Their opportunity to destroy her in the public domain did not exist as Diana had become almost saintly in the eyes of billions of people across the world. Attacks on Diana's character in the media, repeatedly backfired and she seemed invulnerable. Politicians across the West were stunned by the ease of her rise to international stardom. How could an icon be stopped?

On 15th August, Diana flew to Greece for a cruise with her 'good friend' Rosa Monckton, and borrowed Mohamed Al Fayed's private jet to take them there. For one so distrustful of anything and everything to do with the State, it is perhaps a little strange that Diana struck up such a close friendship with Rosa Monckton, given the constant rumours that circulated about her husband's close 'connections' to MI6. But 'friends' they were and Rosa Monckton would later prove to be a greater friend to the British establishment than Diana could ever have imagined.

On 21st August, both Diana and Dodi were back in London, he having returned from Los Angeles, presumably on a fact finding mission to find a suitable property to house the princess. Diana returned briefly to Kensington Palace to freshen up before returning to Battersea Heliport and then back on to Stansted Airport and the refuelled Gulfstream private jet. They headed back to the yacht Jonikal and another holiday together on the Côte d'Azur.

From Nice Airport the loving couple were whisked by car to where the Jonikal awaited them offshore at St. Laurent-de-Var, and while they rested, the yacht's captain Luigi del Tevere, motored south to St Tropez where they anchored at 02.00hrs. Early the next morning they headed to Pamplona Bay where Dodi and Diana joined Mohamed Al Fayed and his wife and four children for lunch. As they left late that afternoon, the Jonikal was being tailed by a small flotilla of press boats.

The presence of the ubiquitous paparazzi didn't faze Diana in the slightest. The next morning, Diana was up and about long before Dodi. Bodyguard Trevor Rees-Jones recalls that she looked stunning in her bathing suit and made absolutely no effort to hide from the rapacious snappers.

During the late afternoon they anchored off St. Jean Cap Ferrat, from where Dodi planned to take Diana shopping and sightseeing in nearby Monaco. On their trip ashore, Dodi's butler René says that they gave their bodyguards the slip while they toured the chic area of Monte Carlo and popped into Alberto Repossi, Dodi's favourite jeweller in the Hermitage Hotel.

In his book, Trevor Rees-Jones denies a visit was made to Repossi's even though Mohamed Al Fayed obtained the CCTV footage of the couple actually in the store. Rees-Jones denial is irrelevant: the ring, which Dodi would collect from the Paris branch a week later, was real enough.

Off Portofino in Italy, the next day, the young lovers chose to stay aboard the Jonikal as the paparazzi were visible in force on the shore. The pair showed no embarrassment about being seen kissing and cuddling during their sunbathing sessions on deck. Even when they were in full sight of the paparazzi, their intimate displays of affection did not abate in the slightest. They were loving every moment of it and the world's press lapped it up and their readers were insatiable for news of the princess and her exotic lover.

By Friday, 29th August, they were anchored off Cala di Volpe, a private resort in Sardinia, where they slipped ashore unseen by the hunting press pack. The paparazzi attention was suffocating and the couple decided to move on. The decision to fly to Paris was made early that evening. A flight plan was filed from Sardinia's Olbia Airport for the next day. Staff were instructed that the couple would spend a day in Paris before going on to London.

The Ritz Hotel was advised from the Fayed nerve centre in London that the couple would be arriving in Paris on the Saturday afternoon, a copy of the memo went to acting head of security Henri Paul! He immediately cancelled a planned weekend away with close friends and put himself back on the rota to be in charge of the reception at Le Bourget Airport.

The main reason for going to Paris, Dodi advised the Harrod's HQ in London, was to pick up a ring. Dodi told his step-uncle, Hussein Yassin, a former press attaché at the Saudi Embassy in Washington, who was stayed at the Ritz that weekend: "Diana and I are getting married. You'll know about it officially very soon." And Hussein's niece, also in Paris, received a similar call that fateful Saturday evening. A gushing Dodi told her, "Our marriage will be founded on true love."

A formal announcement was planned, Dodi told them, after the princess had broken the news to her two sons when they were reunited the following day. It was already decided that the ring he was collecting from Repossi, in the Place Vendôme, would be her engagement ring.

The £130,000 ring Dodi bought for Diana from Repossi Jewellers, Part of the 'Tell Me Yes' range. Dodi was set to propose engagement to Diana on the night they were killed in the Alma Tunnel.

Speaking to the Paget Investigation of Sir John Stevens, Dodi's butler René Delorm said: "In the book I explain how Dodi told me to have Champagne on ice ready for when they returned from dinner on 30th/31st August 1997. He told me that he was going to propose to the Princess and showed me a ring. I will explain this incident in greater detail later in my statement. What I left out of that story was that later that evening I went to enter the living room; I coughed to announce my presence and saw the Princess sitting on the coffee table. Dodi was on one knee in front of her, caressing her belly and she was looking at her hand. The only thing I heard, was her say the word 'Yes.'"

By the time the Gulfstream private jet set down at le Bourget Airport in the northern environs of Paris at 15.22hrs, Diana was as confident as she would ever be that she was truly in love with a good man and more importantly, ready to tell the whole world about it. When their door opened onto the area reserved for private aircraft, the contrast with the Côte d'Azur could not have been greater. There was not the slightest hint of a wind, everything was still, eerily so and the temperature was already soaring in the high eighties.

The British Embassy was not informed that Princess Diana was arriving but waiting by the runway, unbidden, but provided by a 'considerate' government, were the motorcycle outriders and black cars of the French diplomatic protection service – Service de Protection des Hautes Personnalité.

Normally, the princess would have been entitled to a phalanx of SPHP officers and protocol would have made it impossible to refuse them. But Diana had made her feelings perfectly clear to Dodi. The SPHP were not needed and Diana by then had a profound distrust of everything to do with government and state, particularly the British State.

Dodi Fayed was a passive man and readily agreed to almost anything Diana proposed or imposed. Dodi politely refused the SPHP and insisted, on Diana's instructions, that his own personal bodyguards were more than capable of protecting them both. He would ensure the princess's safety and his own. In this of course he was mistaken, disastrously so, as events were to prove. His bodyguards were not used to the frenetic press pack and blows were soon exchanged between the paparazzi and the Fayed security team.

And at Le Bourget a veritable army of photographers were waiting for the princess and her lover, forever hungry for the slightest morsel of newsworthy material. With photographers making vast sums for even grainy shots of the couple together, it was understandable they would gather en masse to ghost Diana everywhere she went. The paparazzi had already earned a new title as the 'stalkerazzi' and were living up to their notoriety.

Diana rejected a final offer of SPHP protection, a decision borne of her distrust of government security officers. Diana's fear of official 'security' personnel by far outweighed her dislike of the stalkerazzi, whose preferred transport in Paris, she would learn, was motorcycles and scooters. Their persistence and sheer aggression, would make the antics of their Mediterranean cousins seem almost benign by comparison.

In London, palace courtiers were going on the offensive, briefed by MI6 that the official announcement of Diana and Dodi's engagement was imminent, the royal hangers-on briefed the press that the Queen was about to strip Harrods of its Royal Crest. This was a direct attack on Mohamed Al Fayed and a punishment for his son daring to propose marriage to Diana, who had done more to bring about a British Republic without trying, than those who had.

Behind the scenes in Paris, officers of the British Secret Intelligence Service, unbeknown to the Queen, put the final touches of their operation into action. They had shadowed Diana and Dodi all day and into the late evening. Several spooks were among the crowd of photographers outside the Ritz Hotel. Their remit was not the 'protection' of Princess Diana and her Egyptian playboy lover, son of the hated enemy of the British Establishment.

Across the English Channel, the Sunday newspapers were about to print anti-Al Fayed smear stories from the lips of royal courtiers. At 23.30hrs in London, the Sunday newspapers can be bought from vendors in and around Kings Cross. The first edition of the Sunday Mirror carried the story below: -

QUEEN 'TO STRIP HARRODS OF ITS ROYAL CREST'

Sunday Mirror, Aug 31st, 1997 by Andrew Golden

The Royal Family may withdraw their seal of approval from Harrods ... as a result of Diana's affair with owner's son Dodi Fayed. The top people's store - with its long and proud tradition of royal patronage - may be about to lose the Prince of Wales royal crest.

Senior Palace courtiers are ready to advise the Queen that she should refuse to renew the prestigious royal warrants for the Knightsbridge store when they come up for review in February.

It would be a huge blow to the ego of store owner Mohammed Al Fayed - and would infuriate Diana, who was yesterday understood to be still with Dodi aboard his yacht, near the Italian island of Sardinia. But the Royal Family are furious about the frolics of Di, 36, and Dodi, 41, which they believe have further undermined the monarchy. Prince Philip, in particular, has made no secret as to how he feels about his daughter-in-law's latest man, referring to Dodi as an "oily bed-hopper".

At Balmoral next week, the Queen will preside over a meeting of The Way Ahead Group where the Windsors sit down with their senior advisers to discuss policy matters. MI6 has prepared a special report on the Egyptian-born Fayeds which will be presented to the meeting.

The delicate subject of Harrods and its royal warrants is also expected to be discussed. And the Fayeds can expect little sympathy from Philip. A friend of the royals said yesterday:

"Prince Philip has let rip several times recently about the Fayeds - at a dinner party, during a country shoot and while on a visit to close friends in Germany.

"He's been banging on about his contempt for Dodi and how he is undesirable as a future stepfather to William and Harry. Diana has been told in no uncertain terms about the consequences should she continue the relationship with the Fayed boy. Options must include possible exile, although that would be very difficult as, all said and done, she is the mother of the future King of England.

"She has also been warned about social ostracism. But Diana's attitude is if that means not having to deal with the royals and their kind, then she would be delighted." There are some who believe Diana may be past caring and has decided to look towards those who can afford to keep her in the lifestyle to which she became accustomed. The Fayed family have all the trappings of vast wealth... wherever it originated from.

And Dodi has told Diana what he has told many of his other beautiful girlfriends in the past: *"It's my father's store and you can have what you want. Charge it to my account and I'll just sign the bill."* But now the Royal Family may decide it is time to settle up.

QUEEN 'TO STRIP HARRODS OF ITS ROYAL CREST'

By Andrew Golden

THE Royal Family may withdraw their seal of approval from Harrods ...as a result of Diana's affair with owner's son Dodi Fayed.

The top people's store — with its long and proud tradition of royal patronage — may be about to lose the Prince of Wales royal crest.

Senior Palace courtiers are ready to advise the Queen that she should refuse to renew the prestigious royal warrants for the Knightsbridge store when they come up for review in February.

It would be a huge blow to the ego of store owner Mohamed Al Fayed — and would infuriate Diana, who was yesterday understood to be still with Dodi aboard his yacht, near the Italian island of Sardinia. But the Royal Family are furious about the frolics of Di, 36, and Dodi, 41, which they believe have further undermined the monarchy.

Prince Philip, in particular, has made no secret as to how he feels about his daughter-in-law's latest man, referring to Dodi as an "oily bed-hopper".

At Balmoral next week, the Queen will preside over a meeting of The Way Ahead Group where the Windsors sit down with their senior advisers to discuss policy matters.

MI6 has prepared a special report on the Egyptian-born Fayeds which will be presented to the meeting.

The delicate subject of Harrods and its royal warrants is also expected to be discussed. And the Fayeds can expect little sympathy from Philip.

A friend of the Royals said yesterday: "Prince Philip has let rip several times recently about the Fayeds — at a dinner party, during a country shoot and while on a visit to close friends in Germany.

"He's been banging on about his contempt for Dodi and how he is undesirable as a future stepfather to William and Harry.

"Diana has been told in no uncertain terms about the consequences should she continue the relationship with the Fayed boy.

"Options must include possible exile, although that would be very difficult as when all is said and done, she is the mother of the future King of England.

"She has also been warned about social ostracism. But Diana's attitude is if that means not having to deal with the royals and their kind, then she would be delighted."

There are some who believe Diana may be past caring and has decided to look towards those who can afford to keep her in the lifestyle to which she became accustomed.

The Fayed family have all the trappings of vast wealth... wherever it originated from.

And Dodi has told Diana what he has told many of his other beautiful girlfriends in the past: "It's my father's store and you can have what you want. Charge it to my account and I'll just sign the bill."

But now the Royal Family may decide it is time to settle up.

By the time of the Sunday Mirror's second edition, the story had been dropped. A terrible 'accident' involving Diana and her lover Dodi Fayed, first-born son of Mohamed Al Fayed, the owner of Harrod's, happened minutes before the second edition was about to go to press. The news filtered in to every newsroom in London and the nation waited breathlessly for the wheels of history to turn, not daring to believe for a moment that anything could have happened to the Peoples' Princes.

Chapter 3

Destiny in Paris

The Ritz Hotel, nerve centre of the Fayed business empire in Paris, had sent two cars to collect Dodi and his party from Le Bourget Airport. One was a luxury black Mercedes 600 limousine with classic tinted windows, driven by Philippe Dourneau, who was on a permanent contract as Dodi's chauffeur.

The other, Dodi's personal black Range Rover was driven by Henri Paul, the acting head of security at the world renowned hotel. Diana had met the balding and bespectacled security chief on her previous visit to the hotel with Dodi and she and her lover stood chatting with him for several minutes before boarding the Mercedes.

Strictly speaking, Henri Paul should not have been there. He had scheduled himself off the rota for the weekend for a planned trip to the countryside with close friends. But as soon as he learned that Diana was coming to Paris with Dodi, he cancelled his planned weekend excursion to Lorient to see his parents.

Trevor Rees-Jones, as bodyguard, a former paratrooper in the British Army, was delegated to travel with Dodi and Diana in the front passenger seat of the Mercedes. It was noted by Philippe Dourneau that Dodi and Diana did not fasten their seat belts in the back of the car. And yet Diana was renowned for fastening her seat belt, urging her boys the princes to do the same whenever they got into a car before a journey.

The Al Fayed security team did not insist that the couple fasten their seat belts, conforming to their training and this was due mainly to the fact that Dodi did not favour fastening rear seat belts. Instructions to fasten seat belts would likely have been countermanded by Dodi and so the issue, vitally important, was dropped.

Dourneau was a skilled driver and soon shook off the pursuing swarm of stalkerazzi, as he drove the Mercedes around the réphérique, the circular Paris motorway to the Bois de Boulogne exit ramp to the west of central Paris. Their first stop, twenty-five minutes' drive from the airport, was the Villa Windsor. Like love-struck teenagers the couple are said to have toured the house where the Duke of Windsor was exiled with Wallis-Simpson.

Some twenty years earlier, Mohamed Al Fayed had acquired the lease on the Villa Windsor from the French government and had spent a fortune refurbishing it. Dodi tried to persuade Diana that this was one of the houses they should make home but Diana was not entirely impressed. She thought the place was far too gloomy and filled with ghosts – the curse of the Windsors, who had brought her so much grief, loomed over the property.

As the lovers toured the house, Henri Paul had taken René, the butler and two female members of the Jonikal crew and the luggage to Dodi's apartment in central Paris. From there he drove to the Villa Windsor flanked by the second bodyguard, Alexander "Kez" Wingfield, to rendezvous with Dodi and Diana.

After spending just twenty-eight minutes, according to CCTV footage, at the villa, Diana and Dodi climbed back into their car for the short drive to the Ritz Hotel in the Place Vendôme. Henri Paul followed behind in the Range Rover, forming a small convoy. A number of stalkerazzi were already there to take pictures, having received a tip-off from 'sources' that the couple were about to arrive.

When the convoy arrived at the Ritz, the stalkerazzi were out in force. Mingling with the photographers were several MI6 field officers. CCTV footage from the Ritz, studied after the crash shows the operatives but they have never been traced nor accounted for. They blended in perfectly with the photographers and well-wishers and no one guessed at anything untoward.

Despite the hue and cry at the Ritz, the couple and their security team entered the hotel shortly after 14.30hrs and Dodi and Diana were again safely installed in the Imperial Suite. One of Diana's first tasks was to telephone friend and confidant, Richard Kay of the London Daily Mail. In his report, of that telephone call, Kay revealed what Diana told him: "I have decided to radically change my life." She would honour her obligations to her charities and would then, around November, completely withdraw from public life.

Richard Kay confided to his readers that "Diana was as happy as I have ever known her. For the first time in years all was well with her world." Kay also confirmed that Diana was in love with Dodi and she believed that he was in love with her and the he genuinely believed in her.

But Kay did not speculate on why Diana intended to change her lifestyle, but others, who had for weeks heard much discussion about Diana's bulging figure, suspecting she was pregnant, took Diana's outpouring to Kay that she was indeed expecting a baby and that Dodi was the father.

After making her call to Kay in London, Diana went down to the hotel's hairdressing salon by the swimming pool to have a wash and blow-dry before dinner, and Dodi went to collect the ring from Repossi's jewellery boutique. It was no more than 100 yards' walk across the Place Vendôme to the store but Dodi chose to drive there in the Mercedes flanked by Trevor Rees-Jones. Claude Roulet and Kez Wingfield followed on foot and the three bodyguards waited outside while Dodi went inside to collect the £130,000 ring from the 'tell me yes' range.

Left, Repossi Jewellers, Paris Branch. Dodi and Diana had selected their engagement ring together.

At approximately 19.00hrs, the couple were ready to leave the Imperial Suite and transfer to Dodi's apartment where they would change for dinner and where butler René had chilled wine and caviar waiting. The couple had already reserved a table at Diana's favourite Paris restaurant, Chez Benoit on the periphery of Les Halles. Their bodyguards and servants could not help but notice that Dodi choreographed the evening perfectly as a build-up to a formal proposal of marriage to arguably the most beautiful woman in the world.

Philippe Dourneau continued as their driver in the Mercedes 600 but for this penultimate journey they would be without their bodyguards Rees-Jones and Wingfield. It has been argued that lack of professionalism caused them to break one of golden rules of close protection work. To give the couple sometime to themselves was the real reason at the insistence of Dodi. The bodyguards travelled in the back-up Range Rover which was driven by Jean-Francis Musa, the owner of Etoile Limousine company, based at the Ritz.

If the two vehicles had become separated, the result could have been disastrous. As it was, their journey to the rue Arséne Houssaye, near the junction of the Champs Elysées and the Arc de Triomphe was smooth and successful. But on arriving outside the apartment, it was absolute bedlam as the entourage clashed with waiting stalkerazzi. Rees-Jones and Wingfield believed that the photographers had been tipped off in advance and there was clearly a leak in their security team.

Bodyguard Kez Wingfield of the Al Fayed security team.

Both Wingfield and Rees-Jones had suspected that 'someone' was leaking their every move to the press and stalkerazzi. But in the heat of the frenetic movements they were involved in, there was little or no time to identify and plug the gaps. They were out of their depth and urgently needed to bolster their ranks to deal with the aggressive, ubiquitous snappers. They were taken aback by the ferocity of the snappers and blows were exchanged outside Dodi's apartment.

Even Diana, who had years of experience with photographers, was frightened by the unbridled savagery of this frenzy, each paparazzo aware of the fact that huge sums of money were at stake for the right pictures. Total security in the eye of this contrived storm was practically impossible. And events were intensifying greatly.

Diana had long coexisted with oppressive press attention or intrusion that came with the mantle of royalty, but as the royal mantle slipped away, the press had become less concerned about intruding her privacy. Some of the antics of the photographers who stalked her around London were appalling and they often referred to her as "the loon" among many unpleasant names they hurled at her to provoke a profitable response.

Now only the über-celebrity remained, the royal title had been stripped following her divorce the previous year and it was open-season on Diana and her every move was of interest to the insatiable press and millions of avid readers across the globe. Diana had become vulnerable and she knew it but her innate distrust of government security officers had perversely left her wide open to attack. There was no longer a royal protection officer on hand with the authority to ward off the press and tell them when they had gone too far.

When Dodi and Diana finally reached his luxurious apartment, he was white-hot with anger and deep frustration and perhaps also a hint of humiliation that the Al Fayed security team was not proving as effective as he had boasted it would be. Shaken, but physically undamaged, the couple tucked in to caviar and a superb chilled white wine, and soon were smiling again as the unbridled happiness of their loving relationship won through the adversities contrived quite deliberately by the press and their 'secret sources' of information on the couple's whereabouts.

Soon it was time for them to change for dinner and Diana chose calf-hugging, white Versace jeans with high-heeled Versace black slingbacks with a sleeveless black top under a black Versace blazer. The final decoration was a pearl necklace given to her by Dodi, complemented with gold earrings and a Jaeger Le Coultre watch.

Dodi attired himself in Calvin Klein blue jeans over brown cowboy boots, a grey Daniel Hechter leather shirt, sported outside his jeans and with which he was unable to wear Diana's latest gift of cufflinks that had belonged to her late father. Dodi slung on a casual brown, suede jacket and looked every inch the stylish playboy for which he was renowned. His jewellery included a Cartier watch and a metal identity disk, engraved with 'Fayed. Blood Group B Positive.'

He also took with him cigars, a cigar cutter and his mobile phone, none of which was found in the destroyed Mercedes after the crash. It is likely that some clue was contained in the mobile phone's flash memory, of a call he made that needed to be covered up or maybe these personal items were simply plundered by the rescue workers. Mohamed Al Fayed would later buy back the phone from an unnamed person but the contents of the phone's memory, if not forensically wiped beforehand, have not be released by Al Fayed.

A little after 21.30hrs, they again ran the aggravating gauntlet of jostling and aggressive photographers, by now richly deserving the title of 'stalkerazzi'. Rees-Jones and Wingfield again decided to follow in the Range Rover. Defying security protocols yet again, a lead car and a rear car should have shadowed the Mercedes. The whole expedition, fast becoming an escapade, was heading to a disaster of historic proportions which in just several hours time would shake the whole world.

Dodi soon took the view that with so many photographers on the streets hunting them, a quiet dinner at Chez Benoit was out of the question and cancelled the reservation on his mobile phone. He then called Rees-Jones in the back-up Range Rover to advise him that they were returning directly to the Ritz Hotel. Rees-Jones was aware that the temporary hotel boss Claude Roulet was outside the Chez Benoit waiting for them and there was no one else on duty to call for back-up security.

They were already turning onto the Place Vendôme, when into sight came the spectre of over one-hundred photographers and assorted 'tourists' thronging outside the hotel entrance. The Ritz CCTV security cameras noted that several of these 'people' had been there all day, observing from the very edge of the crowd but could not be classed as either 'tourists' or photographers.

Former Scotland Yard detective chief superintendent John McNamara, who led the Ritz-Fayed investigation into the 'accident', later identified them as British and foreign service intelligence officers. To this day not one of them has been traced using sophisticated track and trace methods including facial recognition. They have simply disappeared off the face of the earth or it is has been made to seem this way.

The small-convoy ground to a halt outside the Ritz. Immediately the two bodyguards rushed forward to the limousine, the crowd closed in on all sides and flashbulbs popped at an alarming rate. The whole experience was stressful and aggravating and quite disorientating. When Rees-Jones opened the door of the Mercedes, Dodi climbed out but made no response, he just sat there frozen, overawed by the nauseating event which greeted him.

In fact, no one in the car moved for several seconds as the passengers seemed gripped like rabbits in the headlights of an oncoming truck. The advantage was lost, the element of surprise work in reversed. When Diana, who obviously saw the situation deteriorating, emerged from the car, she was almost immediately engulfed. She wore an expression of terror and she jumped over people's legs and ran forward, swaying from side to side, heading to the Ritz front door. With some good fortune and athleticism, she made into the hotel and collapsed on a chair in the foyer.

Dodi, assisted by Wingfield and Rees-Jones, was just moments behind her lead. The Harrods heir was raging mad and as Rees-Jones threw a photographer back into the street he exploded at his bodyguards: "How the fuck did this fiasco happen?" He clearly blamed his security team but in reality the cause was being in a relationship with the hottest celebrity in the world and the press wanted their morsels for the next day's front pages.

Wingfield was also livid and as he admitted later, was close to landing a punch on his boss. He retorted forcefully to Dodi: "You never told us where we were going in time. If you had, we'd have been able to phone ahead and get it sorted out." And Wingfield, a consummate professional was entirely right. Dodi's replete contraindications had led to this debacle outside the Ritz but even he should not be blamed too much. They had never before confronted such a numerous mass of pushy and aggressive photographers.

Dodi backed off, realising the situation had come to a head and he was responsible in large part for the resulting fiasco. He walked over to Diana and gave her his full attention, leading her into the hotel's prestigious L'Espadon restaurant. Wealthy onlookers sat gawking at the couple, almost amazed at the scene before them. Diana was in tears and asked to be taken up to the hotel's Imperial Suite so they could eat in private. Even so, they still intended to return to Dodi's flat when the carnival outside the Ritz calmed down – how naïve....

Instead of calming down, matters heated up considerably. Outside the Ritz there was a strange sort of barely controlled madness swimming around the rapacious paparazzi. Rumours circulated that Diana was pregnant, and the paps' had come from all over Europe to feed at the rich trough of Princess Diana. A shot depicting Diana with a small bump, perhaps indicating pregnancy could fetch in excess of £1 million. The stakes were of the Everest order.

The princess had been snapped in swimsuit which showed a slight bulge in her tummy. She had told a friend that the bump was excess fat and that she planned to have it removed by liposuction treatment in London. But the press and their freelance paps' remained unconvinced. They had, apparently, compelling 'sources' of information to indicate Diana was indeed pregnant and all they needed was hard photographic proof – 'a picture tells a thousand words'.

Still littered among the frenetic crowd of 'tourists' and paps' were the same British, French and American intelligence officers. They were picked up later under forensic examination of the Ritz's close-circuit television tapes. It was also later confirmed that the personal secretary of Britain's MI6 (Secret Intelligence Service) had spent the entire weekend in Paris. No credible explanation has ever been given to explain why the intelligence officers were mingling with the crowd outside the hotel.

But dissident former MI6 officer, Richard Tomlinson states that an unusually high number of his former colleagues were in Paris that night and certainly not for the purpose of 'protecting' the princess. He said that they included two senior MI6 officers and went on to add: "I believe either, or both of them would have detailed knowledge of events affecting Princess Diana that night".

Shortly after 22.00hrs, Henri Paul arrived back at the Ritz. He had been called in at Dodi's summons, by his night security manager, Francois Fendel. "Dodi is on top of the world but he would appreciate you coming in. It would help calm things down," Fendel told his boss. And so the man who cancelled his weekend break to see his parents, without any knowledge that he would be called up at short notice by Dodi, found himself in a position to 'influence' the most crucial event of the evening.

Henri Paul's first move was to join up with Rees-Jones and Wingfield, who were getting ready to eat at the hotel's restaurant bar. They chatted casually and Henri Paul had two drinks before going off to do his security rounds in the Ritz. Following his return, the responsibility for security in the hotel automatically passed to him. Rees-Jones and Wingfield remember, and are absolutely clear, that Henri Paul was relaxed and in no way drunk. His behaviour, entirely characteristic, caused no one any alarm.

Taken from the Ritz records that night, it was shown that Henri Paul had imbibed just two pastis – a spirits-strength drink taken with five parts of water to one of pastis. They were the only alcoholic drinks Paul consumed during his two hours and ten minutes at the hotel. It has not been established where he was or what he was doing between 19.00hrs and 22.00hrs, the period during which he left the hotel and then returned following Fendel's urgent call.

But it is also important to note that no-one, including his friends saw him at any of his frequented haunts during that time and it is therefore, entirely reasonable to assume that he was at home. Paul certainly did not run the risk of turning up for work drunk and the equal risk of being dismissed from his £20,000 a year job. Losing his job would also cost him the £35,000 a year bounty he made from the international intelligence community for whom he spied. Richard Tomlinson said, "And as an agent of MI6 he probably had an even better reason to remain sober."

During the day, Henri Paul had acquired £2,000 in cash which he was carrying in his pocket and which sum the police discovered was still on his body after the crash. According to investigative journalist Gerald Posner, quoting a CIA intelligence officer, the Ritz acting security chief was with agents of the French DGSE (Direction Général de la Sécurité Extérieure) in the hours before he returned to the hotel.

And the sum of £8,000 had been paid into several of Paul's bank accounts in the past few weeks – the same few weeks during which Dodi and Diana had become a loving couple. This was only a part of the £100,000 plus which he had squirreled away in seven bank accounts in the past few years. The Paget Inquiry, headed by Sir John Stevens later discovered that most of the payments had been made into the accounts from London-based clearing houses, a favoured method of MI6.

Richard Tomlinson suspects that the £2,000 found on Paul's body was payment for the Breton's 'efforts' during the course of the weekend but that Paul had no idea at all that he was being used as a patsy. It is suggested that Paul persuaded Dodi which route to follow that night and that he should return to his apartment, despite being safe at the Ritz. Dodi would take little persuading to go back to his apartment, as he planned to propose to Diana there and his plans were already laid before Paul could influence matters.

Paul's close friend and neighbour Claude Garric said: "I knew all along that Henri did work for intelligence agencies. He was in touch with the British secret service and the Israelis and others. The hotel had important clients from all over the world." And intelligence agencies have long targeted the security managers of top hotels who have close access to targets of interest to the spooks. The Paget Inquiry disregarded Claude Garric because he postulated facts uncomfortable to the British Establishment.

Friends of Paul were also ignored by the French police, tasked with 'investigating' the 'accident' in the Alma Tunnel. No one who knew Paul has said that he was a heavy drinker, prone to drunkenness. The cover-up conducted by the French and British simply suggested that Paul was skilful at hiding his drunkenness and if true, he must rank as the only person in the world who could defy the laws of physiology.

Just three days before the crash Paul had taken his annual medical as a private pilot and passed all the tests, including urine, reflexes, hand-eye coordination and mental health. He had never had a health or drink problem in the twenty-five years since he had been attracted to a flying club close to his home town of Lorient in Brittany. He obtained his pilot's licence when he was sixteen and often piloted Dodi's light aircraft.

Rees-Jones and Wingfield saw him on several occasions in the two hours after he returned to the hotel and at no stage did they report him as being drunk or unfit to drive. It was perfectly clear from the mass of evidence provided by CCTV footage at the Ritz and eyewitnesses at the scenes that Henri Paul, unequivocally was not drunk nor even modestly inebriated! At one stage he is even seen bending down to tie a shoe lace, not a hint of poor coordination.

Henri Paul was a favourite of Dodi's and well liked. It was clear that Paul had Dodi's confidence and was entrusted with driving them back to his apartment. A little before 22.30hrs, Dodi had spoken to the hotel night manager, Thierry Rocher and told him that it was their intention to return to the apartment. He asked Rocher to tell Henri Paul to contact him in the Imperial Suite for a pre-journey conference and to receive instructions.

Dodi's family say that he had already formally proposed to Diana and in a telephone call to his father, the princess is said to have confirmed they were to marry and that she had found a man to make her happy in the shape of his son. *The Sunday People* newspaper later arranged a taped interview with Mohamed Al Fayed in which he reiterated what he claimed Diana told him. The recording of the interview was tested by Dr Steven Laub, America's leading criminologist, using the latest lie-detecting equipment. After several hours of tests, Dr Laub reported, **"I am convinced he is telling the truth."**

It might explain why Dodi and Diana were so keen to return to the familiar intimacy of his apartment rather than consummate their engagement in the impersonal environment of the Imperial Suite, regardless of how luxurious it might be. An hour later Dodi told Rocher that they would be leaving from the back entrance in the rue Cambon. Dodi was satisfied that Henri Paul was the right man to perform the task of driving them safely back to the apartment. If Paul was drunk both Diana and Dodi would have spotted this and had another driver taken them there but they had no such concerns about Paul.

Dodi told Rocher to organise an extra car to be taken to the rear entrance on rue Cambon after midnight. The two vehicles used earlier would remain outside the front entrance to act as decoys when the moment came for departure. At 23.30hrs, Henri Paul went to the Imperial Suite, where Rees-Jones and Wingfield were seated outside waiting for further instructions and told the stunned bodyguards that they would not be travelling with Dodi and Diana.

Henri Paul alone would be responsible for driving them to the apartment and he would also ensure their safety. Dodi had been persuade by Henri Paul to use the bodyguards as a decoy to the paparazzi. This flew entirely in the face of Al Fayed security regulations. One instruction, covering the movement of VIPs, stated that the personal bodyguard and upwards to several other trained bodyguards must operate within the immediate area of the VIP and responsible for his or her safety at all times.

Indeed, whenever Mohamed Al Fayed moved, he used an armoured limousine, a back-up car and eight bodyguards. Dodi was proposing to take the most famous woman in the world across Paris in a single car with no bodyguard, all on the assurance of his friend and acting security chief of the Ritz Hotel. Paul informed Rees-Jones and Wingfield that no bodyguard was needed nor a back up car and added abruptly: "We will be leaving in half an hour. And you will be with the decoy vehicles." The die was cast.

Was this the Henri Paul and Ritz employee talking or was he speaking as a paid lackey of MI6, arranging a 'surprise' for Dodi and Diana. And was he also being set up as a patsy by MI6? Certainly, he would not have taken the route or driven the car at all if he knew what was planned. It is clear that Paul was sold a ruse, being assured that the redirected route was for the princess's 'safety'.

Wingfield went apoplectic at Paul's diktat: "No fucking way is he leaving without a bodyguard. No way in a million years it's going to be without me. I'll be coming with you if we go with this [plan]," he screamed at Henri Paul. Wingfield also said that he would have to "clear this with London" but Paul assured him that Mohamed Al Fayed had already agreed the plan.

The bodyguards find themselves in a difficult situation. There was no simple way to double-check Paul's statement without causing offence and calling his integrity into question, possibly causing them both to be sacked. Yet all this was anathema to their close protection training and vast experience as professional bodyguards.

Almost instantly, Dodi emerged from the Imperial Suite to rubber-stamp Henri Paul's instructions. One car would leave from the back with Paul driving and the bodyguards would leave from the front of the Ritz to act as decoy. But Wingfield persisted and told his boss, "You aren't leaving without security. I'll be coming." Dodi refused to budge and Wingfield again insisted, "There's absolutely no way you're going without security."

Dodi seemed to waver: "OK. One of you can come in the car, in the front." Wingfield had got his way but Dodi refused to relent on the issue of the back up car. This was the most fatal error of the entire night. With a back up car, there was little chance that their Mercedes could be intercepted by the stalkerazzi or even worse elements. But Henri Paul had won over Dodi to the lone-car plan.

Wingfield called up Philippe and Musa, on standby in the Etoile Limousine office opposite the Ritz, and told them to organise an extra car. As he briefed them, Claude Roulet, unexpectedly returned to the hotel and joined in. He had clearly, already spoken to Dodi or Paul and instructed Musa to lay on another car immediately. The car would be driven by Henri Paul....

The Ritz security manager was qualified on his ordinary licence to drive a Mercedes S280 – the chosen replacement car. But in France the police insist on a special licence to drive a limousine for hire. Claude Roulet was unconcerned that Paul may need a special licence to drive the Mercedes S280 and was satisfied that Paul would be able to get Dodi and Diana home safely. He did not quibble over back-up security.

Back at the Imperial Suite, Wingfield was attempting to change Dodi's mind and accept the two-car plan but Dodi would have none of it, insisting to his bodyguard, "It's been OK'd by my father." Mohamed Al Fayed would later deny he knew anything about Henri Paul's plan to drive his son back to his apartment. It is possible that Paul even hoodwinked Dodi into believing that he had spoken to his father.

left, Dodi and Diana begin to feel the oppressive heat as the pack of hunting photographers surround their limousine. Dodi's expression tells a thousand words....

Al Fayed is clear that he told his son to stay in the Imperial Suite if he had any concerns about his safety. The Harrod's mogul has gone on record many times stating, "Paul convinced my son that he should go to the apartment. That all their things were there. He said they should leave from the back entrance and he would get them home. He changed Dodi's mind and persuaded him to go along with him. That it was safe." Clearly, Paul had not "OK'd" the plan with Al Fayed.

On several occasions Paul appeared at the Ritz's front entrance to tease the photographers that Diana would be coming out shortly. This was all part of the decoy plan to fool the paps' into following the decoy car driven by Wingfield. The plan failed and anyone who has had dealings with the press will know not to treat them as fools, particularly when big money is at stake and it was!

Just after midnight, Frederic Lucard, who worked as a chauffeur with Etoile Limousine, drove a Mercedes S280 bearing the registration plate 688 LTV 75, to the back entrance on the rue Cambon. The limousine was a standard type with no tinted windows and armour. At 00.14hrs, Dodi and the princess departed the Imperial Suite, laughing and relaxed despite the day's epic events. They had relaxed with wine and the princess's tears of just two hours before had dried up.

Left, a sober Henri Paul makes small talk with Dodi and Diana.

Below, Dodi leaves the back entrance followed by Rees-Jones.

She was happy with her chosen man. They walked down one flight of stairs which led them to the back entrance and waited in a narrow service corridor. The press had not yet latched onto their decoy plan. A smiling Henri Paul made small talk with them while Wingfield kept watch for the Mercedes S280 limousine. As the bodyguard looked out, he vividly remembers seeing a light-coloured hatchback car, possibly a Fiat Uno and a scooter and several journalists. The press had by then been tipped off.

At approximately 00.19hrs, the Mercedes S280 arrived, the security cameras captured Dodi sliding a hand gently to the small of Diana's back, a gesture of affection and reassurance. The changeover went without incident. Lucard handed the keys to Henri Paul and he slid comfortably behind the wheel. Rees-Jones escorted Dodi and Diana to their seats in the rear of the car as flashbulbs popped around them and then took his seat in the front passenger seat next to Paul.

Rees-Jones alerted Wingfield in the Mercedes at the front of the hotel that they were about to leave. Two minutes later the original Mercedes and the Range Rover sped off as decoys but the plan had already gone wrong and should have been aborted immediately, their security was compromised. The press had already uncovered the decoy plan, having been tipped off again from impeccable 'sources'.

At 00.20hrs. Henri Paul pulled away from the rue Cambon, flashbulbs firing in a crazy explosion of artificial light as they pulled off from the back entrance of the Ritz. One of the last things Rees-Jones remembers is the light-coloured or white Fiat Uno car following them. He also recalls that Henri Paul was calm, sober and completely in control of the Mercedes S280 as they sped off to meet their destiny in Paris.

Chapter 4

'There is a God'

As the Mercedes S280, carrying Diana, Princess of Wales and Dodi Fayed, sped off down the rue Cambon, the paparazzi were still snapping away at the car and its golden occupants. Many of the paps' were already mounting their scooters and motorbikes to give chase to their valuable quarry. The couple believed they had only five more minutes to endure the press pack frenzy before arriving safely at Dodi's apartment, just over a mile away from the Ritz.

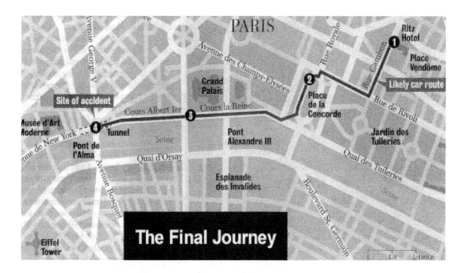

As Henri Paul swung the big car into the rue de Rivoli, many of the paparazzi from the front of the Ritz in the Place Vendôme, were pouring out of the rue de Castiglione into the same major thoroughfare just 150 yards behind the limousine. Henri Paul was taking his time to drive carefully, doing nothing stupid and all it required was for him to drive straight up the Champs Elysées.

The very worst that could happen, it seemed, was if they were forced to stop at traffic lights, the paps' may get a few more shots of the car, taken sideways. The Champs Elysées is the widest, straightest and best policed road in the whole of Paris – what could possibly go wrong in these perfect driving conditions?

Yet dissident MI6 officer Richard Tomlinson is of the opinion that Henri Paul was marching to the well-drilled drumbeat of the

British Secret Intelligence Service and thus he was ordered to take the route leading under the Alma Tunnel, a completely unnecessary manoeuvre. Paul who had been duped was about to experience a finale he had not been promised.

At the traffic lights outside the Crillon Hotel he turned the car left into the Place de la Concorde. But instead of going immediately onto the Champs Elysées, he continued south along the west side of the square, past the Paris twin of Cleopatra's needle in London and almost as far as the River Seine. There he jumped the traffic lights on red and threw the Mercedes S280 onto the Cours la Reine, a fast freeway.

This new direction lead him parallel to the river and at an angle fifty degrees at odds with his intended destination and he was speeding up with every passing motion of the engine. Diana and Dodi had not fastened their seatbelts and nor had the hapless Paul. Hervé Stephan, the judge appointed to investigate the crash never bothered to determine why Paul had chosen a completely different route to the one he should have taken.

Immediately after joining the Cours la Reine they entered the first of a series of tunnels which are designed to keep traffic on this central city freeway moving efficiently and smoothly. By the end of the first 300-yard tunnel, which underpinned the two bridges of Pont des Invalides and Pont Alexandre III, Henri Paul had put a considerable distance between himself and the chasing paparazzi and did not need to go any faster, he was way ahead of the game and began to slow down.

Unlike the safer Champs Elysées, this new route was dimly lit and was not an ideal environment for photographers to take pictures. The flashbulbs would simply bounce off the windows and distort the shots with excessive lens flare. And most of the pursuing paps' had broken off the chase, guessing they were heading back to Dodi's apartment and had begun massing at the site to await the lovers arrival. Wingfield was also busy driving the 'decoy' to the apartment on the rue Arséne Houssaye.

One other vehicle, at the very least, was heading in the same direction as the Mercedes S280, a white Fiat Uno, likely the same Fiat Uno spotted by Rees-Jones earlier in the rue Cambon and in the Place Vendôme, almost certainly driven by leading paparazzo and freelance fixer to the International intelligence community, James Andanson. He had been on Diana's case since the middle of August, even hiring a helicopter to take shots of the loving couple aboard the Jonikal down in the Mediterranean.

Andanson would later lie about being in the Alma Tunnel that night. At the time of the crash he was under investigation by the French Special Branch, implicated in the 'suicide' of former French Prime Minister Pierre Bérégovoy. Andanson was a millionaire with a dirty and murky past, often turning up nearby to the deaths of famous people he knew, as I will explore later.

Curiously, though the Fiat Uno was in front of the Mercedes not the usual position an intercept car would take to off-road another vehicle, if that was its purpose. Richard Tomlinson believes that Andanson did not need to follow the Mercedes because he knew exactly which route the car would take.

As he passed the last turnoff on the Cours Albert 1er, 350 yards before the Alma Tunnel, Henri Paul was cruising at a comfortable speed of 64 miles per hour, although it would take several more years to ascertain this information from a speed-camera printout and photograph in the tunnel's roof. It should be noted that French police repeatedly denied the existence of this data but were caught out lying and not for the first time!

Paul could have turned off at this point, up the slip road leading on to the Avenue George V which led almost directly to Dodi's apartment almost a mile away. People have speculated that Dodi instructed him not to but Rees-Jones heard no such instructions from his boss to Henri Paul. They had travelled a mile by this time and each extra yard travelled now would take them farther from their destination. And the paparazzi, those who remained in pursuit, were well behind them.

A witness would later state that a motorcyclist dressed in black jeans and leather jacket, wearing a crash helmet, had blocked the entrance to the Cours Albert 1er, but even so Paul made no attempt to take the slip road and so it was assumed he had predetermined 'other plans'. The motorcyclist has never been traced by either the French or British 'investigations'....

Just yards from the entrance to the Alma Tunnel, the Mercedes S280 pulled into the left-hand lane of the outside freeway. Paul was obliged to do this in order to pass the Fiat Uno, still ahead of them in the right-hand lane. It had been crawling along just before the tunnel entrance and had begun to pick up speed at the sighting of the Mercedes. French and British police have refused to say if it was also photographed by the speed camera which logged the Mercedes.

Just before they arrived in the Alma Tunnel, a motorbike passed them with a pillion passenger and took up a lead position in front of the two cars. The motorcyclist and the passenger were never identified and it is not known if they were photographers. The nearest paparazzi were travelling half a mile behind them.

As the Mercedes reached the tunnel and was about to cross the notorious hump at its entrance, two things happened, almost in synchrony: first a speed camera set in the tunnel roof, photographed the Mercedes and the second, the Fiat Uno, still gaining speed, slipped left into the path of the Mercedes.

The Fiat Uno had dawdled in the approach to the tunnel, some witnesses say it was zigzagging, but suddenly increased speed and swerved into the path of the oncoming Mercedes, precisely on the threshold of the most dangerous blackspot on the river freeway. It was at this exact point that the driver of the Fiat Uno could be assured to cause the maximum damage and then be so positioned to speed away without stopping to offer any assistance to the crashed vehicle.

Henri Paul, seeing the Fiat Uno swerve into his path, was forced to swerve violently to his left to avoid a serious collision with the smaller car. He was not fast enough and clipped the left-hand side of the Uno's rear bumper and red taillight with his right wing mirror, wing and front door as the cars swept down into the dip road which follows the hump.

It was at this moment that Rees-Jones, realising the immediate danger they were in, held his seat belt across his chest to prepare for impact – he would survive the crash as a result of his quick thinking. He also says that he told the three other occupants to fasten their seatbelts but they ignored him.

The Mercedes was now angled toward the centre of the dual freeway, which at this point began to bend quite sharply to the left. Henri Paul's flick of the left wheel to avoid the smaller car might have been slightly dangerous but certainly not enough to be fatal. But these were not normal circumstances. The Fiat Uno had deliberately swerved into the path of the Mercedes, an action which caused the limousine to crash.

Almost simultaneously a bright, blinding light erupted from a lead vehicle, momentarily blinding Paul, he lost control and the Mercedes slammed into the thirteenth pillar at approximately 64 miles per hour. Some witnesses say the blinding flash came from the Uno, others say the pillion passenger on the lead motorbike fired the flashlight at Paul. It is suggested by Tomlinson that MI6 used an Anti-Personnel Device of the type favoured by the SAS to bring down helicopters.

Just as likely and perhaps more so, the light was that from a powerful flashbulb fired from a photographer's camera (see photograph above). Either way, the combination of the flashlight and the collision with the Uno was enough to throw Paul's concentration completely, he swerved uncontrollably, spun to his left violently and in a second or so he was dead, crushed horribly in the mangled wreckage of the limousine. The wheels of history had turned and ground to a halt.

The last picture taken of the Mercedes S280 as it passes through the tunnel, seconds to impact. Henri Paul can be seen smiling, Rees-Jones looks bemused, Diana peers out of the back window. This picture was taken from a 'vehicle' in front of them not from the speed camera in the tunnel roof.

The devastating impact threw Diana forwards and sideward to her left. Dodi slammed into the back of the driver's seat and almost instantly shared Henri Paul's fate. Rees-Jones was crushed, his face torn and disfigured but he was alive. The Fiat Uno sped off not stopping once to lend assistance to the destroyed vehicle it had helped to off-road. From the rear mirror the Fiat Uno's driver would have seen the impact.

Smoke, steam and water hissed from the broken car and its shattered engine and the haunting blast of the horn screamed eerily down the tunnel. The Fiat Uno and the motorbike were exiting the tunnel at the far end. The wheels of history had turned and in an instant ground to a halt and a 20th Century icon lay dying. But the palace courtiers, so desperate to get rid off Diana, would fail completely to eradicate her memory.

Richard Tomlinson states that, "Everything happened in an instant, exactly as specified in the MI6 plan to kill Slobodan Milosevic." Unless Rees-Jones recovers his memory or more likely decides to speak out, no one will ever know for sure, the exact details of the murder of Princess Diana, Dodi Fayed and Henri Paul. And Rees-Jones, it should be remembered, a former paratrooper, is still subject to the Official Secrets Act and worse.

One other man could have given a full description of what happened, but James Andanson was found dead in a burned out car three years later. Apparently, according to the police, he poured twenty litres of petrol over himself, locked the doors of his BMW from the outside and burned himself to death.... Just how stupid do the French police think we are!?

The Mercedes was travelling only at 64 miles per hour, as the French police know only too well. And yet they continue to perpetuate the myth that the car was travelling much faster. In 2004, Scotland Yard detectives in the Paget 'Inquiry', asked an 'unnamed' racing car driver to go through the tunnel at 75 miles per hour. The racing car driver refused, saying it was "much too risky". The French police suggest the Mercedes was doing in excess of 75 miles per hour, an impossible feat that even professional drivers would not attempt. But stretching the bounds of belief has always been the purpose of the British and French authorities.

It is clear that had it not been for the intervention of the Fiat Uno swerving into Henri Paul's path and the subsequent flashlight blinding him, he would not have crashed the Mercedes S280. Diana, Dodi and Paul would have lived and returned safely to Dodi's apartment on the rue Arséne Houssaye. Witness Eric Petel, was driving towards the Alma Tunnel when he was overtaken by Diana's Mercedes.

Petel states: "The car was going quite fast and after it passed me I heard a sort of implosion. As I had just bought the motorbike, I thought the noise may have come from my exhaust and that I had a problem there. So I slowed down, thinking the bike had gone funny. Then I heard a much louder noise: the sound of a car crashing at speed. Ahead I saw the Mercedes which had exploded head-on into a heavy concrete pillar in the centre of the dual freeway.

"It had spun around and was facing back the way it had come. The horn was still blaring. I went to the car and saw a woman in the back. She had fallen against the seat in front and was bent over. I tried to ease her back and her head flopped back and I saw a little blood was coming from her nose and ear. That's weird, I thought. I know this person."

Petel said his first instinct was to call for help but he did not have a mobile phone. "I don't like them," he said. Instead he went to a public telephone off the Place de l'Alma and called the emergency services. Of the remarkable number of witnesses he was one of the few who tried to call for help.

It is certain that Petel is a key witness to the events immediately leading up to the crash. He explained to the operator that a car carrying Princess Diana had crashed in the Alma Tunnel but the operator mistook him for a crank caller and ignored his plea for help. Not to be outdone, Petel set off for a police station nearest to his home. He headed for the commissariat at Avenue Mozart.

At the police station he received a frosty reception and was again mistaken for a 'crank'. Obviously feeling he was being ignored, Petel threw a pile of police papers on the desk on to the floor. The police tried to calm him but he became even more upset, again feeling he was being ignored. Eventually the police lost patience with him and forcibly restrained him with handcuffs and sat him in an office on his own. He waited between 30 to 45 minutes before he was seen again.

The police came back and told him he would be taken for questioning to the Quai de L'Horloge. The public are seldom admitted to this building, the police HQ. He waited for almost 30 minutes before he was seen by police inspectors who were disturbed of his talk of an 'implosion' at the scene. He was seen by more police inspectors but refused to change his story. The door behind him opened and there stood a strange man.

He said: "A senior official came and he said it would be best if I did not make myself known. He only issued this threat. I didn't know then who he was." The senior official's intonation was threatening and Petel was relieved when the autocrat ordered him to be released. Petel had just met the rather sinister Préfet of Paris police, Philippe Massoni. The cover-up was already swinging into action, hence the threat to Petel that he should "forget" what he had seen.

That night French journalists were told by the police to ignore Petel. They alleged, falsely, that he was a 'junkie and had a long criminal record.' In fact he had one minor offence for fraud as a teenager. He was now a grown man, in full-time employment. Clearly the police were desperate to discredit him from the outset.

Brian Anderson, an American businessman from California was travelling in a taxi and saw a motorbike with two riders pass the Mercedes on the left. He said: "My attention was drawn away until the cab came to a sudden stop and I saw an object in front of us, crossing over. Sparks were flying, there was dust, there was a lot of dust, there was a lot of noise and it happened very quickly and the car came down and rested on its tires. In that instant the horn went off." The riders on the motorbike have never been traced.

François Levistre from Rouen in Normandy was interviewed by the Reuters Office in Paris just four days after the crash. He and his wife Valerie were in the capital for a night out and were driving into the Alma Tunnel when he noticed lights approaching from behind in his rear view mirror.

He said to his wife: "There must be a big shot behind us with a police escort. Then I went down into the tunnel and again in my rear view mirror I saw the car in the middle of the tunnel with a motorbike on its left with two people on it which then swerved to the right directly in front of the car.

"As it swerved there was a flash of light. It was an explosion of light, like a searchlight but then I was heading out of the tunnel and heard, but did not see the impact. I immediately pulled my car over to the curb but my wife said "we should get out of here it may be a terrorist attack." Such was their impression of that they perceived the 'accident' in the same genre of a 'terrorist' attack.

Another witness, Brenda Wells, a forty-year-old British secretary, was returning home from a party and told police that as he neared the Alma Tunnel she had been forced off the road by a motorbike with two men on it, travelling at speed. She said: "It was following a big car. After in the tunnel, there were very strong lights, like flashes. I saw the big car had come off the road and I stopped. After that, five or six motorbikes arrived and people started taking photographs.

French policeman David Laurent made a statement in June 1998. He remembers that he was driving toward the Alma Tunnel when a white Fiat Uno sped past him. As Laurent drove into the tunnel he again saw a white Fiat Uno creeping along very slowly. The car, he states, had come to a near standstill in the inside lane just before the tunnel, clearly waiting for the Mercedes to catch up. The trap was almost closed.

At around 00.26hrs, photographer Romuald Rat got off his motorbike in the tunnel and left his driver to park up. He ran towards the Mercedes and quickly took three pictures. He looked into the car and recognised Dodi Fayed. Smoke was still billowing out of the car. He said: "At that point I was shocked because it wasn't a pretty sight. I drew back for a few seconds."

Rat was clearly shocked but soon got a grip and observed that Dodi's eyes were half open. He said: "I could see nothing more could be done for him. The princess was on the floor, between the two seats, her back to me. I said to her in English: 'Be cool, the doctor is coming.' She said, 'My God, my God.'" He then saw Rees-Jones shudder violently and assured him too that the doctor was coming.

Later, revulsion would sweep around the world as Rat revealed that he put his fingers on Diana's neck to take her pulse. His action was entirely natural but he was hated nonetheless and it was unfortunate for him that he had the surname 'Rat', which has so many negative semantics in the Anglo-Saxon world. He claimed not to have taken pictures of the car and its dead and dying occupants but this was an outright lie. French police confiscated his camera and revealed that the first four frames on his reel were of the wrecked car and the dead, badly injured and dying.

The next to arrive on the scene was another paparazzo Christian Martinez, whose 'reputation' was as bad as Rat's. It is argued that Martinez is ruthless, violent and mean-spirited. A tussle ensued between the two hard case photographers as Diana lay dying. They were bickering over who would get the best shots. At this time it is extremely difficult to feel nothing but contempt for these 'men'.

Other paparazzi joined the sickening scrum, a feeding frenzy of awful proportions and which would forever blacken the name of the press. Serge Arnal, David Oderkerken and Serge Banamou were soon in the scrum, jostling for position, flashbulbs popping, poking their cameras through shattered windows, torn metal and steam and smoke at the torn bodies.

By a strange quirk of fate a doctor arrived at the scene, Dr Frédéric Mailliez, who was off duty that night. He had been driving in the opposite direction on the way back from a party and decided to stop his car and lend much-needed assistance. The paparazzi, astonishingly, carried on taking pictures as Mailliez tended the crash victims.

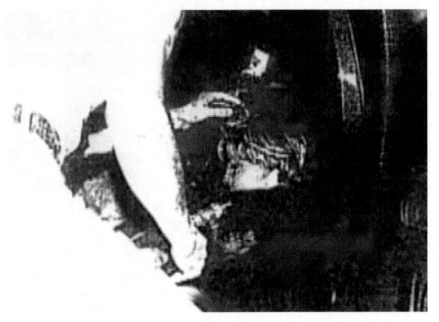

Princess Diana, seriously injured, receiving 'attention' in
the back of the wrecked Mercedes S280

Dr Mailliez forced his way past them, who he said, "Seemed to have lost all leave of their senses." He ran back to his car, using his mobile phone he twice tried to ensure that two ambulances were on the way. "I told them there were two severely injured people." His second call was to request cutting equipment which was needed to cut Rees-Jones free of the wreckage.

He returned to the wreck to find two off-duty firemen who had also been driving in the opposite direction, had also stopped to help. Damien Dalby and Sébastien Pennequin had gone to the aid of the trapped bodyguard, holding up his badly injured head so as to help him breathe.

Dr Mailliez said that there was very little he could do to help Diana. Through the back door he tilted her head back to help her breathe and clear her upper respiratory passage and fix an oxygen mask over her nose and mouth. He said: "I sought to unblock the esophagus. This seemed to ease her breathing and made her more animated."

As Dr Mailliez worked on the princess, the paps' carried on taking pictures. The first police arrived at the scene at 00.30hrs, a couple of minutes before the fire brigade. The police also had to force their way through the snapping paparazzi, who were taking shots from every angle. It was sickening and an argument soon broke out between the police and the paparazzi who demanded to be allowed to 'work' unhindered.

Police officers Lino Gagliardone and Sebastian Dorzee were on patrol nearby, when they were told by passers-by that there had been an accident. Immediately they called for reinforcements. Gagliardone and Dorzee, without success, tried to stem the tide of baying photographers and arguments ensued. These scenes were certainly very ugly but would soon become far worse.

Gagliardone tried to hold back the paps' but with little success. At the same time, his colleague Dorzee checked on the wrecked car and its occupants, radioing the information back to base. Dorzee noticed that Diana was still alive and mumbling. As the princess turned to look at Dodi's body she said quite clearly, "Oh my God."

Dorzee recounts vividly: "She was moving slightly and her eyes were open. She was in pain, I think. She turned her head toward the front of the car and saw the driver. I think she understood better then what had happened. She became quite agitated, then she looked at me and closed her eyes and let her head rest back." Officer Gagliardone said: "The photographers were virulent, objectionable and pushy, continuing to take photos and wilfully obstructing an officer from assisting the victims."

At 00.32hrs, two teams of firemen arrived in vehicles 94 and 100. The officer in charge at the scene, Xavier Gourmelon, evaluated the situation and he decided that his main priority was to cut the roof wreckage from the vehicle so that Rees-Jones could be extracted. The injured bodyguard appeared to everyone to be more seriously injured than Diana and he was prioritised for medical treatment.

Meanwhile, paparazzo Christian Martinez hurled abuse at the police, shouting: "You make me sick, let me do my job. In Sarajevo the police at least let us work." Subsequent checks on Martinez by the police and media revealed that he had never worked in Sarajevo, at least not officially. This mystery has caused some people to suggest that Martinez was in the employ of French intelligence but there is no supporting evidence at this time to prove the allegation against him.

Within minutes, Madame Maude Coujard, the duty prosecutor, arrived at the scene. When someone dies violently in France, the first person to be informed is the prosecution office, which in Paris is the Palais de Justice. Madame Coujard was driven to the scene by her husband on his BMW motorbike. She would oversee the French investigation into the crash and appoint other judges and officials.

Her first decision was to appoint the Criminal Brigade to investigate the accident. The Criminal Brigade usually deal with terrorist incidents and sudden deaths that cannot be explained. Commander Jean-Claude Mules, soon placed his trust in Martine Monteil to head the Criminal Brigade's investigation. She was the first female head of the Brigade, having been appointed in 1996.

The duty judge that night was Hervé Stephan and he was ordered to the scene by Madame Coujard. Two days later she appointed him to conduct the full investigation into the crash. At the same time as judge Stephan was being ordered to the scene, a similar order went out to Paris chief of police Philippe Massoni, who had by then attempted to silence witness Eric Petel. Ostensibly, at least, the police were dealing with an 'accident' and yet Massoni had tried to silence the distraught Petel....

Massoni had conferred with minister of the interior Jean-Pierre Chevénement, who in turn informed the British ambassador Sir Michael Jay. The French foreign minister and the Elysée Palace had also been fully briefed on the unfolding tragic events in the Alma Tunnel. From the outset, both French and British officials were determined to declare the incident an accident, end of story.

And a scapegoat presented itself in the shape of the harassing paparazzi who would soon shoulder the blame for a crash they did not cause. When the Mercedes collided with the thirteenth pillar in the Alma Tunnel, having first collided with Andanson's Fiat Uno and the disorientating white light, the pursuing paparazzi were over a quarter of a mile behind and did not see the crash. Logically, how could they be blamed for an 'accident' they had not even witnessed?

But within days the French authorities would offer the scapegoat press an escape route, by shifting the blame onto a supposedly drunken Henri Paul. The press, particularly in Britain responded to the offer and lambasted the unfortunate Paul who could no longer defend himself. In Britain, the press were taking a hammering from the public. When Henri Paul was offered up as bait the press snatched at it and have towed the line ever since, effectively silencing all lines of inquiry.

In the ten years since the crash, the might of the British puppet media has been diverted away from asking the vital questions that the British and French 'investigations' have covered-up. The ease with which the British press swallowed the tales of the French authorities is best summed up by Piers Morgan, former editor of the Daily Mirror.

Piers Morgan meets with Diana in 1996. The former Daily Mirror editor had got to know Diana fairly well after his personal audience with her at Kensington Palace in 1996. On 1 September 1997, Morgan infamously exclaimed 'there is a God' when news was leaked that Henri Paul was allegedly drunk and to blame for the 'accident' and the press were let off the hook.

On hearing the news from the French Authorities that Henri Paul was allegedly drunk, he exclaimed in the newsroom, "There is a God." He saw that the press had an opportunity to get off the hook and took it immediately. So much for his so-called 'friendship' with Diana. And in 2005, Morgan got his comeuppance when he was duped into publishing fake photographs, which depicted British soldiers apparently abusing

Iraqi prisoners. Morgan was set up by MI6 and the Ministry of Defence and was forced to resign, his career in tatters.

On Page 169 of his book, *The Insider*, Morgan writes: '*31 August 1997 – There were bound to be paparazzi chasing them [Diana/Dodi] around and everyone's going to think they nearly killed them and start demanding a privacy law again.*

By the next day Morgan was feeling ebullient again, writing on Page 171 of The Insider: *The media, and tabloid newspapers in particular, have been getting hammered on the airwaves. We are being, as I feared, directly blamed for the accident and the repercussions are going to be unprecedented. People in my office are already talking of us never buying paparazzi photos again.*

Monday, 1 September 1997 – 'There is a God'. Henri Paul, driver of the Mercedes, was reported in France to have been three times over the drink limit, and going at 121mph. 'Drunk, speeding Fayed driver kills Diana' is a lot better than 'paparazzi kill Diana'. The press, desperate to switch the blame from ourselves, have immediately turned our collective turrets on to Henri Paul. This is going to get uglier and nastier as the days go on.

(Computer generated image of what the blinding white flash would have looked like to Henri Paul)

Chapter 5

The Deadly Delay

Shortly after Martine Monteil's arrival at the scene and after consultation with prosecutor Madame Coujard and a radio discussion with Commander Mules, it was decided to place the blame for crash on the paparazzi alone – they opted for the easy route. The paps' had clearly harassed the princess and Dodi throughout their sojourn in Paris and down in the Mediterranean.

The evidence from all the key witnesses proved that the paparazzi had not caused the crash. But this did not deter the French authorities from pursuing this official, highly convenient and snap judgment, that endures to this day, in government corridors at least but it is rejected by the wider public.

Romuald Rat, Stéphane Darmon, Christian Martinez, Jacques Langevin, Serge Arnal, Laslo Veres and Nikola Arsov were shepherded away from the crash by the police and immediately taken into custody. The Paris prosecution department would ask for an inquiry to be opened against the forenamed paparazzi. Others were arrested later for failing to give assistance to persons in danger, an abuse of the French good Samaritan law.

Sergeant Gourmelon designated Philippe Boyer, one of his 95 strong team, to take over from Dr Mailliez, to take care of Diana until the emergency service (SAMU) arrived to take over. Boyer fixed a surgical collar around Diana's neck. He stayed until SAMU doctors took over. Two firemen were assigned to extract Rees-Jones from the wrecked car. They held his head up from the dashboard, administered oxygen and attached a cervical collar around his neck in case of suspected spinal damage.

At 00.44hrs, the camion de désincarcération (can-opener) arrived under the command of Armand Forge and in short order he had spotlights focused on the wreckage and began cutting the roof from the car. At the same time, Dr Jean-Marc Martino, a resuscitation expert, had taken over treating Diana. Another medical team led by Dr Le Hote was attending to Rees-Jones.

Dr Martino attached a drip to Diana's arm to sedate her, as she was still agitated and occasionally crying out. He said that she was "confused and agitated" and so he had no choice but to sedate her. He directly supervised the firemen and medics who hoisted her slim body out of the back of the wrecked car. They took great care lifting her out as she was partly wedged against the floor, the back seat and the passenger seat in front. Dr Martino judged her state as "Severe but not critical".

Diana was also talking but not coherently. As she was being transferred onto a stretcher she went into cardiac arrest and the full severity of her condition became very clear to the medics. Dr Martino administered respiratory ventilation by inserting a narrow tracheal tube down her throat, whereupon he applied heart massage. All this was done with professional haste given her seriously deteriorating condition. All this activity took place on a roadside stretcher.

Eventually, Dr Martino was able to revive Diana and he instructed ambulance driver Michel Massebeuf to transfer to the ambulance stretcher where work continued on her broken body. The inside of a French ambulance is akin to a small operating theatre but even the abundance of medical equipment was not enough to save the princess. She had suffered her first heart attack and more would follow.

By 01.30hrs, the bodies of Henri Paul and Dodi Fayed had been removed from the wreckage and laid on the road. Medics had worked for a good 30 minutes on Dodi, applying external heart massage but history was the master of this situation and his name had become indelibly engraved in British royal history. Within hours, his princess would join him in the next life.

Diana was then ferried to Pitié-Salpêtrière hospital just four miles away. In Britain the practice is to get a trauma victim to hospital quickly to be treated by expert medical staff but the French have a different system. Their ambulances are equipped with the finest medical equipment available and the practice is to stabilise the victim before going to a hospital for treatment. Conspiracy theorists claim that Diana's ambulance was 'intercepted' by intelligence agents and thus slowed down to ensure she died. The truth tells a very different story.

It was 01.30hrs, when the ambulance carrying Diana left the Alma Tunnel en route to Pitié-Salpêtrière. The journey began slowly and continued in the same vein all the way to the hospital, flanked by two police cars and two police motorcyclists. No intelligence agents were in the ambulance and they played no part in slowing down the journey either. The ambulance driver Michel Massebeuf explains that he had to drive so slow to prevent passage over bumpy road surfaces from aggravating the patient's condition.

As they were crossing the Austerlitz bridge, Diana's heart appeared to have stopped again for the second time, her blood pressure was low and Dr Martino instructed the convoy to stop so as to administer emergency treatment. By now they had passed two major hospitals and were parked up outside the botanical gardens, just half-a-mile away from Pitié-Salpêtrière. In Britain the practice would be to dash for the hospital but as I have explained the French have a different system.

Dr Martino decided to treat Diana himself instead of rushing to the hospital. To many it is baffling that he would stop for a further ten minutes to try and revive Diana but they were the conditions under which he was working and he was in temporary charge of his patient. Again he applied external heart massage and injected a large dose of adrenalin directly into the heart. He succeeded to revive Diana, she was now clinging to life.

News of the crash had already spread around the world and it was confirmed that Dodi Fayed had been killed and Diana was seriously injured. At the hospital, senior politicians, police and the British ambassador Michael Jay were gathered at the entrance. Paris police chief Philippe Massoni had driven to the hospital directly from the Alma Tunnel but still the SAMU ambulance had not arrived. Later Massoni admitted that at one stage he believed that the ambulance may have got 'lost'.

But the ambulance did not lose its way, it arrived at the Pitié-Salpêtrière at 02.06hrs and was greeted by Professor Bruno Riou, the hospital's head of intensive care. He immediately took over care for Diana and the dying princess was rushed into theatre. Despite the fact that the SAMU ambulance had notified the hospital that Diana had suffered two heart attacks in the space of 30 minutes, there was no specialist cardiac team there to meet them. Nor was a heart-lung bypass machine available.

The French were bungling the treatment of Diana and would later make every attempt to conceal their incompetence and much else. Diana was unconscious on arrival at the hospital and completely unaware of the drama unfolding around her almost lifeless body. But her heart, wounded so many times in bitter clashes with the House of Windsor, was still beating, her fighting spirit shining through again. X-rays revealed both massive internal haemorrhaging and severe internal injuries.

She was being drained of the blood which had seeped into her chest cavity, when at 02.10hrs, she had another cardiac arrest. Professor Bruno ordered duty surgeon Maniel Daloman to open up her chest on the right side while he swiftly applied external heart massage. With the surgical procedure well progressed, heart surgeon Professor Alain Pavie was summoned to take charge.

Pavie quickly ascertained that the internal bleeding was coming from a ruptured pulmonary vein, the centrifugal link between the heart and lungs. Pavie sutured the 2.5 centimetre incision while heart massage continued. And a nurse was administering injections of adrenalin the whole time to keep Diana's heart going. The medics were battling desperately to save the 'queen of hearts' but the delay in getting to hospital was proving to be irreparable. An astonishing total of 150 5ml doses of adrenalin were injected into Diana but to no avail.

At 03.00hrs, Professor Pavie extended the incision and massaged the heart by hand. This development was explained to the interior minister and Sir Michael Jay at 03.30hrs by Professor Riou. But the immediate prognosis was desperate and the medics had little faith that Diana could be saved. The pressure they were under was enormous. This was the Princess of Wales, after all, and if she died in the care of French doctors... the whole world would never forget and probably never forgive them.

Repeatedly, the defibrillator (electric-shocks) attempted to revive Diana's heart. Through hand-held terminals fixed to Diana's chest, shock after shock, shook through her body but not enough to shock her heart back to life. Finally, with mutual consent, all attempts to resuscitate her were abandoned and the Princess of Wales was officially pronounced dead at 04.00hrs on the 31 August 1997. History had come to pass and with Dodi and Henri Paul, she will live on for as long as human beings retain historical records. The official statement, signed by both Professors, Pavie and Riou, stated: -

The Princess of Wales was the victim of a high-speed car crash tonight in Paris. She was immediately taken by the Paris SAMU emergency services which carried out initial resuscitation. On her arrival at Pitié-Salpêtrière hospital, she had massive chest injuries and haemorrhaging, followed rapidly by cardiac arrest. An emergency thoracotomy revealed a major wound on the left pulmonary vein. Despite closing this wound and two hours of external and internal cardiac massage, circulation could not be re-established and death occurred at 4 o'clock in the morning.

Diana also had a puncture wound in her hip, for which no explanation has ever been offered and a broken arm. Seeing the need to manage public relations, Dr Goldstein, vice-president of SAMU said: "We can't do the impossible. Diana had no chance of making it. The accident was too violent. The internal injuries she suffered were incompatible with life."

On the contrary, if Diana had been taken to a hospital immediately she was pulled from the wrecked Mercedes S280, she would likely have lived and made a full recovery. The French were incompetent and to this day still refuse to accept the fact. Condemnation of the French emergency system would soon pour in from across the world. It was felt that the 'People's Princess', as Tony Blair would later attribute to her, had been let down by the French and the French were only too aware of the need to dumb down the furore and Henri Paul would provide the perfect scapegoat.

The public announcement of Diana's death was made at 05.45hrs, by Sir Michael Jay. By this time pictures of Diana receiving 'treatment' in the wrecked Mercedes had been flashed across the world by photo agencies looking to make a 'killing' out of a killing. The Laurent Sola agency, had already received offers totalling £1 million alone from the British press. Piers Morgan summed up the mood perfectly in his memoir *The Insider*: -

I got to the office by 5.45am and there was controlled pandemonium. My picture editor, Ron Morgans, a brilliant veteran operator, immediately led me to a screen where he had photos of Diana lying dead in the back of the car. She looked serene, like she was asleep. There was a trickle of blood running from her lip but otherwise no visible sign of injury. I stared at the screen for minutes, just saying 'fuck me' repeatedly. I had never seen more sensational news images.

Then I realised the enormity of what I was looking at. I ran to the phone and called the boss of the agency who had sent the pictures in. 'Retrieve those fucking photos from everywhere you have sent them right now, or you will be out of business by the end of today.' He sounded panicky. 'What do you mean, why?'

He was a good operator who ran a good business, but he hadn't quite got to grips with this yet. 'Listen, mate, Diana's possibly been killed by the bloody paparazzi and you are trying to flog me pictures of her still warm corpse. Think about it, for fuck's sake.'

'It's too late, they've gone out,' he said, his voice trembling a bit. 'No, it isn't, ring everyone and say there's been a terrible mistake and these photographs are not for publication. They will all understand. Then if I were you, I'd turn your machines off and leave the country until it all blows over. Because if people find out what you were doing they will come and get you.' He thanked me for the advice and withdrew the pictures.

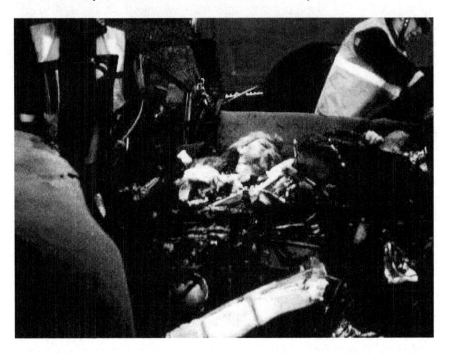

Other picture agencies with photographs from the crash scene, showing the dead, dying and the injured, also withdrew their pictures from tender. In the end, not one of pictures was sold and the victims of the orchestrated crash, at least, retained a little dignity in death. The only survivor was bodyguard, Trevor Rees-Jones, who had horrible injuries, particularly to his head and face which would leave him disfigured for life.

At 01.30hrs, Kez Wingfield, having been updated about the crash and that Dodi had been killed, telephoned Paul Handley-Greaves, chief of Mohamed Al Fayed's personal security, in London. The lights flashed on in Barrow Green Court, the Surrey farmhouse home of Al Fayed, who listened to Handley-Greaves compassionately breaking the news that his dearly beloved eldest son, Dodi (the one you can depend on) was dead and that Princess Diana was critically injured.

Mohamed Al Fayed ordered his bodyguards to transport him to Gatwick Airport, just twenty miles away, where he boarded his private helicopter and took off, bound for Paris. He could not have known then, distraught with grief at his son's death, that he was embarking on a journey to battle for truth and justice which will likely last to his own dying days.

As his private helicopter flew over Surrey, over in Paris it had already been decided that his son's death was a terrible accident, caused by the harassing paparazzi and soon Henri Paul, stone cold dead and unable to defend himself, would also be blamed. Al Fayed was heading into a battle royal, literally, and his vast fortune would be needed to uncover the truth.

The Foreign Office telephoned the switchboard at Buckingham Palace to break the news and a call was patched through to Prince Charles at Balmoral Castle. The Prince of Wales was woken immediately and with mounting horror listened to the news being broken to him. The heir to the throne, then telephoned his mother to break the news. The persistent thorn in the side of the House of Windsor had been pruned forever.

A little before dawn, the ashen-faced Prince Charles went to an audience with his mother and told her it was his firm intention to fly to Paris at first light. He proposed to the Queen, that he would bring home his ex-wife's body aboard an aircraft of the Queen's Flight. The Queen refused the use of her aircraft and explained that following the divorce of Diana and Charles the previous year, Diana was no longer a Royal and should be brought home in body bag, just like any other British citizen killed abroad.

Charles was livid and at one point on the telephone told Sir Robert Fellowes, the Queen's private Secretary to go and "fucking impale yourself on a flagpole". A royal equerry explained to the Queen that it would not do to have the body of the Princess of Wales retuned in a "Harrod's van". Charles was not for compromising and by breakfast, after bitter arguments with his mother and Prince Philip, the Queen relented and Charles got his way. Prince Edward, when told of Diana's death, said, "It was only the way it was going to end. It was amazing it took that long for it to happen."

In Paris, Kez Wingfield and Claude Roulet drove to Le Bourget airport in the northern environs of the city, arriving at 04.55hrs.

Almost in perfect synchrony, the Harrod's helicopter hovered overhead. It touched down as the Range Rover and Mercedes drew up on the tarmac. At that very moment, Wingfield fielded a call from the British Consulate: "Princess Diana is dead!"

Al Fayed stepped from the helicopter flanked by two bodyguards to be greeted by Wingfield, who had never touched his boss before, put his arm around his shoulder and explained that he had more bad news for him. Al Fayed intuitively asked: "The princess?" Wingfield nodded and said: "They're all dead."

The Al Fayed convoy immediately made its way into Paris and as it neared the centre of the city, Wingfield, sat in the front seat of the car, witnessed the Harrod's mogul suddenly erupt. "I hope the British government is satisfied now," he exclaimed, understandably frothing at the bit. Wingfield replied: "Nobody could have wished this, sir," but Al Fayed was inconsolable, he slumped in his seat and made no reply. It was clear from the outset that Al Fayed believed British Intelligence had a hand in his son's death.

Their small convoy arrived at the front entrance of the Pitié-Salpêtrière shortly before the official announcement was made that Princess Diana was dead. Al Fayed decided not to go into the hospital itself and was met by an official. Immediately, the official showed him to the morgue, where a hearse was waiting. Under Islamic law, the dead have to be buried within a day of death.

There was a short delay while the official searched for keys to let them in to the morgue. Al Fayed stood there, rooted like a statue, unmoving and unspeaking, simply stunned by what had happened. But good news came in the form of Rees-Jones, who was still alive and doubtless would be able to explain some of what had happened. The bodyguard was in bad shape though and would need weeks of intensive care to pull through.

It took a little over ten minutes to collect Dodi's body from the hospital morgue, whereupon the Al Fayed convoy sped off for Dodi's apartment to collect Diana's already packed luggage. From there they headed back to the airport and flew back to Surrey. As the Harrod's helicopter took off from Le Bourget airport, the Alma Tunnel was being swept clean by the municipal street cleaner.

On the baffling orders of the Criminal Brigade, the tunnel was swept with detergent, a little over four hours after the crash. All forensic evidence was destroyed apart from the small amount collected beforehand. It is stunning that in a car crash in which three people died, so little attention to forensic analysis was paid. But the French and British authorities had decided from the outset that the crash was an accident. Vital forensic evidence was thus destroyed and deliberately so!

As much as it was a clean up, it was also the beginning of the cover-up. The stretch of road where the Mercedes S280 crashed was swept twice with detergent, just to make sure nothing of value was left behind. By the time a crash expert was despatched to the scene, the clean-up was done and there was nothing left to inspect. If a normal visiting VIP had been killed in the same manner, the road would have been closed for a minimum of 24 hours but there was a calculated haste to clean-up.

Just six hours after the crash, stunningly, the tunnel was reopened to traffic. The only clue to the terrible accident was a chunk of concrete missing from the foot of the thirteenth pillar. *Newsweek's* Paris correspondent Christopher Dickey said: "I went there at seven o'clock to view the scene, and was stunned to find it already reopened. I would have thought that for an accident of that magnitude, involving the death of such a famous individual, the police might have kept it closed for days in their search for evidence."

The Paris traffic police made an elementary examination of the scene and no more, there was no detailed forensic examination. The Criminal Brigade's Martine Monteil was clear that she had no interest in reading the report. There was no cooperation between the two police departments at any time and this continues to be the case today. Judge Herve Stephan did not ask to see the 'report' either.

Mercedes-Benz offered to send engineers to examine the wrecked car and determine possible causes of the crash but the Criminal Brigade rejected the offer. It is clear that Mercedes-Benz engineers were best qualified to conduct such tests on one of its own cars but the police could not run the risk of 'something' being found which did not support their impetuous theory of 'accident'. The cover-up was in full swing, involving both British and French governments. The British could have brought diplomatic pressure to bear against the French to conduct a proper investigation but nothing was said.

That morning saw many unusual decisions taken of a highly suspicious nature. The most controversial of which was the priority order from London to conduct a partial embalming of

Diana's body, from the waist up, before a full post mortem could be done. Why were the legs not embalmed? It is still not known who ordered the partial embalming but more likely than not the order came from a royal courtier. Well placed sources suggest it was Diana's bother-in-law, Sir Robert Fellowes but this allegation remains unproven.

(The destroyed Mercedes S280 surrounded by police in the Alma Tunnel, shortly before being removed, just four hours after the crash. The tunnel was then swept with detergent, thus destroying most of the forensic evidence at the scene)

The order was relayed to the French authorities by Sir Michael Jay on behalf of St James's Palace. The inescapable fact is that under French law an embalming can only be ordered by the deceased's next of kin. Charles and Diana were divorced the previous year and St James's Palace had no business in this matter. The French, however, eager to comply, did not complain and the partial embalming was done.

The French also turned a blind eye to their own law prohibiting embalming where a post mortem is to be conducted. The primary constituent of embalming fluid is Formaldehyde, which completely corrupts toxicology tests. Therefore any subsequent test to determine if Diana was pregnant was not possible because the embalming fluid rendered the test useless. Mohamed Al Fayed, to this day, insists that Diana told him she was pregnant just hours before she died.

Commander Mules of the Paris police department insists that the instruction to embalm came from an higher authority, he said: "The decision was taken by a higher authority than myself, before the body was released." Likely, the objective of the embalming was to render useless any pregnancy test. It also severely limited the chances of there being a successful full post mortem in France or England.

To this day, Professor Dominique Lecomte, who carried out the partial embalming, insists that she did nothing wrong. With Professor Andre Lienhart, she had only carried out a partial embalming and not a full post mortem. Both professors merely confirmed the nature of the injuries which caused Diana's death. A copy of their report was given to the French authorities but it was removed from Judge Stephan's 'inquiry'. For a simple 'accident', a great deal was being covered up and blocked.

According to Robert Thompson, an assistant at the Hammersmith and Fulham mortuary in West London, where a post mortem was performed on Diana's body, "There had been some wadding inserted into the body. I presume it had been soaked in Formaldehyde or Formalin, because I could get the smell." Later, the mortuary's blood results came through and revealed that no alcohol was anywhere in Diana's body, despite the fact that Thompson said her stomach contents reeked of alcohol!

If the mortuary was able to defy the laws of physics regarding the alcohol content of Diana's stomach, what else was covered up? Thompson says that he and his colleagues reacted to the smell of the alcohol, it was so strong, he said, "It permeated the whole room." And yet, the toxicology 'test' showed there to be no alcohol. It must also be noted that the Queen 'insisted' that Diana was taken to the Hammersmith and Fulham mortuary.

Thompson also says that at one point during the autopsy, forensic pathologist Dr Chapman (safe pair of hands) announced that Diana was not pregnant. But Thompson did not see any hard evidence of this remark and so it must be dismissed. Thompson said: "Another 'person' who was present, just as categorically told me that the princess was expecting a baby when she died." The evidence of this has been lost or deliberately eradicated. The lying game had begun in earnest.

And other, seemingly inexplicable things, happened just twenty-fours after the crash. Two incidents took place at separate addresses across London, which bore remarkable and almost identical similarities.

At 03.00hrs, a London-based photojournalist, Lionel Cherruault was woken up at his home in Mowbray Road. His wife's screams had alerted him. She had looked down the stairs to discover, to her sheer horror, that the front door was wide open – they had locked it before going to bed. Lionel checked his studio, where he kept his photographic equipment and computers, to find that they had been robbed, almost as if by ghosts or spooks, because they had heard nothing at all. This brings to mind *Spycatcher*, Peter Wright's famous statement: "We bugged and burgled our way across London."

The only thefts from his studio were computer disks and storage media for saving and transmitting photographs. He had a vast library of royal pictures and these were the principal targets of the silent raiders, who wafted in and out, just like spooks in the night. One can imagine the terror that they rightly felt.

The previous morning, a few hours after the crash in Paris, Lionel Cherruault was offered pictures of the crash in the Alma Tunnel but after Diana died, the deal collapsed because the pictures were deemed too sensitive to publish. Cash, credit cards and jewellery were on open display to the raiders but they took nothing and concentrated only on the computer equipment and storage media containing Cherruault's library of royal pictures. Expensive cameras and lenses were also ignored.

Cherruault explains that the computers had their hard disk drives removed by the raiders, first turning off the computers. They had made virtually no noise and had not woken the couple but what could have happened to them had they woken to find the spooks rifling through their property? Would they also have been taken out? Tomlinson, former MI6 officer, says that the spooks will stop at nothing, including assassination, as long as they can get away with it.

The next day Cherruault was visited by a man wearing a grey suit who also had grey hair. He told Cherruault that he had been targeted not burgled and suggested possible government involvement. He said: "You can call them what you like – MI5, MI6, MI7, MI9, Special Branch or local henchman – anything you like. But that person who came to your house had a key into your house and knew exactly where to go. But not to worry, you lives weren't in any danger."

The word on the media circuit, from reliable sources, is that the Metropolitan Police Special Branch (MPSB) were behind the raid and they had been ordered by MI5 to remove the stolen material. This also shows sister-service cooperation in the events after the hit on Diana. It must also be remembered that Metropolitan Police 'detectives' made up the Paget Operation led by their former Commissioner Sir John Stevens. But of course they would have us believe that they were 'impartial'.

Lionel Cherrault and his London home 'burgled' by spooks on 31.08.1997

By 03.00hrs on 31 August, Darren Lyons, Australian boss of Big Pictures, had received pictures of the crash in the Alma Tunnel. This demonstrates that a large surveillance operation was in full swing, monitoring the internet and mobile phone traffic of every photo agency in Paris. The spooks were able to track all outbound communications from the photo agencies and knew where and to who, pictures of the crash had been sent.

It is vitally important to note that if the spooks were not involved in causing the crash in the Alma Tunnel, why were they monitoring the communications of Paris-based photo-agencies? Spooks do nothing for no reason – surveillance costs time and big money. Their operation was in full swing and any loose ends had to be tied up and eliminated. GCHQ has the technology to locate a transmission in the deserts of Australia if needs be but Paris is a soft target, right on the doorstep....

At approximately 23.45hrs on 31 August, the office of Big Pictures in west London was broken into, again by Metropolitan Police Special Branch 'enforcers', who appeared to be mysterious raiders. Lyons explains, "When I returned to the office that night at 00.30hrs with colleagues I found I couldn't turn on any of the lights. It seemed as though we had suffered a power cut but other offices in the same building and in other buildings nearby, remained alight, and the street lights were working. I heard an indistinct noise, like ticking, and thought a bomb was on the premises, so I told everyone to get out and called the police."

Lyons then told police that he was convinced that secret-service agents had raided his office and either searched the place and/or planted audio and video surveillance devices there. I have worked with Big Pictures several times in the past and I have experience of similar strange goings on in relation to matters of 'State'. I believe Darren Lyons to be a man not easily spooked and not prone to exaggeration either. Big Pictures, clearly, had a big let off. And yet his sudden memory loss at the quasi-inquest is something only Lyons can and should explain to the public....

Chapter 6
The Oxbridge Gang

In December 2003, Daily Mail journalist Sue Reid, with whom I have worked in the past investigating the 'suicide' of Dr David Kelly, quoted a source, who insisted on remaining anonymous, saying that Diana went to a leading London hospital, days before she joined Dodi on holiday, to undergo a pregnancy scan. The result is unknown and the test was conducted in the utmost secrecy.

But then Diana's self-confessed 'best friend' Rosa Monckton, claims that Diana menstruated only a week before the crash while they were on holiday in Greece. It is clear that Monckton believes she cannot be challenged on this issue but former MI6 officer Richard Tomlinson alleges that Rosa's husband, Dominic Lawson, former editor of the Sunday Telegraph newspaper and Spectator magazine, provided journalistic cover for MI6 officers while he was editor of the Spectator.

Rosa's brother, the Honourable Anthony Leopold Colyer Monckton, a diplomat, was also an MI6 spy according to Tomlinson. It should be noted that Dominic Lawson has never sued any publication or person for alleging he was an MI6 stringer. Dominic Lawson, is of course, the son of former Tory Chancellor Nigel Lawson and brother of famous TV 'kitchen goddess' Nigella Lawson. The very same Nigel Lawson who detested Mohamed Al Fayed for besmirching the Tories.

Tomlinson alleges that Dominic Lawson provided cover for an agent named ironically 'Spencer', who was put on the case of a young Russian diplomat, Pluton Obukhov, in Tallin, capital city of Estonia. In an excerpt from Tomlinson's 'banned' book (*The Big Breach*) published in Pravda, it was revealed that Spencer, returning from a visit to Information Operations (I/Ops), which plants stories or propaganda in the British press, remarked, "Flippin' outrageous. They've got the editor of the Spectator magazine on the books. He's called 'smallbrow'. He's agreed to le me go to Tallin undercover as a freelancer for his magazine. The only condition is that I have to write an article which he'll publish if he likes it' the cheeky bastard wants a story courtesy of the taxpayer."

The allegations that Dominic Lawson was a paid asset of MI6 have also been made in parliament but he has always denied ever having been an agent. How likely is it that he would admit it? Again, I reiterate that Lawson has brought no libel action against any publication alleging he was an MI6 asset, or a 'stringer' planted on newspapers by the spooks to further their covert propagandist agenda.

Rosa Monckton   Dominic Lawson

Other disturbing aspects of the unlikely 'friendship' between Diana and Rosa were raised by Paris-based journalist Jane Tawbase in a EuroBusiness investigation into Monckton and Lawson. She wrote: 'Rosa Monckton, a generation older, made an odd friend for the often unhappy princess. A svelte sophisticate and a wealthy working woman, her first relationships and loyalties lay, almost from when she was born, with the Queen. She was a regular visitor to the royal household all her life and was, for that reason, more given to loyalty to the crown than to an unhappy and disruptive outsider, one who was seriously damaging the public image of the royal family.'

On closer inspection, the relationship between Monckton and the 'disruptive' Diana, is somewhat inexplicable, perhaps very odd. Diana was a fashion goddess and fitness fanatic whose delighted in shopping and modern music. Monckton, by contrast, is a highly cerebral woman of the world, married to a man with links to MI6 that no journalist or newspaper editor should ever have.

Jane Tawbase also raises two further questions on this murky subject and throws more light on the matter than most before or after her. She wrote: 'Whether Rosa Monckton introduced her brother to the princess and whether he was part of the MI6 operation. It was almost unthinkable that he was not.'

In her second point she wrote: 'Did MI6 ask Rosa Monckton to do the key job of moving into the princess's inner circle and become her confidante? It would certainly have made the job easier.'

Dissident MI6 officer, Richard Tomlinson, who has been harassed for years by the French and British authorities, is certain that Monckton's brother is a spy. It should be noted that Anthony and Rosa's grandfather worked for Edward VIII and kept a close watch on him for the security services throughout the abdication and beyond.

Like Diana, the British Establishment were determined to rid themselves of Edward VIII. The Queen Mother, however, said that Diana was a greater threat to the monarchy than Wallis-Simpson and Edward VIII put together. Tawbase concludes that, 'It would indeed be ironic if history had repeated itself and Rosa Monckton performed the same role for MI6 with regard to Princess Diana.'

Richard Tomlinson, former MI6 officer, has offered up credible evidence of the involvement of British Intelligence in the death of Princess Diana. Consequently, he has been pilloried in the puppet press and harassed by the British State. If there is no truth in what he has said, why take such desperate measures to silence him?

In these circumstances, it is perhaps understandable that Rosa Monckton declared that Diana was not pregnant. It must also be noted that no one else can give witness to Monckton's suggestion that Diana menstruated while they holidayed in Greece, nor should her statement be regarded as fact, it is opinion. Monckton simply expects everyone to believe her version of events because she was Diana's 'friend'. And again, it must be stated that Diana abhorred everything to do with the State and was convinced that hired assassins were trying to kill her. It is puzzling why Diana formed a friendship with Monckton.

We must turn to the testimony of Richard Tomlinson, who has been deliberately ignored by the French authorities. His affidavit, reproduced below, to judge Herve Stephan was dismissed. Stephan showed no interest in Tomlinson's affidavit but the British certainly did and MI6 led a campaign of arrests and harassment against its dissident officer across the world to disrupt his life and attempt to silence him.

Affidavit of Richard Tomlinson

(to Judge Herve Stephan)

I, Richard John Charles Tomlinson, former MI6 officer, of Geneva, Switzerland hereby declare:

1. I firmly believe that there exist documents held by the British Secret Intelligence Service (MI6) that would yield important new evidence into the cause and circumstances leading to the deaths of the Princess of Wales, Mr Dodi Al Fayed, and M. Henri Paul in Paris in August 1997.

2. I was employed by MI6 between September 1991 and April 1995. During that time, I saw various documents that I believe would provide new evidence and new leads into the investigation into these deaths. I also heard various rumours, which though I was not able to see supporting documents I am confident were based on solid fact.

3. In 1992, I was working in the Eastern European Controllerate of MI6 and I was peripherally involved in a large and complicated operation to smuggle advanced Soviet weaponry out of the then disintegrating and disorganised remnants of the Soviet Union. During 1992, I spent several days reading the substantial files on this operation. These files contain a wide miscellany of contact notes, telegrams, intelligence reports, photographs etc, from which it was possible to build up a detailed understanding of the operation. The operation involved a large cast of officers and agents of MI6. On more than one occasion, meetings between various figures in the operation took place at the Ritz Hotel, Place de Vendome, Paris. There were in the file several intelligence reports on these meetings, which had been written by one of the MI6 officers based in Paris at the time (identified in the file only by a coded designation). The source of the information was an informant in the Ritz Hotel, who again was identified in the files only by a code number. The MI6 officer paid the informant in cash for his information. I became curious to learn more about the identity of this particular informant, because his number cropped up several times and he seemed to have extremely good access to the goings on in the Ritz Hotel. I therefore ordered this informant's personal file from MI6's central file registry. When I read this new file, I was not at all surprised to learn that the informant was a security officer of the Ritz Hotel. Intelligence services always target the security officers of important hotels because they have such good access to intelligence. I remember, however, being mildly surprised that the nationality of this informant was French, and this stuck in my memory, because it is rare that MI6 succeeds in recruiting a French informer. I cannot claim that I remember from this reading of the file that the name of this person was Henri Paul, but I have no doubt with the benefit of hindsight that this was he. Although I did not subsequently come across Henri Paul again during my time in MI6, I am confident that the relationship between he and MI6 would have continued until his death, because MI6 would never willingly relinquish control over such a well-placed informant. I am sure that the personal file of Henri Paul will therefore contain notes of meetings between him and his MI6 controlling officer right up until the point of his death. I firmly believe that these files will contain evidence of crucial importance to the circumstances and causes of the incident that killed M. Paul, together with the Princess of Wales and Dodi Al Fayed.

4. The most senior undeclared officer in the local MI6 station would normally control an informant of M. Paul's usefulness and seniority. Officers declared to the local counter-intelligence service (in this case the Directorate de Surveillance Territoire, or DST) would not be used to control such an informant, because it might lead to the identity of the informant becoming known to the local intelligence services. In Paris at the time of M Paul's death, there were two relatively experienced but undeclared MI6 officers. The first was <u>Mr Nicholas John Andrew LANGMAN</u>, born 1960. The second was Mr Richard David SPEARMAN, again born in 1960. I firmly believe that either one or both of these officers will be well acquainted with M Paul, and most probably also met M. Paul shortly before his death. I believe that either or both of these officers will have knowledge that will be of crucial importance in establishing the sequence of events leading up to the deaths of M. Paul, Dodi Al Fayed and the Princess of Wales. Mr Spearman in particular was an extremely well connected and influential officer, because he had been, prior to his appointment in Paris, the personal secretary to the Chief of MI6 Mr David Spedding. As such, he would have been privy to even the most confidential of MI6 operations. I believe that there may well be significance in the fact that Mr Spearman was posted to Paris in the month immediately before the deaths.

5. *Later in 1992, as the civil war in the former Yugoslavia became increasingly topical, I started to work primarily on operations in Serbia. During this time, I became acquainted with Dr Nicholas Bernard Frank Fishwick, born 1958, the MI6 officer who at the time was in charge of planning Balkan operations. During one meeting with Dr Fishwick, he casually showed to me a three-page document that on closer inspection turned out to be an outline plan to assassinate the Serbian leader President Slobodan Milosevic. The plan was fully typed, and attached to a yellow "minute board", signifying that this was a formal and accountable document. It will therefore still be in existence. Fishwick had annotated that the document be circulated to the following senior MI6 officers: Maurice Kendrick-Piercey, then head of Balkan operations, John Ridde, then the security officer for Balkan operations, the SAS liaison officer to MI6 (designation MODA/SO, but I have forgotten his name), the head of the Eastern European Controllerate (then Richard Fletcher) and finally Alan Petty, the personal secretary to the then Chief of MI6, Colin McColl. This plan contained a political justification for the assassination of Milosevic, followed by three outline proposals on how to achieve this objective. I firmly believe that the third of these scenarios contained information that could be useful in establishing the causes of death of Henri Paul, the Princess of Wales, and Dodi Al Fayed. This third scenario suggested that Milosevic could be assassinated by causing his personal limousine to crash. Dr Fishwick proposed to arrange the crash in a tunnel, because the proximity of concrete close to the road would ensure that the crash would be sufficiently violent to cause death or serious injury, and would also reduce the possibility that there might be independent, casual witnesses. Dr Fishwick suggested that one way to cause the crash might be to disorientate the chauffeur using a strobe flash gun, a device which is occasionally deployed by special forces to, for example, disorientate helicopter pilots or terrorists, and about which MI6 officers are briefed about during their training. In short, this scenario bore remarkable similarities to the circumstances and witness accounts of the crash that killed the Princess of Wales, Dodi Al Fayed, and Henri Paul. I firmly believe that this document should be yielded by MI6 to the Judge investigating these deaths, and would provide further leads that he could follow.*

6. *During my service in MI6, I also learnt unofficially and second-hand something of the links between MI6 and the Royal Household. MI6 are frequently and routinely asked by the Royal Household (usually via the Foreign Office) to provide intelligence on potential threats to members of the Royal Family whilst on overseas trips. This service would frequently extend to asking friendly intelligence services (such as the CIA) to place members of the Royal Family under discrete surveillance, ostensibly for their own protection. This was particularly the case for the Princess of Wales, who often insisted on doing without overt*

personal protection, even on overseas trips. Although contact between MI6 and the Royal Household was officially only via the Foreign Office, I learnt while in MI6 that there was unofficial direct contact between certain senior and influential MI6 officers and senior members of the Royal Household. I did not see any official papers on this subject, but I am confident that the information is correct. I firmly believe that MI6 documents would yield substantial leads on the nature of their links with the Royal Household, and would yield vital information about MI6 surveillance on the Princess of Wales in the days leading to her death.

7. I also learnt while in MI6 that one of the 'paparazzi' photographers who routinely followed the Princess of Wales was a member of "UKN", a small corps of part-time MI6 agents who provide miscellaneous services to MI6 such as surveillance and photography expertise. I do not know the identity of this photographer, or whether he was one of the photographers present at the time of the fatal incident. However, I am confident that examination of UKN records would yield the identity of this photographer, and would enable the inquest to eliminate or further investigate that potential line of enquiry.

8. On Friday, 28 August 998, I gave much of this information to Judge Herve Stephan, the French investigative Judge in charge of the inquest into the accident. The lengths, which MI6, the CIA and the DST have taken to deter me giving this evidence and subsequently to stop me talking about it, suggests that they have something to hide.

9. On Friday, 31 July 1998, shortly before my appointment with Judge Herve Stephan, the DST arrested me in my Paris hotel room. Although I have no record of violent conduct I was arrested with such ferocity and at gunpoint that I received a broken rib. I was taken to the headquarters of the DST, and interrogated for 38 hours. Despite my repeated requests, I was never given any justification for the arrest and was not shown the arrest warrant. Even though I was released without charge, the DST confiscated from me my laptop computer and Psion organiser. They illegally gave these to MI6 who took them back to the UK. They were not returned for six months, which is illegal and caused me great inconvenience and financial cost.

10. On Friday 7th August 1998 I boarded a Qantas flight at Auckland International airport, New Zealand, for a flight to Sydney, Australia where I was due to give a television interview to the Australian Channel Nine television company. I was in my seat, awaiting take off, when an official boarded the plane and told me to get off. At the airbridge, he told me that the airline had received a fax "from Canberra" saying that there was a problem with my travel papers. I immediately asked to see the fax, but I was told that "it was not

possible". I believe that this is because it didn't exist. This action was a ploy to keep me in New Zealand so that the New Zealand police could take further action against me. I had been back in my Auckland hotel room for about half an hour when the New Zealand police and NZSIS, the New Zealand Secret Intelligence Service, raided me. After being detained and searched for about three hours, they eventually confiscated from me all my remaining computer equipment that the French DST had not succeeded in taking from me. Again, I didn't get some of these items back until six months later.

11. Moreover, shortly after I had given this evidence to Judge Stephan, I was invited to talk about this evidence in a live television interview on America's NBC television channel. I flew from Geneva to JFK airport on Sunday 30 August to give the interview in New York on the following Monday morning. Shortly after arrival at John F Kennedy airport, the captain of the Swiss Air flight told all passengers to return to their seats. Four US Immigration authority officers entered the plane, came straight to my seat, asked for my passport and identity, and then frogmarched me off the plane. I was taken to the immigration detention centre, photographed, fingerprinted, manacled by my ankle to a chair for seven hours, served with deportation papers (exhibit 1) and then returned on the next available plane to Geneva. I was not allowed to make any telephone calls to the representatives of NBC awaiting me in the airport. The US Immigration Officers – who were all openly sympathetic to my situation and apologised for treating me so badly – openly admitted that they were acting under instructions from the CIA.

12. In January of this year, I booked a chalet in the village of Samoens in the French Alps for a ten day snowboarding holiday with my parents. I picked up my parents from Geneva airport in a hire car on the evening of 8 January, and set off for the French border. At the French customs post, our car was stopped and I was detained. Four officers from the DST held me for four hours. At the end of this interview, I was served with the deportation papers below (exhibit 2), and ordered to return to Switzerland. Note that in the papers, my supposed destination has been changed from "Chamonix" to "Samoens". This is because when first questioned by a junior DST officer, I told him that my destination was "Chamonix". When a senior officer arrived an hour or so later, he crossed out the word and changed it to "Samoens", without ever even asking or confirming this with me. I believe this is because MI6 had told them of my true destination, having learnt the information through surveillance on my parent's telephone in the UK. My banning from France is entirely illegal under European law. I have a British passport and am entitled to travel freely within the European Union. MI6 have "done a deal" with the DST to have me banned, and have not used any recognised legal mechanism to deny my rights to freedom of travel. I

believe that the DST and MI6 have banned me from France because they wanted to prevent me from giving further evidence to Judge Stephan's inquest, which at the time, I was planning to do.

13. Whatever MI6's role in the events leading to the death of the Princess of Wales, Dodi Al Fayed and Henri Paul, I am absolutely certain that there is substantial evidence in their files that would provide crucial evidence in establishing the exact causes of this tragedy. I believe that they have gone to considerable lengths to obstruct the course of justice by interfering with my freedom of speech and travel, and this in my view confirms my belief that they have something to hide. I believe that the protection given to MI6 files under the Official Secrets Act should be set aside in the public interest in uncovering once and for all the truth behind these dramatic and historically momentous events.

[The above testimony was made to the French inquiry into Princess Diana's death, headed by Judge Herve Stephan and subsequently ignored by both the inquiry itself and the Establishment's puppet media. Since testifying, Britain's security establishment has hounded Tomlinson to the point where he now lives in virtual exile in Cannes, France. The embattled former spook has not entirely disappeared and now keeps a weblog detailing his ongoing skirmishes with both French and British authorities. But on 8 March 2007, three days after the pre-Inquest hearing at the High Court, his weblog was again taken down by MI6, desperate to prevent him testifying at the Inquest.]

Tomlinson also revealed that during his time with MI6, he learned that there was an informal but direct link between certain MI6 officers of senior rank and royal courtiers. St James's Palace and Buckingham Palace are easy access points for the spooks through the back-channel process. Many of these 'men' share an Oxbridge background with royal courtiers and the relationship continues for life. They would all have known of the CIA eavesdropping operation against Diana and certainly shared the 'product'.

In the Paget Report, Sir John Stevens alleges that MI6 and MI5 were not aware of the CIA operation. Indeed, he salaciously goes as far to say that the CIA were only interested in Diana's 'contacts' and prime among which were Mohamed Al Fayed and his murdered son Dodi Fayed. By definition, if the CIA were watching Diana's contacts, then Diana was also being watched. Obviously, Sir John Stevens, the faithful Establishment plod, knows this but at the same time, he must presume the general public to be completely stupid. His tale is defeated with elementary logic.

British intelligence certainly would have been told of the

surveillance operation on Diana and her contacts and highly likely also, they would have been given access to the product of the eavesdropping. It is also perfectly cleat to anyone with experience of modern surveillance that Diana would have been tracked through the signal from her mobile phone. Such signals allow the target to be pinpointed to within a metre of their location. The same is also true of Dodi Fayed, Wingfield, Rees-Jones and Henri Paul etc.

As a 'reward' for his indiscretions, Tomlinson was arrested at gunpoint by the French DST (Direction de la Surveillance du Territoire) at his home. He suffered a broken rib in the operation against him despite the fact that he has no record of violence. The DST agents were ordered to go in hard to teach him a lesson. The whole arrest was designed to shake him to the core and think better of opening his mouth in future. And this is an interesting point which requires further analysis.

By their very nature, 'fantasists' or people who make things up, are ignored, not arrested at gunpoint and violently assaulted. Again, if Tomlinson was at least mistaken, or indeed lying about the matters he revealed, there would have been no need to arrest him and he could simply have been dismissed as a former employee with a furtive imagination. The fact he was arrested in such brutal fashion, proves that Tomlinson has revealed too many truths that powerful people would prefer to remain hidden. It is also noteworthy that Tomlinson has not been accused of being a 'conspiracy theorist' by his detractors.

In the event, Tomlinson was questioned for over eighteen hours at the Paris HQ of the DST to discourage him from giving evidence to the Stephan inquiry. But he did appear before Stephan and told him, **"As long as they [MI6] can get away with doing something then that's their only limit about what they will do. This includes assassination."**

Diana's decision to embrace Islam and highly likely produce a mixed-race brother or sister to the heirs to the throne of England, and her anti-landmines campaign were enough to warrant her elimination. But there is more still in the shape of the 'secrets' she held in her little box of treasures at Kensington Palace.

Paul Burrell, often referred to as 'Diana's rock' was aware of the box and most if not all of its contents. Following his arrest on the grounds that he unlawfully took over 300 items from Kensington Palace, after the princess's funeral, he was interrogated again and again by Scotland Yard detectives, who shook him up quite badly but failed to break him.

In his book *A Royal Duty*, he relates his experience of the arrest and what the political police were looking for: 'Then DS Milburn asked me two bizarre questions: **"Do you have a manuscript of the memoirs you are writing?"** If there was one moment when I knew the officers were stabbing in the dark, that was it. No such manuscript existed.'

Burrell then explains the events of the following morning: 'The next morning, DS Roger Milburn returned. On instructions from Andrew Shaw, I said nothing to his volley of questions. **Again, his curiosity seemed to focus more on the contents of a box, sensitive paperwork and a manuscript.'**

Burrell's trial was a landmine for the monarchy and they Queen could not risk her former butler, revealing some of what he saw. In open court, just before the trial collapsed, a truly revealing encounter took place that gave the world some insight of what was in Diana's box of treasures.

Burrell wrote: 'The full picture emerged with the judge's approval. Scotland Yard was looking for a signet ring given to the princess by Major James Hewitt; a resignation letter from her private secretary Patrick Jephson; **letters from Prince Philip to the princess; and a tape, which became known after the trial as the Rape Tape.**

It was a recording made by the princess in 1996 when she informally interviewed former KP orderly and ex-Welsh Guardsman George Smith. He had alleged that after a night of heavy drinking he had been raped in 1989 by a male member of staff who worked for Prince Charles. It all came to a head because George who had worked at Highgrove, St James's Palace and KP, had been suffering nightmares, was drinking heavily, and his marriage was falling apart. He blamed it all on an incident that he said he was bottling up.'

'The princess knew the member of staff in question. From that moment on she loathed him. "I know what that evil bugger did. I know what he did to George, and I will never forgive him for that," she seethed, after her futile attempts to bring about justice. He [George Smith] never returned to work, and accepted a settlement [Fiona Shackleton] at the end of his employment of around £40,000.'

'The princess ensured that the tape never saw the light of day. But the mystery of its whereabouts, and the threat its contents posed, emerged during the police investigation of my case. Lady Sarah McCorquodale had asked that Scotland Yard 'ascertain' the contents of the box. In court, DS Milburn said: "**I was looking for the contents of that box. All of a sudden, the undertones behind the raid on my home became clear.'**

As the trial wore on it was obvious Burrell would have to take the stand. The prospect of 'Diana's rock' hurling highly explosive stones at the British Establishment was enough to prompt the Queen to recall a conversation she had with Burrell in December 1997 at Buckingham Palace in which Burrell told her that he was taking a number of the princess's items into safekeeping.

The exchange was a chilling encounter for Burrell. He wrote of it: 'As the meeting neared its end, the Queen said one more thing to me. Looking over her half-rimmed spectacles, she said: **"Be careful, Paul. No one has been as close to a member of my family as you have. There are 'powers' at work in this country about which we have no knowledge,'** and she fixed me with a stare where her eyes made clear the **'do you understand?'.**

'She [Queen] **might have been referring to the domestic intelligence service MI5 because, have no doubt, the Queen does not know of its secret work and 'darker practices' but she is aware of the power it is capable of wielding. Like the royal household, the intelligence services are given carte blanche to act in whatever way is considered to be in the best interests of state and monarchy.'**

'At my December 1997 meeting with the Queen and as my statement had made clear: '**I feared at the time of the princess's death that there was a conspiracy to change the course of history, and erase certain parts of her life from it.** Mrs Frances Shand Kydd spent two weeks shredding personal correspondence and documents.'

Piers Morgan in his own memoir, *The Insider*, explains that he tried to help Burrell and have the quasi-case against him dropped, he wrote: -

17 January 2001 - I rang Mark Bolland at the Palace.
'You guys are mad, Mark. Burrell could say anything in the stand.'
'I know, I know,' he replied despondently.
'It's a mess.'
'Well, end it now, before it's too late.'
'We can't, the police are running the case now.'

A cornered Burrell could be a very dangerous beast. This will go on for weeks, and can only be damaging to the Royal Family. They must be mad allowing Burrell to potentially take the stand. Cornered and desperate, he might say anything, and he knows the lot because he was there. There's also no way he stole Diana's stuff, anyone who knows him knows that. He could make more money from what's in his mind than he ever could from a few of her trinkets.'

Paul Burrell at the launch of his bestselling memoir A Royal Duty. In the book he confesses, **'In writing this book, I continued to protect the darkest, most intimate secrets.'**

The Establishment were again courting disaster by trying to silence Burrell. In reality, the tactic worked in reverse, virtually ensuring that Burrell, facing five years in prison if convicted, would open up before the glaring eyes of the world to save his own skin.

By 16th September 1997, bodyguard Trevor Rees-Jones had opened his eyes. The worry for the British Establishment was the strong possibility that he would remember what happened in the moments before the Mercedes crashed. Rees-Jones can certainly remember fastening his seatbelt just seconds before the car crashed but claims that he cannot remember anything after that. But again, further clarification comes in the shape of Piers Morgan and his memoir *The Insider*.

Morgan wrote: *'Tuesday, 16th September 1997 – I had a brief chat with Fayed today and he said that Rees-Jones is awake, and having flashbacks of the crash. 'Can we have the first interview? Fayed was anxious. 'He needs to tell us what happened first, that is the most important thing. Then perhaps he can talk to you. But we must be careful Piers, he is in a very bad way.'*

Naturally, Rees-Jones, who suffered terrible injuries, claims that he can remember nothing. Can he remember coming round in the hospital in the presence of Al Fayed and having 'flashbacks of the crash'? I do not wish to be offensive to Rees-Jones, particularly given the injuries he suffered, but I do not think his story holds up in the slightest under examination. He can remember some things but not others, selective memory loss not amnesia....

For instance, Rees-Jones can remember leaving the Ritz Hotel on the rue Cambon and that a white Fiat Uno was tailing them. He then recounts that he saw a white Fiat Uno again on the approach the Alma Tunnel. He also recalls that he fastened his seatbelt and encouraged the others to do the same moments before impact. At the very moment he fastened his seatbelt, the white Fiat Uno was careering into the path of the Mercedes but Rees-Jones does not remember that.

His memory falls apart when it comes to events in the Alma Tunnel. He can remember belting up, not verbally at that time, but cannot remember seeing the white Fiat Uno in the tunnel nor a blinding white flash. If he can remember fastening his seatbelt, he can remember what happened in the very next seconds involving the white Fiat Uno and the blinding flash of light and the escaping motorbike.

It is little wonder that the majority of people do not believe Rees-Jones. I will go further and state that he is lying about not being able to remember the juicy bits, the crucial events immediately before the Mercedes crashed. Either that, or he has made it all up about seeing a white Fiat Uno and fastening his seatbelt and encouraging the others to do the same. But then why would he do that?

This man wants his cake and to eat it but the majority of people do not swallow his version of events. Rumours are rife in the media world that Rees-Jones has been threatened by British intelligence. If he opens his mouth and suddenly remembers what happened in the crucial seconds to impact, he might not be so lucky a second time. Rees-Jones is also still subject to the Official Secrets Act and government lawyers can make that mean whatever they want it to mean.

I have signed the Official Secrets Act and could, in theory, be prosecuted under the OSA for revealing anything the State wanted kept secret. Theoretically, the OSA should apply only to the period one was in service but the strictures of the Act apply for the rest on one's life and Rees-Jones knows this only too well. He has however played the sympathy ticket for all its worth and been protected to the hilt by the British Establishment. Although no one should be surprised by this 'protection' because Rees-Jones is an asset and providing he goes on changing his story to confuse people, his 'protection' will remain intact.

There is also the fact that in Northern Ireland, Rees-Jones, a former paratrooper with experience of putting enemy targets under surveillance, worked closely at times with British Army intelligence and he will know only too well what the Force Research Unit, MI6 and The Increment are capable of. On his testimony that he cannot remember the vital seconds before I impact, Rees-Jones should not be believed. The claim is that he suffers from amnesia, only in part mind you, and that we should have sympathy for him.

I sympathise with the fact that he suffered terrible injuries in the crash but one must remain logical and rational and not succumb to emotional impulses. In his book, The Bodyguard's Story, he repeats the same old tale, over and over again: he cannot remember the 'juicy bits' but has no problem dishing out all the old crumbs of information he wants us to know. And I know people in the media world, who are certain that Rees-Jones has been silenced by British intelligence and I have come to share this view.

An important note to end this chapter on, comes in the form of a quote from former MI6 officer, Richard Tomlinson: **"There is an arrogant faction in MI6, part of the Oxbridge clique, which doesn't try to hide dedication to the royal family and their self-appointment as defenders of the realm."** And spooks excel at the lying game, as par for the course of their 'training' and ethics by prerequisite, are irrelevant.

In the selection process for MI5 and MI6, applicants are asked if they have moral qualms about doing 'certain things' to enemies of the State. If the applicant answers 'yes' and demonstrates a strong degree of morality and principle, that applicant is eliminated from the recruitment process. The unassailable fact proves nothing that emanates from the British Intelligence community can be believed. A fact redoubled by the appalling concoction of 'evidence' by MI6 with Alastair Campbell and Tony Blair to 'justify' the illegal invasion of Iraq in 2003.

The 'dodgy dossier' as it has come to be known, would certainly sparked opposition from Princess Diana, particularly if she had married Muslim Dodi Fayed. But with Diana dead and buried, the principle opposition to the illegal war from official quarters came from Dr David Kelly, who apparently committed 'suicide' because he could not cope with the 'strain' of telling the truth about the 'dodgy dossier' and exposing the lies of the New Labour criminal gang.

The message is perfectly clear that any statement coming from British Intelligence must be dismissed as pure fantasy in whole or at least in part. At the quasi-inquest, former MI6 Controller Sir Richard Dearlove said MI6 had a licence to kill but had not used it for decades. Obviously, the key players or prime malefactors in the secret dirty war in Northern Ireland would be able to tell a different story and indeed many have done just that.

But those who have told the truth have disappeared off the scene, been murdered, committed 'suicide' under strain or been harassed into silence. Journalists who have 'dared' to cover the sinister activities of British Intelligence in Ulster have also been intimidated and harassed and bullied into silence. Liam Clarke at The Sunday Times is arguably the best example of this State-sponsored hate campaign. The overriding message is that the British Establishment are the biggest organised criminal gang in the UK and Mohammed Al Fayed never stood a chance of beating them.

Chapter 7

French Farce

Final report by Paris prosecutor's office
Diana crash inquiry report

Examining Magistrate:
Mr Hervé STEPHAN
Ms Christine DEVIDAL

Substitute:
Ms Maud MOREL COUJARD

COURT OF THE FIRST INSTANCE

Public Prosecutor of the French Republic

Dept. : P5 GENERAL CRIMINAL LAW
No. of entry: GG
No. of case: 97 245 3009/9
No. of preliminary investigation: 65/97

PUBLIC PROSECUTOR'S LEGALLY BINDING JUDGEMENT OF NO GROUNDS FOR PROSECUTION

The Public Prosecutor of the French Republic, at the court of the First Instance,

Having examined the following enquiry against:

1) ARNAL Serge
D.O.B. 10th August 1961 in PARIS 12th district
Parents: Elie and Suzanne GENTILLET
Nationality: French
Freelance Photographer
Residing at:

Charged: 2nd September 1997 (D796)
Placed in custody: 02/09/97 to 21/10/97

2) ARSOV Nikola
D.O.B. 20th April 1959 in SKOPJE (Yugoslavia)
Parents: Jordan and Ladjdovska ARSOV
Photographer
Residing at:

Charged: 2nd September 1997 (D797)

3) DARMON Stéphane
D.O.B. 27th May 1965 in PARIS 1st district
Parents: André and Suzy GUEZ
Messenger
Residing at:

Charged: 2nd September 1997 (D806)
Placed in custody: 02/09/97 to 21/10/97

4) LANGEVIN Jacques
D.O.B. 21st September 1953 in LAVAL (MAYENNE)
Parents: Marcel and Georgette AGUILLE
Freelance photographer
Residing at:

Charged: 2nd September 1997 (D803)
Placed in custody: 02/09/97 to 13/10/97

5) MARTINEZ Christian
D.O.B. 15th May 1954 in PARIS 12th district
Parents: François and Jeanine MORAND
Press photographer
Residing at:

Charged: 2nd September 1997 (D813)
FREE SUBJECT TO LEGAL RESTRICTIONS PENDING TRIAL
Date of order: 2nd September 1997

6) RAT Romuald
D.O.B. 17th September 1971 in LE RAINCY (SEINE SAINT DENIS)
Parents: Michel and Marie-France GAUTREAU
Photographer
Residing at:

Charged: 2nd September 1997 (D809)
FREE SUBJECT TO LEGAL RESTRICTIONS PENDING TRIAL
Date of order: 2nd September 1997

7) VERES Laslo
D.O.B. 1st December 1943 in BECEJ (Yugoslavia)
Parents: Pal and Ilona SABO
Photographer
Residing at:

Charged: 2nd September 1997 (D800)

8) ODEKERKEN David
D.O.B. 8th March 1971 in CRETEUIL (94)
Parents: Jean and Josiane DEBUYSERE
Freelance photographer
Residing at:

FREE SUBJECT TO LEGAL RESTRICTIONS PENDING TRIAL
Date of order: 2nd September 1997

9) CHASSERY Fabrice
D.O.B. 16th March 1967 in PARIS 12th district
Parents: Jean and Nicole PETON
Freelance photographer
Residing at:

Charged: 5th September 1997 (D1299)
FREE SUBJECT TO LEGAL RESTRICTIONS PENDING TRIAL
Date of order: 5th September 1997

10) BENAMOU Serge
D.O.B. 15th September 1953 in SAIDA (Algeria)
Parents: Paul and Charlotte BENSOUSSAN
Photo-journalist
Residing at:

Charged: 5th September 1997 (D1305)
Placed in custody: 05/09/97 to 22/10/97

Under investigation charged with:

failing to assist people in danger
involuntary homicide involuntary injury,
ITT more than three months

Public Prosecutor's charge of 2nd September 1997 (D792)

PLAINTIFFS

Mr Jean PAUL
Mrs Jean PAUL
represented by : Mr Jean Pierre BRIZAY

Mr Mohammed AL FAYED

represented by: Mr Bernard DARTEVELLE and MR Georges KIEJMAN

Mrs Francis SHAND-KYDD
Mrs Sarah MC CORQUODALE
represented by: Mr Alain TOUCAS

Mr Trevor REES JONES
represented by : Mr Christian CURTIL

WHEREAS THE ENQUIRY HAS ESTABLISHED THE FOLLOWING FACTS:

Initial Findings

(D706 –D709)
At 0.26 hrs on August 31, 1997, the switchboard at Paris fire brigade headquarters received a code-18 emergency call informing them of a serious traffic accident in the Pont d'Alma tunnel in Paris's 8th arrondissement.

(D55)
A few minutes later, a police patrol on Cours Albert 1er consisting of officers Lino GAGLIADORNE and Sebastian DORZEE, patrolling Cours Albert 1er, was told of the accident by passers by and made their way to the scene.

The first Paris fire brigade crew arrived at the scene at 0.32 hrs.

Inside the tunnel, in the Concorde-Boulogne lane, police and rescue services discovered a black Mercedes vehicle, type S280, registration number 680 LTV75. The vehicle was badly damaged and had come to rest against the outer wall of the tunnel, facing in the opposite direction to the normal flow of traffic.

Four people were found inside the vehicle

- Lady Diana SPENCER, who had been sitting in the rear right passenger seat, was still conscious and crouched on the floor of the vehicle with her back to the road.

- At her side, stretched out on the rear seat, was Emad AL FAYED, who had been sitting in the rear left passenger seat and appeared to be dead. Nevertheless, fire officers were still trying – in vain – to resuscitate him when he was pronounced dead by a doctor at 1.30hrs.

- In the front of the vehicle was the driver, Henri PAUL, the deputy security manager at the Ritz hotel, who had been killed immediately and was declared dead on removal from the wreckage.

- The front passenger was Trevor REES JONES, a body guard in the employment of the Al FAYED family, who was still conscious and had suffered serious multiple injuries to the face.

The two forward passengers' airbags had functioned normally.

Three people attended to the casualties: Dr Frédéric MAILLEZ, a doctor with "SOS Médécin", and two volunteer fire officers, Dominique DALBY and a second who is unnamed. All three had been driving in the opposite direction, and on seeing the wrecked car, had stopped to go spontaneously to the aid of its occupants.

In the tunnel, among the onlookers who had gathered around the vehicle, several photographers were in action.

(D1602 – D1606)
The two police officers, GAGLIARDONE and DORZEE, had trouble keeping the onlookers at bay in order to secure the scene and all the first witnesses reported that the photographers, who had arrived at the scene almost immediately, had pushed around the vehicle for the sole purpose of taking pictures of the casualties.

Autopsy Conclusions

(D789 – D6858)
Autopsy examination concluded that Henri PAUL and Emad AL FAYED had both suffered a rupture in the isthmus of the aorta and a fractured spine, with, in the case of Henri PAUL, a medullar section in the dorsal region and in the case of Emad AL FAYED a medullar section in the cervical region.

(D6833 – D6821)
Lady Diana Spencer received pre-hospital intensive care treatment, both while she was trapped in the wreckage, from which she was finally released at 1am, and during her transfer by ambulance, until her arrival at Pitié-Salpêtrière hospital at   2.06hrs.

However, despite intensive surgical intervention, doctors had no option but to declare her dead at 4am.

The report submitted by professors Dominique LECOMTE and Andre LIENHART concluded that the cause of death was a wound to the upper left pulmonary vein, together with a rupture to the pericardium. The experts believed that it was exceptional for a patient who had suffered such serious intra-thoracic lesions to reach hospital alive, resuscitation had been in accordance with pre-hospitalisation regulations. According to the experts, the surgical team was beyond reproach, and no other surgical, anaesthetic or resuscitation strategy could have prevented deterioration in the condition of the patient.

(D6833)
The same experts pointed to the obviously traumatic origin of the injuries to the three victims, stating that those suffered by the first two were frequently observed in severe crash cases, head-on with extreme deceleration, while those to Lady Diana SPENCER were more unusual and could probably be explained by the victim's sideways position at the moment of impact.

The opening of the enquiry ....

The Paris Prosecution Department, which immediately sent a representative to the scene, entrusted the enquiry of the case to the Paris police crime squad. It is in these conditions that several press photographers: Christian MARTINEZ, from the Angely Agency, Romuald RAT from the Gamma Agency, Stéphane DARMON, his companion, Jacques LANGEVIN, from the Sygma Agency, Serge ARNAL, from the Steels Press Agency, Laslo VERES, independent photographer and Nikola ARSOV, from the Sipa Presse, were taken in for questioning because of their attitude at the scene.

(D792)
By Public Prosecutor's charge dated 2nd September 1997, the Paris Prosecution Department asked for an enquiry to be opened against the above named for failing to give assistance to persons in danger and, against unnamed person, for homicide and involuntary injury.

(D796 - D797 - D800 - D803 - D809 - D813)
However the examining magistrate named to lead these proceeding put under investigation all the people who were brought before him for all the charges listed in the initial charge.

(D1299 - D1302 - D1305)

As three photographers had left the scene before the police arrived, Fabrice CHASSERY, David ODEKERKEN and Serge BENAMOU, all independent photographers, reported to the crime squad offices on 4th September 1997 and, on 5th September 1997, were put under investigation for the same charges by the investigating magistrate.

The paths explored by the enquiry:

-The enquiry, which was finally entrusted to two examining magistrates by the Presiding Judge of the Court of Paris, because of the extent and complexity of the investigations to be carried out, was going to clarify the context in which the photographers had followed the Mercedes in which the couple were travelling and the affect of their presence on the behaviour of the driver of the vehicle immediately before the accident.

-In addition, the preliminary investigation file had to identify and examine the attitude adopted by these same photographers in the moments which immediately preceded the accident.

-The enquiry was also going to look into the conditions in which Henri PAUL had taken the wheel of the Mercedes carrying the couple on the evening of 31st August 1997

(D816 - D828 -D1329 - D1332 - D1342 - D1519 - D1522 - D1524)

On this particular point, numerous experts' reports examined following the autopsy on the body of Henri PAUL rapidly showed the presence of a level of pure alcohol per litre of blood of between 1.73 and 1.75 grams, which is far superior, in all cases, than the legal level.

Similarly, these analyses revealed as those carried out on samples of the hair and bone marrow of the deceased, that he regularly consumed Prozac and Tiapridal, both medicines which are not recommended for drivers, as they provoke a change in the ability to be vigilant, particularly when they are taken in combination with alcohol.

(D1514)

Finally, the amount of transferring in the blood showed a level of 32 UI/l [?], compatible, according to the experts with a chronic alcoholism over the course of at least a week.

-       Finally the investigations which were carried out both at the scene and on the vehicle itself, allowed for the hypothesis of a possible collision with another vehicle.

(D5433 to D5829 - D5969)
The Mercedes S280, in which the passengers were found, belonged to the company Etoile Limousine and had been hired by this company to the Ritz hotel, its only client. It was examined by the experts from the Institut de Recherche Criminelle de la Gendarmerie Nationale (I.R.C.G.N.), then by NIBODEAU-FRINDEL and AMOUROUX, the experts commissioned by the examining magistrates, who all concluded that it had a low mileage and was in perfect mechanical and working order.

(D1023)
Jean-François MUSA, manager of Etoile Limousine, confirmed that, on 31st August, it did not have any trace of accidental damage or scratches.

(D1372-D1835)
Now the investigations showed traces of whitish colour both on the front right wing and on the body of the right wing mirror, found further on in the tunnel.

The additional research carried out by I.R.C.G.N. showed traces, both on the front right wing and on the body of the wing mirror, which came from the same vehicle, whose technical characteristics corresponded to a vehicle make Fiat "Uno", white in colour, built in Italy in the period 1983 to the end of August 1987.

(D1506)
In addition, some red and white optical debris found on the right hand lane, 7 or 8 metres from the entrance to the Alma tunnel were described as also coming from a rear light of a vehicle make Fiat "Uno", built in Italy in the period May 1983 to September 1989.

The arrival in Paris of the couple Diana SPENCER and Emad AL FAYED:

The arrival of the couple in Paris and their movements during the day of 30th August 1997 mobilised a growing number of press photographers.

Lady Diana SPENCER, Princess of Wales, and her friend, Emad AL FAYED, had landed at Le Bourget airport in the morning of the 30th August 1997 from Sardinia, at the end of a Mediterranean cruise, where they had been followed by a great number of the world's press.

The couple were accompanied by two English bodyguards, employed by the private security of the AL FAYED family, Trevor REES JONES and Alexander WINGFIELD.

Two vehicles were waiting for them, a Range Rover which was driven by Henri PAUL, deputy security manager of the Ritz hotel, owned by the father of Emad AL FAYED, Mohammed AL FAYED, and a Mercedes 600, driven by Philippe DOURNEAU, Mohammed AL FAYED's official driver when he was in France.

The Princess had not advised the British Embassy of her presence in France and had not requested any particular protection from the French authorities.

The press was present from their arrival: at the airport were: Fabrice CHASSERY, at the wheel of a charcoal grey Peugeot 205, registration no. 5816 WJ 92, David ODEKERKEN was driving a beige Mitsubishi "Pajero" 4/4, registration no.520 LPZ75, Romuald RAT and his driver, Stéphane DARMON, on a dark blue Honda motorcycle, registration no. 302 LXT75 and Alain GUIZARD, from the Angely Agency, was in a grey-blue Peugeot 205, registration no.3904 ZR 92, accompanied by three press motorcyclists from the same agency.

After a detour to one of the residences of the AL FAYED family, the Windsor villa, situated on the Bois de Boulogne, Lady Diana SPENCER and Emad AL FAYED went to the Ritz hotel.

(D1043 - D2473 -D1052)
During the different journeys, the photographers ended up losing sight of the vehicles and only Alexander WINGFIELD recalled the dangerous behaviour of some of them on the road. Trevor REES JONES and Philippe DOURNEAU, on the other hand, testified that the photographers had always remained behind the Range Rover.

At about 18.00hrs the couple, still in the Mercedes driven by Philippe DOURNEAU, returned to the AL FAYED family hotel, rue Arsène Houssaye, very close to the Arc de Triomphe, while Jean-François MUSA replaced Henri PAUL at the wheel of the Range Rover.

(D2020)
Numerous photographers had again started to follow them at that moment, and, according to Trevor REES JONES, he had asked them not to take photos during the journey, a request which they respected.

(D2173 - D2178 - D1043 - D2020 - D1633)
However there were still more of them as the couple's car turned into rue Arsène Houssaye, and there was then a jostling, followed by an incident between Romuald RAT and the security personnel, an incident

which was quickly resolved by the intervention of Trevor REES JONES and Alexander WINGFIELD.

As well as the photographers who were already present since Le Bourget, there were in front of the building in the rue Arsène Houssaye, Serge BENAMOU and Lalso VERES, who were both riding their scooters, as well as Christian MARTINEZ and Serge ARNAL , who had come in the latter's car, a Fiat black "UNO", registration no. 444 JNB 75.

(D2161)
During this time Henri PAUL, who was not on duty that evening, had left the Ritz hotel at about 19.00hrs, telling the security guard, François TENDIL, that he could always be reached on his mobile telephone.

(D5150)
Claude ROULET, the assistant of Franck Klein, the manager of the Ritz hotel, who was not in Paris at that time, had, at the request of Emad AL FAYED, reserved a table for the couple in a restaurant in the capital, where he had gone to wait for them.

He cancelled this reservation at about 21.00, as Emad AL FAYED informed him that, because of the crowds of journalists they were dining at the Ritz, in the hope of getting some more peace.

Despite these precautions, when the Mercedes and the Range Rover arrived at Place Vendôme, the photographers had followed them from the rue Arsène Houssaye, and in front of the hotel there was a big crowds of curious onlookers and journalists.

As the couple left their vehicle belatedly there was a crush at the moment when they entered the hotel.

(D1043 – D5073)
This situation annoyed Emad AL FAYED, as testified by Trevor REES JONES and Alexander WINGFIELD, who added that, not being made aware of the change of programme until the journey to the Ritz, they were unable to anticipate the difficulties.

(D2473)
Trevor REES JONES even stated: *"Dodi took an active part in security arrangements, he was the boss and in addition we did not know the programme in advance, only he knew the programme."*

(D2136)
Henri PAUL was informed of the incident by François TENDIL, who took

the initiative to return to the hotel, where he reported at 22.07 hrs, as seen by the hotel surveillance camera.

(D2193)
Then he joined the two English body guards at the bar where he consumed two glasses of "Ricard".

The change in the programme: the diversionary tactics decide by Emad AL FAYED:

(D2136)
As soon as he arrived at the Ritz, Emad AL FAYED, for his part, called Thierry ROCHER, the night manager of the hotel to inform him of the situation.

Learning from the latter that Henri PAUL had returned, he asked him to tell him that they needed a third vehicle, placed in rue Cambon, at the back of the building, to return to rue Arsène Houssaye, and that the two vehicles used by the couple during the day would stay in Place Vendôme to create a diversion.

(D1043 - D5073 - D2473)
Trevor REES JONES and Alexander WINGFIELD confirmed that the decision to use a third vehicle had been taken by Emad AL FAYED and that it was he who had asked Henri PAUL to drive it.

Emad AL FAYED had in addition stipulated that Trevor REES JONES should accompany them.

The two bodyguards explained that they had expressed their disagreement with these arrangements, but only in as far as they were to separate.

None of them, however expressed any reservations on the capability of Henri PAUL to drive. They stated that nothing in his behaviour lead them to think that he was drunk and they claimed that they had not seen the types of drinks that he had had.

(D2144 -D2156 - D2159 - D2169 -D2136)
In fact, of the four employees in charge of the bar that evening, only Alain WILLAUMEZ noted that Henri PAUL was drunk; Thierry ROCHER, who went to tell Henri PAUL the instructions from Emad AL FAYED found that his behaviour was completely normal.

He stated that Henri PAUL had replied that *"he was going to finish his "Ricard" with the English"*.

The results of the analyses, notably of the amount of transferring, showed the existence of a certain amount chronic alcoholism and the testimony of one of his closest friends, Dr Dominique MELO revealed that it was not an isolated problem, as the latter had consulted him a year and a half previously about the matter.

The enquiry was not able to establish formally is the employers of Henri PAUL were in a position to know about this aspect of his personality: apart from the testimony of Alain WILLAUMEZ, none of the other professional colleagues of Henri PAUL had heard anything about this subject. He did have the reputation of being someone who "enjoyed life".

He had been employed at the Ritz since 1985 and was well liked by the management.

(D1011 - D1020 - D2213)
On a private level his best friends, his ex girlfriend, his neighbours, all painted a portrait of a man who was both "shy" and at the same time "enjoyed life". No-one seemed to have noticed the existence of a problem linked to alcohol.

In fact, if the appointment of Henri PAUL as the driver poses a problem about the awareness of his state on the evening in question and his intemperance, it should also lead to an examination of the conditions in which it had been decided to resort to a vehicle from the company Etoile Limousine, whose fleet was made up of high powered cars, necessitating to drive them, the possession of a special licence, which Mr Henri PAUL did not possess.

(D1023 - D4936)
On this point the versions of the Ritz management and Jean François MUSA, the manager of Etoile Limousine, diverge : Jean François MUSA claimed that he had expressed reticence when he heard that Henri PAUL would drive the car, notably because he did not have an ad hoc licence, but no witness confirms this point.

Jean François MUSA, who however admitted still allowing the use of the vehicle, despite knowing that Henri PAUL was to drive it, justified this by reason of the fact that he could not refuse what was asked of him.

Now, examining the nature of the commercial links which united the Ritz - Jean-François MUSA used to drive for the Ritz - to the Etoile Limousine company, one can see the total dependence of the Etoile Limousine company on the Ritz, its only client, which put it in competition with another company offering identical services - the MURDOCH company.

Finally, it is worth remembering that during the day Jean-François MUSA had been used to drive the Range Rover for Emad AL FAYED and that the same Jean-François MUSA, who did not belong officially to the staff of the Ritz, had been used on different occasions in the same conditions, as if he were still an employee of the hotel.

From a general point of view, even if Emad AL FAYED and the Princess had not gone down to the Ritz, the management and the staff of the institution as a whole were put at the entire disposal from their arrival in Paris and Emad AL FAYED had, as a last resort, the power to decide all matters.

While the diversionary manoeuvre was being prepared, the photographers were still waiting in front of the hotel, in the Place Vendôme, and several more arrived: notably Alain GUIZARD, Jacques LANGEVIN, who arrived in a grey Golf registration no. 3765PL94, and Nikola ARSOV, driving a white BMW motorbike registration 448 BNE 91.

Towards midnight, Philippe DOURNEAU and Jean-Francois MUSA simulated a fake departure, driving around the Place Vendôme in the Mercedes 600 and the Range Rover.

Several journalists noticed that Henri PAUL was behaving unusually towards them that evening, coming to see them, and announcing the departure of the couple as imminent. Several described him as "laughing, particularly jovial".

Frederic LUCARD, the young valet in charge of driving the Mercedes S280 to the Rue Cambon, confirmed the "jovial" discussions between Henri PAUL and the journalists and even added - although he alone described it - that when Henri PAUL took the wheel of the Mercedes in the Rue Cambon, he heard him say to the journalists present: *"Don't try to follow us, you'll never catch us"*.

Anticipating the possibility of the couple's exit by the rear of the building, Serge BENAMOU, Jacques LANGEVIN, Fabrice CHASSERY and Alain GUIZARD went to the Rue Cambon and watched both the arrival of the Mercedes S280 and the departure of the couple.

They then warned Romuald RAT, Christian MARTINEZ, Serge ARNAL and David ODEKERKEN , who had stayed in front of the hotel.

Jacques LANGEVIN, Fabrice CHASSERY and Serge BENAMOU took a few pictures of the couple, then the Mercedes left at speed.

It was then 12.20am on the hotel's surveillance camera clock in the Rue Cambon.

The drive from the Ritz to Alma:

Among those under investigation, several confirmed they had followed the same path as the Mercedes.

(D1636 – D1720 – D1710 – D1700 – D5033)
Thus, Romuald RAT, Stéphane DARMON, Serge ARNAL and Christian MARTINEZ claimed that after a red light in the Place de la Concorde, the Mercedes accelerated to a very high speed along the river, and that they rapidly lost sight of it.

They had then slowed down at the exit of the first tunnel, thinking that the Mercedes might have turned off, but they continued along the road, only seeing the Mercedes again, this time involved in the accident, as they approached the Alma tunnel.

(D1731 – D5033)
Serge BENAMOU had also followed the river, but rapidly left behind, he had taken the first tunnel exit and arrived at the Place de l'Alma.

(D1688 – D4745 – D5033)
Jacques LANGEVIN meanwhile explained that his car had been parked in the Rue Cambon, and after a detour through the Place Vendôme, he had decided to go to meet friends for dinner. It was by chance, and some time later, that he followed the same road as the Mercedes.

(D1648 – D5033)
David ODEKERKEN found himself behind the Mercedes until the Concorde red traffic light. He claimed he had then decided not to follow further. He saw the Mercedes depart in a whirlwind, followed by Serge ARNAL's vehicle, and he was then overtaken by Romuald RAT and Stéphane DARMON. He explained that to get to his home he had also by chance followed the Mercedes' route.

Consequently, none of the photographers admit that they "chased" the car carrying the couple, nor that they had impeded his progress or taken pictures en route. None of the negatives seized from the photographers show pictures taken on the journey. Nor did any of them admit to having been close enough to the Mercedes to have witnessed in the actual accident.

There were three photographers under investigation who claimed not even to have tried to follow the Mercedes:

Laslo VERES stayed in front of the Ritz and only learned of the accident later in a phone call from Serge BENAMOU. His story was confirmed by the Ritz surveillance cameras, which established that at 12.26am he was still in front of the hotel.

(D1675-D5033)
-Fabrice CHASSERY declared that, in agreement with David ODEKERKEN, he had decided to not follow the car and that from the Place de la Concorde he had taken the Champs Elysées, where a call from David ODEKERKEN informed him of the accident.

-Finally Nicola ARSOV had stayed in front of the Ritz with some other photographers, including Pierre HOUNSFIELD, and had finally followed the Range Rover and the Mercedes 600 until the Champs Elysées, then avenue Wilson, where he had left these two vehicles and turned into Cours Albert 1er to arrive at the Place de l'Alma.

In fact the critical examination of the accounts of the persons questioned does not allow them to be radically called into question . . .

(D5293 – D7087 – D5969)
- In fact, as regards first of all Romuald RAT and Stéphane DARMON, the experts' reports comparing the speed of the different vehicles established that over 1400 metres, or the distance between the Avenue Champs Elysées and the Pont de l'Alma, their motorcycle was slower than the Mercedes.

- As for Serge BENAMOU, who was driving a scooter, the question did not arise, and the same can be said for Serge ARNAL, whose Fiat "Uno" could not be compared with the Mercedes.

(D4911)
The moment's hesitation mentioned by Romuald RAT, Stéphane DARMON, Christian MARTINEZ and Serge ARNAL at the exit of the first tunnel seems logical, in as far as the exit towards the Place de l'Alma allowed access to the Avenue Marceau and to thus follow directly on to

the Rue de Presbourg and the Rue Arsène Houssaye. This was moreover the route, which Philippe DOURNEAU was taking in his Mercedes 600.

(D136 – D1459 – D1087 – D2352 – D141)
In addition, if some witnesses noted the presence of motorcycles behind the Mercedes, or even their annoying behaviour during the journey between the Place de la Concorde and the Alma tunnel, they did not state either the number or the type.

(D1418 – D1426 – D1532 – D1536 – D2377 – D2363 – D1422 – D1448 – D1529)
Finally the witnesses situated, at the moment of the accident, opposite the entrance to the tunnel, definitely noticed a motorcycle, but whereas according to some of them it was following the Mercedes closely, according to others, it did not arrive until after the accident. Above all they proved incapable of describing it with a minimum of details.

- The explanations of David ODEKERKEN and Fabrice CHASSERY were not totally convincing as Romuald RAT, Stéphane DARMON, Serge ARNAL, Christian MARTINEZ and Serge BENAMOU confirmed having seen them behind the Mercedes at the red traffic light at la Concorde.

Furthermore it is difficult to understand why professionals reputed to be "persistent" and who had already waited for hours would have given up in this manner.

But, there again, the presence of the David ODEKERKEN quite distinctive vehicle was, however, neither noticed by the witnesses to the journey nor by the witnesses to the accident.

(D6135)
In addition, on the list of telephone calls made, a call by David ODEKERKEN to Fabrice CHASSERY at 00.24:05, or at a time which corresponds to minutes after the accident, is identified, which would tend to confirm that they had separated, perhaps in order to better "cover" all the possible routes.

- If the statements made by Nikola ARSOV do not correspond to the route described by Philippe DOURNEAU, as being the one that he would have followed, one cannot deduce with certainty that he had set off in pursuit of the Mercedes.

(D2612 –D2392)
On the one hand the testimony of Pierre HOUNSFIELD, another reporter
present in front of the Ritz, confirmed that Nikola ARSOV had left the
Place Vendôme too late to be found immediately behind the Mercedes
and, on the other hand, if a witness, Jean-Louis BONNIN, stated that he
had been overtaken on the right bank [of the Seine] by a motorcycle
with a number plate "91", like that of Nikola ARSOV, he described two
people on the motorcycle, when it has been established that Nikola
ARSOV was driving alone.

(D1057 – D5003)
- As for Jacques LANGEVIN, his position was only called into question by
Alain GUIZARD, who, in his first statement, had explained that he had
seen Jacques LANGEVIN's Golf in the group of vehicles behind the
Mercedes at the traffic light on the Place de la Concorde, but, when
confronted, had not confirmed this statement.

- Finally, the only survivor of the accident, Trevor REES JONES,
  suffering from amnesia, had no memory of the part of the
  journey between the Ritz and the Alma tunnel, and was not
  able to supply precise information on the progress of the
  journey.

(D2473 – D4346)
The only thing he could confirm was the presence behind them leaving
the Rue Cambon of a scooter and a small light coloured car as well as,
at the stop at the traffic lights on Place de la Concorde, the presence of
a motorcycle at their sides, before the Mercedes sped off quickly in first
position.

In conclusion, it is not possible to determine exactly which of the
people under examination who followed the Mercedes for the whole of
the journey right up to the place of the accident, as a doubt exists on
this point with regard to Fabrice CHASSERY and Nikola ARSOV.

As for those who had taken the same route as the Mercedes, their
behaviour on the road nor the exact speed is not known precisely.

And even if it is undeniable that they arrived in the tunnel a very short
time after the accident, one cannot estimate with any certainty what
distance they were away from the Mercedes at the moment where the
latter sped into the tunnel.

Finally, taking account of the technical findings of the I.R.C.G.N.
experts, one can state that none of the vehicles used by the people

under examination corresponds to the Fiat "Uno" which is likely to have been in collision with the Mercedes.

The analysis of the causes and the liability with regard to the crimes of homicide and voluntary [sic.] injury:

First of all, as far as the possible role played in the accident by a Fiat "Uno", the existence of which was revealed by the traces found on the Mercedes, the experts' reports have underlined that, in every hypothesis, its role could only have been a passive one.

(D2359 - D2371)
The driver of this Fiat "Uno" has not been able to be identified, despite extremely long and detailed investigations which have been lead by the enquiry team, who only had, to direct their research the witness statements of a couple of drivers, who, at approximately the time which could correspond to the accident, told of the abnormal behaviour of the driver of a Fiat "Uno" crossing the Place de l'Alma in the direction of Boulogne.

(D2097)
Interrogated about the circumstances of the collision between this unknown Fiat "Uno" and the Mercedes S280, the I.R.C.G.N. experts indicated that it was a collision 'three quarters behind', and that at the moment of contact between the two vehicles the speed of the Mercedes was faster than that of the Fiat "Uno".

(D5433 to D5829)
The experts NIBODEAU-FRINDEL and AMOUROUX, for their part, concluded that the contact between the Mercedes and the Fiat "Uno" only consisted of a simple scrape, which had not lead to a significant reduction in speed by the Mercedes.

The speed at which the Mercedes was travelling was described as very fast by all the witnesses, both during the journey along the banks [of the Seine] and at the moment when it entered the tunnel.

Mr NIBODEAU-FRINDEL and Mr AMOUROUX estimated the speed of the Mercedes, before the collision at a total of between a maximum of 155 km/hour and a minimum of 118 km/hour and the speed, at the moment of the crash on the thirteenth pillar of the Alma tunnel was between 95 and 109 km/hour with a margin of error of more or less 10%.

They attributed the direct causes of the accident to this excessive speed which, taking account of the particular profile of the road, had rendered the vehicle difficult to control, all the more so because of the presence of the Fiat "Uno" at the entrance of the tunnel and the fact that the driver of the Mercedes had a very poor control of his vehicle.

They finally stated that Emad AL FAYED and Lady Diana SPENCER would have survived if they had fastened their safety belts.

Consequently from all of the investigations lead and from the different expert reports it transpires that the direct cause of the accident is the presence, at the wheel of the Mercedes S280, of a driver who had consumed a considerable amount of alcohol, combined with the fact that he had recently taken medication, driving at a speed not only faster than the maximum speed limit in built up areas, but excessive when taking account of the layout of the places and the predictable obstacles, notably the presence on his right of a vehicle moving at a slower pace.

Therefore the loss of control of the vehicle by the driver in the Alma tunnel constitutes the main cause of the accident.

Now, any possibility of pursuing this case is extinguished by the very fact of its previous demise by setting in motion of the public action.

Therefore, in these conditions it remains that the criminal liability of those persons under examination for homicide and involuntary injuries can only be considered in terms of indirect cause since the direct cause of the accident has thus been established.

In other words, the question is knowing whether the fact that a certain number of photographers had undertaken to follow the vehicle carrying Diana SPENCER and Emad AL FAYED played a contributory role, and a clear contributory role, by creating psychological conditions whereby the driver felt constrained to drive at an excessive speed.

This supposes first of all, therefore, that the photographers had "pursued" the vehicle.

Now it is observed that, for the duration of the day, if the growing presence of the photographers did legitimately irritate the Princess and her companion, it was not unexpected, given the extreme media coverage of their relationship, nor, given the amount of means and personnel at their disposal, an event which had left them completely helpless.

The presence of these photographers during the day, although undesirable, had not manifested itself in dangerous practices, nor in recourse to ruses or subterfuges, all the photos taken showing clearly scenes in public.

Taking account of these elements, it is not possible to support the view that this general context constitutes a hounding of the couple by the photographers.

Secondly, this supposes researching how many photographers had followed the couple, their number being able to play an important role in the creation of a psychological effect on the driver, and who from among the photographers had been able to play this role.

In this regard, a rigorous assessment of the charges against each of the people under examination lead to eliminating Laslo VERES from any responsibility, as it has been established that he had not followed the Mercedes and to not uphold that of Fabrice CHASSERY and Nikola ARSOV for whom there remains some doubt on this point.

Finally, with regard to Romuald RAT, Stéphane DARMON, Serge ARNAL, Christian MARTINEZ, Serge BENAMOU, David ODEKERKEN and Jacques LANGEVIN, it is necessary to determine with certainty if, at the moment when the driver lost control of the vehicle, they were within sight of the Mercedes.

The enquiry not having being able to establish this, one cannot therefore state that their presence provoked such a stress in the driver that it definitely explains the speed taken.

In fact, in the hypothesis of a slower speed, or 118 km/hour, it is rather rash to allude to a "fleeing" behaviour.

The speed adopted by the driver can also clearly be attributed to the presence of alcohol in his blood, the effect of which was increased by the medicines, and thereby characterise the psychological effect of a driver who was totally uninhibited at the wheel of a powerful car and sure of having distanced the photographers.

Consequently, it was not shown that at the moment when the driver lost control of his vehicle, he found himself having to drive at speed, rendering the accident inevitable.

One can only state that there is no clear underlying link between the speed of the vehicle and the presence of photographers following the vehicle.

Therefore the charges of homicide and involuntary injury will be judged as no grounds for prosecution with respect to Romuald RAT, Christian MARTINEZ, Stéphane DARMON, Jacques LANGEVIN, Serge ARNAL, Laslo VERES, Nikola ARSOV, Fabrice CHASSERY, David ODEKERKEN and Serge BENAMOU.

-The establishment of an incidental civil claim for damages by Trevor Rees Jones:

(D6927)
On 23rd September 1998, alongside the preliminary investigation of the case opened on 2nd September 1997, Trevor REES JONES' counsel lodged a claim for damages against X for having put in danger the life of another person, by reason of the fact that, by putting at the Ritz' disposal a powerful car without a driver who held a licence as required by the regulations, the managers of the Etoile Limousine company had directly exposed Trevor REES JONES to the risk of death, mutilation or permanent disability.

This claim was followed on 2nd November 1998 by the opening of an enquiry and, by reason of the connection with the enquiry opened 2nd September 1997, a joinder order was made on 30th November 1998.

This claim could not go ahead, in as far as, on the one hand the crime of having endangered the life of another person is only constituted in the absence of harmful result, which is not the case of Trevor REES JONES, as he presented with numerous traumatic lesions following the accident of 31st August 1997 and the experts commissioned to evaluate the gravity [of his injuries] and determine the resulting ITT, concluded on 2nd October 1997 that the initial ITT was still in course and would not be less than six months (D1736).

On the other hand, in order to establish the crime, it is necessary to show that the manifestly deliberate violation of a particular safety or cautionary obligation imposed by law or regulations has directly exposed another person to an immediate risk of death, mutilation or permanent disability.

One cannot sustain in the matter of the non-respect of the provisions of the decree of the 15th July 1955 and the decree of 18th April 1966, which impose for the driving of high powered vehicles, the possession of a special licence, has directly exposed the plaintiff to an immediate risk of death, mutilation or permanent disability, it being a matter of carrying out a relatively short journey in town, i.e. in a secure road environment and on board a vehicle, certainly high powered, but technically accessible to the holders of a Category B driving licence.

Consequently the claim will be judged as there being no grounds for prosecution.

-After the accident: liability with regard to the crime of failing to come to the aid of people in danger:

In order to come to a decision regarding each of the persons under examination on the imputability of the facts with regard to not coming to the aid of people in danger, first of all requires the establishment, with utmost exactitude, of the time sequence of events after the accident occurred, in order to define the exact period during which they can be legitimately charged with voluntary abstention.

Taking account of the multiplicity of sources of information, which cannot be synchronised with certainty, the sequence of the events has been established based on several factors:

The first source comes from the recording of the security cameras at the Ritz hotel, where the internal clock indicated the departure of the Mercedes from the Rue Cambon at 00.20.

Then come the telephone switchboards of the emergency services:

- at the number "18", the number of the main Fire Station, the first call was received at 00.26, the call from Dr. MAILLEZ who arrived on the scene at almost the same period of time;
  - at the number "17", emergency number for the police, the first call was recorded at 00.29:59.

(D6212)
Thirdly, numerous pieces of information were obtained from the listings, supplied by the mobile telephone operators Itinéris and SFR, of all the calls made from a portable telephone on 30th and 31st August 1997, between midnight and one o'clock in the morning, in the Concorde/Vendôme/Alma areas.

(D6135 - D6106)
Thus one finds a first call to "18" at 00.23:43, from Paul CARRIL's mobile, who declared having

called as soon as he heard the crash.

(D6132 - D6134 - D159 - D6131 - D6128 - D6127 - D6126 - D6125)
This first call was followed by a number of others both to "18" and to
"112", the emergency number which is common to Itinéris and SFR.

(D6139)
In addition the listing mentions, at 00.23, a call from Serge ARNAL's
mobile to "12".

(D50)
Finally the emergency services themselves constitute the last source of
information, as the police commander having received the call from the
GAGLIARDONE/DORZEE patrol indicated that it was then 00.30, while
the report established by the fireman mentioned that the first crew
arrived at 00.32.

In spite of an inevitable margin of error, it is accepted therefore that a
short time passed between the departure from the Rue Cambon and the
occurrence of the accident, as well as the existence, in very quick
succession of a large number of calls to the emergency services then
the rapid arrival of these services.

Equally one notes that the call from Dr MAILLEZ to the firemen
happened a very short time after the accident, which is to be
emphasized, as from the moment when the doctor was at the location
and took charge of things, the legal obligation to personally act is no
longer imposed with the same force for any non specialists present at
the scene.

(D1610)
In fact it transpires from the time sequence of the different calls and
from the testimony of Mark BUTT, who accompanied Dr MAILLEZ, that
when Dr MAILLEZ left his vehicle, which was stopped on the opposite
carriageway, to assists the injured, the first policemen had not yet
arrived.

It is consequently in the few minutes preceding Dr MAILLEZ's arrival
that the attitude of the different people under examination can be
usefully considered by piecing together their statements, the analysis of
the photos which they took and the statements of the witnesses most
directly involved.

In fact, the enquiry was able to piece together the existence of a small
group of witnesses present at the scene before the arrival of Dr

MAILLEZ, knowing that other onlookers had equally appeared very quickly on the scene, as seen on the photographs, but without being able to be identified.

(D2396 - D6086)
- Belkacem BOUZID and Abdelatif REDJIL, walking in the Place de la Reine Astrid, explained that they rushed into the tunnel as soon as they heard the crash.

Belkacem BOUZID stated that he then saw four photographers in action, among whom he identified Romuald RAT, while Abdelatif REDJIL claimed that they had been the first on the scene, even before a first photographer, who got off a motorcycle and whom he identified as being Romuald RAT.

It is worth noting that Adelatif REDJIL could only be heard rather belatedly.

However they are both identifiable on different photos, Belkacem BOUZID, dressed in a mustard coloured jacket and Abdelatif REDJIL in blue jeans and a green jacket (D191, D368, D457).

-   Two young people had left a car travelling in the opposite direction to go to the vehicle involved in the accident: Damien DALBY, a voluntary fireman, and his brother Sébastien PENNEQUIN.

(D121 - D1266 - D4928 - D123 - D1259 - D4940)
They explained that at least four photographers were already there, and they identified Romuald RAT, whom they described as kneeling in front of the open back right door, the scene which was found on a photograph by Christian MARTINEZ (DD473).

They heard him shout in the direction of another photographer who was moving away: "she is alive", then saw him push back the other photographers.

After having gone round the car to estimate the state of the injured, Damien DALBY had then seen Dr MAILLEZ, who was taking charge of Lady Diana SPENCER and he himself, together with another unidentified fireman, therefore dealt with Trevor REES JONES (cf. D186, D188, D367, D471, D472 - Damien DALBY being dressed in blue jeans and a blue T shirt and the other volunteer fireman in blue jeans and a blue-grey T shirt).

Sébastien PENNEQUIN stated that he had helped a man to describe the state of the injured, as this man had the firemen on line, thanks to a mobile phone.

(D2367)
This man was James HUTH, who was in a flat in Cours Albert 1er and who explained that he went into the tunnel as soon as he heard the crash.

On photo D470, Sébastien PENNEQUIN appears in a black jacket and black jeans.

(D129 - D132 - D1418)
- Finally Clifford GOOROOVADOO, a limousine driver, who was waiting for his clients at the Place de l'Alma when he heard the crash caused by the accident, stated that at the time he arrived near the vehicle involved in the accident four or five people, of whom three were taking photographs, were near the Mercedes.

He recognised Romuald RAT, whom he described as particularly agitated: *"Romuald RAT was everywhere around the car (. . .), he was moving around in all directions"* (D5018).

He also said he had seen him argue with Christian MARTINEZ.

He spoke in English to the injured to reassure them and, indeed, he also appears on several photographs (D188, D366, D368, D470, D471).

In addition, during the course of the enquiry, Stéphane DARMON, Serge ARNAL, Christian MARTINEZ, Romuald RAT and Serge BENAMOU admitted that they arrived at the scene of the accident before the arrival of Dr MAILLEZ.

(D238 - D243 - D1720 - D5033)
Stéphane DARMON stated that he was the first to enter the tunnel where he had parked his motorcycle about ten metres in front of the Mercedes, Romuald RAT had got off the machine and had gone towards the car when Serge BENAMOU and Serge ARNAL arrived.

Serge ARNAL informed him that he had called the emergency services.

Stéphane DARMON had moved his motorcycle, then he remained apart [from the others], quite distressed, according to his statement.

(D336 - D348 - D340 - D350 - D1636 - D5033)
-Romuald RAT admitted that, as soon as he got off his motorcycle, he had run towards the Mercedes and taken three photographs. Then he had opened the back right door, taken the princess' pulse and had said to her, as well as to Trevor REES JONES, that "the doctor was on his way". He stated that he had not started to take pictures again until after the arrival of the police (D347). He added that at the moment when he saw the injured and realised the severity of their state, he had heard someone shout: *"I have called the emergency services"*.

On a total of 19 photos taken by Romuald RAT in the tunnel there are certainly three photographs which depict just the Mercedes, it must be added that a non-identified individual is in the shot in two of the photographs (D371, D370) and a man who could be Mr BENAMOU on the third (D369).

Finally, on a fourth photo, which did not show either Dr MAILLEZ or the policemen, but already a number of onlookers (D363).

(D4830 to D4867)
According to the expert DEWOLF, Romuald RAT was the second to take photographs of the Mercedes alone and he never put his camera less than 5 metres from the subjects.

(D168 - D172 -D179 - D1710 - D5033)
- Serge ARNAL stated that he had parked his vehicle in the direction of the exit of the tunnel then had immediately called the emergency services, dialling "112" on his mobile phone. He had a contact on line and, despite a very bad reception, had provided the first pieces of information.

He explained that he had then gone down into the tunnel, where Romuald RAT, Christian MARTINEZ, David ODEKERKEN and Serge BENAMOU were already, and he had taken photos of the Mercedes.

He took 16 photographs in the tunnel, of which 8 featured the Mercedes completely alone (D219 to D226).

According to the expert the photo D226 was certainly, of all the photos seized, the first to be taken immediately after the accident, as the smoke coming from the car can be made out, the lights were on and the driver's air bag was still inflated. The seven photographs after that had been taken by going around the vehicle, from the back to the front.

At the time of taking the following photos, Serge ARNAL had never approached the injured by less than 1.5 metres.

(D420 – D428 – D435 – D438 – D1700 – D5033 – D5013)
Christian MARTINEZ stated that he had left the vehicle of Serge ARNAL with his camera, having seen Romuald RAT at the place and heard someone say "I can't get 12". He thought it was Serge ARNAL.

He had taken some photographs before going, with Serge ARNAL, to move the vehicle of Serge ARNAL, then came back and took more photos.

He was the one who had taken the most, 31 in total, and the expert identified him as the one who had come the closest [to the victims], less than 1.50 metres from Lady Diana SPENCER, notably at the moment when Dr MAILLEZ was attending to her.

On four of these photos Dr MAILLEZ did not appear. (D455, D470, D472, D473).

(D1177 – D1188 – D1206 – D1731 – D5033)
Serge BENAMOU stated that, when he entered the tunnel, in the opposite direction to the traffic, as he was coming from the Place de l'Alma, and that Romuald RAT, Christian MARTINEZ and Serge ARNAL were already near the Mercedes, Serge Arnal told him that he had called the emergency services.

(D1207 to D1216)
Both Dr MAILLEZ and the firemen appear on all the photos belonging to him, which were seized belatedly, as he was not questioned that evening.

(D1134 – D1134 – D1166 – D1648 – D5033)
For his part, David ODEKERKEN stated that he had not parked in the tunnel, when he passed by car, he had seen the first four photographers and, going towards the exit of the tunnel, had passed Stéphane DARMON. Then he called Fabrice CHASSERY and explained that he had not called the emergency services at that moment as he had heard people say that they had already been called.

(D5033)
- Finally Jacques LANGEVIN, Fabrice CHASSERY, Nikola ARSOV and Laslo VERES stated they arrived on the scene much later than the arrival of the emergency services.

(D902 – D413 – D862 – D489 to D499)

It is noted that, policemen and firemen appear on all the photos taken by Fabrice CHASSERY, Jacques LANGEVIN and David ODEKERKEN.

As for Nikola ARSOV, he said that he took some photographs, when the emergency services were present, but his flash did not work.

In addition, no witness mentioned their presence before the arrival of the emergency services.

Consequently, since there are no facts which establish the presence of David ODEKERKEN, Jacques LANGEVIN, Fabrice CHASSERY, Nikola ARSOV and Laslo VERES at the scene during the period of time preceding the arrival of the police and the emergency services, and a fortiori that of Dr MAILLEZ, one cannot claim that they failed to offer assistance at the scene.

One must wonder then about the credit that can be accorded to the statements by Serge ARNAL concerning the telephone call to the emergency services, in as far as he explained that he had dialled "112" when, on the listings of calls passed on from the mobile telephones, the call that he made at 0.23 had been to "12", the number for telephone information.

(D230 – D6126 – D7218)

During his detention by the crime squad, the investigating officers had ascertained the last 10 numbers dialled in his mobile telephone memory. They found the "112" just before a call to his Chief Editor, Franck KLEIN, this last communication being found, in the same order, on the listing of mobile calls.

Consequently, the inconsistency existing between the reading of his calls in his mobile and that of the general listing cannot constitute an offence. [there being none]

Serge ARNAL, having acted to call the emergency services, cannot be held in custody.

Then with regard to Stéphane DARMON, Christian MARTINEZ, Serge BENAMOU and Romuald RAT, one must note that, if the law requires you to offer to people in danger immediate and personnel assistance, or to call for assistance, that which each of them was able to do, as they all had a mobile telephone, it remains that the offence cannot be said to have occurred in the absence of intent.

This can be deduced from the establishment of the facts, consequently it is not proved that Stéphane DARMON, Serge BENAMOU and Christian MARTINEZ, who were informed by Serge ARNAL that he had made a call to the emergency services, had, by refraining from making a call themselves, the intention of not proffering assistance to the passengers of the vehicle involved in the accident.

Finally, with regard to Romuald RAT, the few seconds that he took to take three photos, before approaching the vehicle involved in the accident, do not appear in themselves likely to represent criminal intent.

On the one hand, he also maintained that he had heard someone shout that the emergency services had been informed, an assertion which is not improbable, given the telephone call by Serge ARNAL. On the other hand, it emerges from the different testimonies and the photos seized that he had stopped taking photos as soon as he had reached the vehicle and was able to ascertain the state of the injured, and did not resume until after the arrival of Dr MAILLEZ.

The conduct which he adopted in this period of time, crouching down in front of the back passenger door, calling another photographer to tell him that the Princess was alive, then arguing with the other photographers, was liable to several interpretations, favourable or not according to whether you considered that, in the panic of the moment, he had tried to intervene, albeit clumsily, or whether he was acting as a professional cynic, calling his colleagues for a "scoop", then pushing them away to organise his own room for manoeuvre.

In these conditions, it does not appear that the constituent elements of the crime of not assisting a person in danger were identified, the charges weighing on the various aspects of the case under examination being insufficient to justify their referral to a tribunal entertaining jurisdiction.

The critical view which could be brought on the manner in which the various people under examination have, during the course of the night in question, exerted their professional activity can only be recorded within the circumstances of the moral appreciation or the code of ethics which govern the profession of journalist or photo-journalist.

CLAIMS OF NO GROUNDS FOR PROSECUTION:

Whereas within the terms of the enquiry, there are insufficient charges against the following: **ARNAL Serge, ARSOV Nikola, DARMON**

Stéphane, LANGEVIN Jacques, MARTINEZ Christian, RAT Romuald, VERES Laslo, ODEKERKEN David CHASSERY Fabrice and BENAMOU Serge of having committed the crimes of involuntary manslaughter, involuntary injury, having incurred an ITT of more than 3 months and of failing to assist people in danger, of which they are charged, neither against all other charges of homicide or involuntary injury having incurred an ITT of more than 3 months.

Whereas there are also insufficient charges against any of having committed the crime of endangering the life of another person: In accordance with articles 175, 176 and 177 of the Code of Penal Procedure;

The examining magistrates find that there is no case to answer in the case of the state versus the above named of the charges of involuntary homicide, involuntary injury incurring an ITT of more than 3 months and of failing to assist a person in danger and against any of the charges of involuntary homicide and injury which have incurred an ITT of more than 3 months and of endangering the life of another person.

Signed at the Public Prosecutor's Office, on . . . .
Head of the Prosecution Dept. at Courts of the First Instance.

Judge Stephan exonerated the paparazzi of all criminal negligence in the deaths of Princes Diana, Dodi Fayed and Henri Paul. The paparazzi had served their purpose, taking the initial blame and diverting the world's attention onto the rat pack pursuing Diana. From the outset, as I have shown, the French and British authorities decided the crash was an accident, end of story, no room for negotiation, no tolerance of evidence that did not fit in with the 'great accident theory' and theory it is.

The hapless Henri Paul was now the figure of hate. Apparently he was three times over the drink driving limit in France, speeding at close to 100mph and all of which caused him to lose control of the car and crash it into the thirteenth pillar in the Alma Tunnel. A multitude of witnesses tell a different story and it should be remembered that none of the government officials who have promulgated the accident theory were at the scene. However, in their arrogance and contempt for the public, these officials and 'experts' know best and therefore the testimony of witnesses is not relevant.

Things would run in much the same vein at the whitewashed Paget Inquiry and the Inquest of Dame Butler-Sloss. Only the high and mighty, none of whom were at the Alma Tunnel on the night, can deal with such matters. Irritating little witnesses who refuse to confirm the neat 'accident theory' must be overlooked. 18 such witnesses were overlooked both Judge Stephan and Sir John Stevens.

Controversy about the blood samples that apparently showed that Henri Paul was drunk and under the influence of drugs when he drove the car on the night that Diana and Dodi Fayed were killed in Paris, saw the BBC duped by the French investigators whose mishandling of the samples is now the subject of a criminal 'investigation' in France. 'How mighty are the fallen.'

The incontrovertible and inescapable truth is that the blood samples which showed a high level of Alcohol and the presence of drugs have not been shown to be those taken from Henri Paul. These samples were never tested for DNA. There is no provable link between them and Henri Paul. We simply have take the word of 'paid experts' tasked to prove the accident theory, that there is a link. And, of course, governments and their paid officials, never lie, do they!

It is entirely possible that the incriminating samples were taken from another person in the morgue where the tests were carried out. That person was highly likely a suicide victim who had used alcohol, drugs and Carbon Monoxide to take his or her own life. Mohamed Al Fayed has maintained throughout the long investigation he has caused to be undertaken into all the circumstances of the crash.

On the morning on which Henri Paul was killed, an autopsy was carried out by Professor Dominique Lecompte. The 'procedure' was carried out in the presence of Commander Mules. Five samples of blood were allegedly taken from Paul's body, and, according to Commander Mules they were all processed and dealt with in precisely the same way two of the samples were sent off to different laboratories for testing, and the remaining 3 were kept at the Institute where the autopsy was carried out. The two samples tested both allegedly showed identical and excessive samples of Alcohol. One of those same samples was also tested for Carbon Monoxide and showed a staggering level of 20.7%

Although it was said in the report made at the time that the unused remains of the samples actually tested would be stored and preserved, it was eventually claimed during recent court proceedings initiated in Paris by Al Fayed that in fact there is nothing left of those two samples. Consequently, there have been no DNA tests on the two samples which were used as the basis for the Alcohol levels and as the basis for the allegation that Paul was drunk.

The French authorities and the Paget Inquiry team have failed to come up with any credible explanation for the level of 20.7% Carbon Monoxide level found in the sample of blood which was not only tested for alcohol but also for Carbon Monoxide. All the international experts retained by Al Fayed, as well as those retained by the police accept that Henri Paul could not have had such a staggeringly high level of Carbon Monoxide.

The recorded volume of Carbon Monoxide is consistent more with someone who died in a fire or committed suicide as a result of inhaling exhaust fumes and drinking. That is why virtually every expert who has been involved say that it is most unlikely that this blood could have come from Henri Paul. Three   unused and untested samples of blood allegedly taken from Henri Paul's body on the night of 31 August should still remain.

But in the recent Paris Court proceeding, Professor Lecompte has confirmed on oath and under examination that in fact she only took three samples of blood from Henri Paul's body on 31 August and Commander Mules supervised the process. Why did the record books made under his supervision show five samples if only three were taken from Henri Paul – where did the other two come from? Has the figure been altered to make things look good for the police?

No one has been able to explain this aberration. Were these additional ones the two that were sent off for testing and which not only showed the high Alcohol level but also the impossibly high Carbon Monoxide level. If Henri Paul had actually had that combination of Alcohol and Carbon Monoxide level, he could not have stood, let alone driven a car. Professor Lecompte is now the subject of an official criminal investigation in France by the Criminal Brigade on the instruction of the supervising judge.

The three unused samples which were never sent for testing probably did come from Henri Paul. These are probably the three which Professor Lecompte admits she took. It is one of those samples which has been tested for DNA which is why the tests show that it almost certainly came from Henri Paul. The ones sent in 1997 for Alcohol testing do not exist and have never been tested for DNA.

A further sample of blood was taken from Henri Paul's body 4 days later (on 4th September 1997) in front of the French investigating Judge, Herve Stephan. This was sent off to Dr Pepin, the same toxicologist who had carried out the original Alcohol/Carbon Monoxide test, and who in fact owned the laboratory.... Apart from the four day time difference, this blood sample was taken using a different method and taken from a from a completely different part of the body.

Top International experts agree that, under those circumstances, no one should have obtained a closely similar or identical alcohol reading to the blood taken on 31st August, 2007. But amazingly, the person to whom they were sent, the very same Dr Pepin, allegedly obtained an almost identical figure, which is impossible. Even more incredible is the fact that the unused remains of that blood also allegedly no longer exist and so cannot be tested for Henri Paul's DNA.

Mules is also wrong when he claims that the process of taking the blood and labelling it was all done correctly. The samples allegedly all taken at the same time from Henri Paul are in different sorts of bottles, some have typed labels and some have handwritten labels. There is even evidence of someone else's name having been scratched out on one and Henri Paul's name written in. This could be further evidence that Paul's blood samples were mixed up or swapped.

Detailed analysis by independent experts show many other reasons for believing that the blood tested is most unlikely to have come from Henri Paul. As far as the speed of the car goes, it has been claimed that Henri Paul was driving at 100 mph. This is utterly and provably untrue. Scotland Yard have acknowledged that it was in fact travelling at about 60mph at the time of the crash. Incredibly, none of the eyewitnesses to the crash have been seen or interviewed as part of the Paget Inquiry and no one has been able to trace the two missing cars and at least one motorbike which went into the tunnel at the same time as Henri Paul but have never been seen since.

Dr Jim Sprott, pictured above, offered the Surrey Coroner expert evidence of what could have caused such a high blood sugar reading, in the sample apparently taken from Henri Paul's body. He said: "It is well known that post mortem generation of alcohol by microbiological activity can form ethanol (alcohol) from sugars in the blood, and therefore no meaningful evidence can be drawn." The British and French, with lesser experts to rely on, decided to ignore the internationally renowned Dr Sprott.

And an even more controversial decision has been the refusal of French authorities to even consider that James Andanson was in Paris on the 30th/31st August 1997. Sir John Stevens, while he looked into the matter, also concluded that there was, in effect, no case for Andanson to answer. This is not surprising given the fact that Andanson was found dead in his burned out BMW in 2000. And it is to Andanson that I turn next.

Chapter 8

Another Suicide?

(James Andanson, driver of the white Fiat Uno, found dead in
his burned out BMW in the south of France in May 2000)

In the final few days of Diana and Dodi's lives, one of the most
aggressive photographers hunting them was James Andanson.
Unlike the other snappers he was not content simply to follow
them around, he wanted the best shots money could buy. He
hired a helicopter and hovered above the yacht Jonikal to get a
better view. Diana was particularly distressed by this latest
technique of press intrusion into her soon to be ended life.

In the aftermath of the crash, Mohamed Al Fayed brought in
his security chief John McNamara (pictured below) to head a
private investigation, at the behest of the Harrod's chief. Using
unique sources and excellent contacts, it did not take McNamara
long to discover that Andanson owned a white Fiat Uno and that
he usually kept it on his farm in Lignières in Central France.

McNamara states that when he found this shabby white Fiat
Uno, his sharp-witted investigators noted the fact that the car
had been fitted with a new rear tail, which would be logical if

the taillight had been seriously damaged in an accident. Andanson sold the white Fiat Uno a month after the crash. McNamara's agent found the car in a garage but was immediately arrested for interfering with the police 'investigation'. The police limited the hunt for the Fiat Uno to the outskirts of Paris and ruled out that it could be found anywhere else in France.

(John McNamara, former Detective Chief Superintendent, Metropolitan Police and Al Fayed security chief)

French police were alerted by McNamara and his team of the existence of the white Fiat Uno and that it was owned by a man who had been following Diana. Rees-Jones, with what remaining memory he claims to have, recalls seeing a white Fiat Uno on the rue Cambon as they pulled off on the fateful journey. Andanson's recently sold white Fiat Uno had been re-sprayed and there was no documentation to confirm the date of the re-spray.

One might have thought the Paris police would be grateful for the information gleaned from McNamara's team of investigators. On the contrary, the former Scotland Yard detective was assured that if he 'interfered' with the 'investigation' again, he would be charged with a criminal offence. Quite apart from the fact that the French were not having a British detective to be seen upstaging them, it was clear that Andanson was a non-issue, in much the same way that it was decided by senior officials in the Alma Tunnel to stick to the 'accident' theory.

James Andanson, who Richard Tomlinson states was on the books of MI6 as a paid freelancer, was also something of a mystery in the same genre as Henri Paul. Andanson's real name was Jean Paul Gonin but he took the name of Andanson when he married his wife Elizabeth. He flew a Union Jack on his farmhouse, saying he "loved" Britain and the British national flag. This is an odd aberration for a Frenchman, given the traditional 'rivalry', to put it mildly, between France and Britain.

Andanson was a co-founder of the SIPA photo agency and in 1997 he was one of the richest photographers in the world. But he was hated by many people, who disliked his bulling attitude and aggressive manner. Some of his 'targets' have described him as a 'thug with a camera', which indeed he used as a weapon to carve out a very comfortable living.

Filmed as part of a documentary, Andanson was seen to cherish his white Fiat Uno, which was old and shabby, just as witnesses at the Alma Tunnel confirmed and were ignored by both French and British authorities, who had for once forgotten their ancient 'rivalries'. In the documentary Andanson explains that his faithful car had taken him over a colossal distance of 325,000 kilometres.

In the Riviera resort of St jean Cap Ferrat, he 'casually' bumped into the owner of Fiat, the industrialist Giovanni Agnelli. The following day, Agnelli recognised Andanson in the town and struck up a short conversation. Andanson, desperate to impress, as usual, explained how he loved his Fiat and how it had been such a reliable vehicle. Agnelli, eager to play the magnanimous billionaire, promised he would give Andanson a brand new Fiat Uno when his shabby old car had done 500,000 kilometres.

Andanson, could not resist the temptation to brag about Agnelli's generous offer. And yet, so proud of the reliable white Fiat Uno, for which he was promised a brand new replacement on completing the requisite 500,000 kilometres, just a month after the crash at the Alma Tunnel, he sold his 'pride and joy'. As already explained, the car was refurbished with new rear tail light and re-sprayed. All the common signs of covering up 'accidental' damage. But the French police, incorrigibly bent on the accident theory, were not interested in Andanson and his white Fiat Uno....

Super-rich business mogul Giovanni Agnelli promised James Andanson a brand new Fiat Uno free of charge.

One of Andanson's colleagues at the SIPA photo agency in Paris, confirmed that Andanson had often boasted of working for French and British Intelligence services. This would fit in with Andanson's boastful, arrogant nature, a man who believed he was untouchable. He would also boast to friends and neighbours that he was at the Alma Tunnel on the night of the crash and that police were not "clever enough to catch me."

The arrogant braggart boasted to friends and neighbours that he even photographed and taped the last moments of Diana (see photo on page 43) in the tunnel. The French Special Branch believe that Andanson's role for the intelligence services was to harass, intimidate, watch and sometimes eliminate a personality. The French Special Branch were investigating Andanson at the time of his death on the grounds that he was suspected to have played a leading role in the 'suicide' of former French Prime Minister, Pierre Eugène Bérégovoy in 1993. French Special Branch believe Bérégovoy did not kill himself and was instead murdered.

Bérégovoy, apparently, had committed suicide by shooting himself 'twice' in the head; the second bullet was attributed to a nervous reflex, said French police, again playing the guessing game, and his death was ruled a 'suicide'. Yet again, the Bérégovoy case is one of an 'extraordinary' personality defying the mechanics of human physiology by shooting himself twice in the head, the first bullet not being enough to kill him.

Former French Prime Minister, Pierre Bérégovoy, 'another suicide', in the 'suicidal' life of James Andanson. The exit wound in his head was too small for that associated with a .357 Magnum, the alleged 'suicide' weapon. He left no note or letter explaining why he was going to kill himself.

French Special Branch state that there are witness statements to put Andanson in Nevers, central France, on the day Bérégovoy killed himself a couple of miles away. Andanson's widow Elisabeth also confirms that he was in Nevers on the day Bérégovoy was found dead. Forensic evidence shows that Bérégovoy was shot from long distance and which contradicts the police report that he shot himself twice in the head. French Special Branch also reveal that Andanson was present on the day that Diana and Dodi died and he was present on the days of the deaths of Lolo Ferrari, porn star, Dalida, singer, Bernard Buffet, the painter and the pop star Claude François, who sang the French version of 'if I had a hammer'.

Andanson certainly had an uncanny habit of approaching people who died suddenly and he was always in the immediate vicinity on the same day. The French Special Branch say that he had an 'intuition' that certain people were going to die and he just happened to be nearby. Of course, no one is suggesting that Andanson was clairvoyant but rather that he had inside-knowledge that someone was about to die and was probably more accurate than a clairvoyant.

And rumours abound that Andanson took the last picture of the Mercedes S280 (page 43) from his white Fiat Uno and that final burst from his powerful flashbulb blinded Henri Paul, causing him to crash. A multiple burst from a flashbulb of the type used by professional photographers can cause epileptic fit and is just as strong as an Anti-Personnel Device flashgun. The crash could indeed have been accident, caused by the multiple burst from Andanson's flashbulb but if Andanson did not intend to off-road the Mercedes, why swerve into its path?

And there is also the issue of who was driving the white Fiat Uno? Certainly, Andanson could not have driven the car and fired his camera at the same time. Witnesses say that two people were in the white Fiat Uno and one looked like he was hiding his head under a tartan blanket.

Former senior detective John McNamara explains the subject in this way: "You have a Mercedes that's done a 180 degree turn, having crashed into the thirteenth pillar and yet the Fiat Uno survives everything, which suggests to me that that was a very professional driver. I can well believe, as a detective with 24 years experience, why Mr Al Fayed believes that his son Dodi and Princess Diana were murdered."

French Special Branch also discovered from Andanson's diary, that he spent part of the day of 23 August on the yacht Jonikal at the same time as Diana and Dodi. Commentators have spoken of the abnormality of him being on the yacht but Commander Mules suggests that Andanson had made a deal with Diana to photograph her in a high-cut swimsuit. It should be noted that Andanson once made £100,000 for a single photograph of Prince Charles with a suspected 'mistress', presumed to be his nanny Tiggy.

And two weeks after the crash, the Criminal Brigade finally admitted that red-and-white optical debris found in the tunnel entrance in the right-hand lane came from the rear light of a Fiat Uno built in Italy between May 1983 and September 1989. This matched the paint deposits on the front right wing mirror and body panels of a white Fiat Uno made in Italy between 1983 and

1989. Andanson's white fiat Uno was made during the same period.

But the Criminal Brigade limited the search for the white Fiat Uno to two departments (districts) the Paris, near to the Alma Tunnel and the remainder of France was ruled out of the investigation. When John McNamara's team of detectives found Andanson's white Fiat Uno, they were arrested and McNamara was warned that he would be charged with a criminal offence if he interfered again with the 'investigation'. McNamara's team clearly had done a professional job and were not interested in limiting their search area to a couple of Paris suburbs. But French police did not want to take the matter any further and Andanson knew only too well that the police would not be able to touch him.

In effect, McNamara and his team of professional investigators were warned off because they were doing a better job than the French Criminal Brigade or more likely that they had got too close to the truth by finding Andanson's white Fiat Uno. But the ever so mercurial Andanson was living on borrowed time. He bragged often to friends and neighbours, who were used to his boasts, that he was at the Alma Tunnel on the night of the crash. He also bragged to work colleagues that he was in the employ of French and British Intelligence – he was a "loose cannon". But before he was put out of action permanently, he had much wriggling to do.

Andanson may have denied to the police that he was in Paris on 30/31 August, chasing Diana but he boasted to a neighbour of having not only been in Paris, but that he was present when Diana was killed and that he filmed and taped the incident and that could only have been from inside his white Fiat Uno, which was not driven by him. Confidential police forensic reports hidden in Judge Stephan's report, put Andanson at the Alma Tunnel but the matter went no further and Lord Stevens has also ignored this fact.

Even though his son, James said he thought his father was grape harvesting that particular morning in Bordeaux. Apparently, he had left home at 04.00hrs to travel to Bordeaux, over three hours after the crash and more than enough time to get back home from Paris, a couple of hours' drive away, before setting off to pick grapes and cement a cover story for future reference.

In the Paget Report, John Stevens wrote: *'The initial contact between the French police and James Andanson was by telephone on 11 February 1998. Lieutenant Eric Gigou of the Brigade Criminelle tried to arrange an appointment to interview him. This was as a result of the police becoming aware of his ownership of a white Fiat Uno. The exchange was somewhat terse. Lieutenant Gigou reported that James Andanson said 'He does not have the time to waste with the police' and that he 'Refuses to receive policemen in his manor and that he has no time to give.' During this telephone call Lieutenant Gigou recorded '...on the day of the accident he was in Saint-Tropez and that he therefore had nothing to do with the case' (French Dossier D4546-D4547).'*

A very simple text book case for the French police. Andanson says he was not there [Alma Tunnel] and that is it, no further investigation into his implausible claim. Criminals across the world must be hoping for the same treatment. 'I was not there, I was somewhere else, sir, when that person was killed,' would seem to be the ideal alibi to prevent a thorough investigation. In reality the reverse is always true.

Of course, everyone knows that in criminal cases, alibis are thoroughly tested and investigated. But the French and British authorities decided from the outset that the fatal crash was an accident and there would be no criminal investigation. In the Paget Report, Stevens adopts the same dismissive stance and has only skimmed the surface of available witness testimony, which was his purpose from the outset. The faithful Establishment plod, had not intention of upsetting the apple cart from which he draws his own succour.

In essence, the paint scratches found on the Mercedes came from a white Fiat Uno but Judge Stephan ruled that the Uno played only a "passive" part in the crash. The reality is that the Mercedes was thrown off course by the Uno swerving into its path and with the combination of a series of near-blinding flashes of white light, Henri Paul slammed into the thirteenth pillar.

But it all became academic in 2000, when Andanson was found dead in his BMW, 400 miles away from his home in Nant, central France, on the site of a French army training area. Andanson's skeleton was, in fact, found by French soldiers, who had seen smoke rising on the horizon and gone to investigate the burned out wreck in the woodland. Andanson was so badly burned that he could only be identified by DNA tests. And the location in itself was something of a mystery.

Research shows that when people know they are dying, they find a primitive urge to return to the place of their birth or their favourite home. But Andanson, supposedly, threw human nature aside, drove 400 miles away from home, drove a further two miles along a potholed lane, scraped another mile along cow pastures, into dense forest, found a clearing few local people knew existed, which begs the question how he knew it existed, and set in motion the process of killing himself.

Andanson, again supposedly, doused himself with over 20 litres of petrol, enough to drown him, fixed his seatbelt, locked the doors of his BMW from the outside, crossed his arms, and torched the car from the inside. When his skeleton was found his arms, what remained of them, were still crossed. One has to imagine the sheer agony and terror of burning to death. He would have thrashed around like a madman in the final minute or so of his life but he was found, as if sitting comfortably, which is completely unbelievable.

Christophe Pelat offered to testify at the Diana Inquest to the effect that he saw bullet holes in the skull of James Andanson. But his 'testimony' was not required.

Police believed he had killed himself, but a French fireman, Christophe Pelat, who attended the burning wreck of the car, says he appeared to have a bullet hole in his skull. Pelat has since declined to comment on whether he has been interviewed by Stevens' detectives. Along with everything else, the police immediately decided that Andanson had committed suicide in the most implausibly horrific circumstances. I have never come across a case of anyone committing suicide by burning to death in car. Why not just use pills or a gun?

Conveniently, of course, the inferno destroyed all valuable forensic evidence in the car and there was little left of Andanson's skeleton and he left no suicide note. Almost reminds one of the 'suicide' of Dr David Kelly during the prelude to the illegal Iraq war. But, right on cue, came Sir John Stevens, during the press release of the Paget Report, to tell us that he had once attended an almost identical 'suicide' and that we should not think it strange that Andanson killed himself in this manner. It should also be noted that Stevens did not mention the name of the victim or the incident, time, date etc. so the media could investigate the matter and we must therefore assume his **tiresome little tale** was produced simply for effect....

Andanson's family and particularly his widow did not accept the 'suicide' fantasy pushed by French police and insisted a criminal investigation should be conducted but the police, true to form, said that the possibility that Andanson was murdered was "fantasy". And part of the "fantasy" is that no one has ever found the keys to his locked car. Was Houdini present?   Did Andanson lock the doors from the outside and by act of magic, disappear the keys into thin air? More likely that his killers in the DST made the mistake of taking the keys with them. Nominalization dictates that there will always be one mistake. The biggest mistake of the French police is deluding themselves that anyone with a rational brain could possibly believe their tales which defy the laws of logic.

The view in the intelligence community is that Andanson had been talking too much and someone decided to silence him *ad infinitum* before he revealed seriously damaging information in the murders of Princess Diana, Dodi Fayed and Henri Paul. There is also clear evidence, from his colleagues that he threatened to come clean about what happened that night and was prepared to release the photographs and that was quite simply a 'bridge too far' for his handlers.

Andanson's friend François Dard said, "He told us that he was there. He was behind them. He was following behind. He saw the accident and all but he wasn't stopped by the police. He left. It is impossible that he committed suicide. We are convinced of it. To be burned alive in a car – we don't believe it at all." In fact, no one with half brain cell believes that Andanson committed suicide in the circumstances ascribed.

(The burned-out wreck of James Andanson's precious car in remote French woodland near a 'military' firing range)

And a week after his death, the SIPA photo agency in Paris, which he co-founded, was raided by three armed men, wearing balaclavas. They shot a security guard in the foot and held dozens of employees hostage for several hours. Staff phoned the police but they did not turn up. A member of staff said: **"They seemed to know exactly what they were looking for and were confident enough to remain in a busy building for several hours, though they stole nothing of real value."**

Indeed, the 'raiders' disabled the CCTV cameras in the offices and did not seem stressed about the police turning up. For armed 'robbers' they were incredibly relaxed about the whole thing. And yet again, they took computer hard drives, laptops, cameras and the storage media for photographs. They knew exactly what they were looking for. SIPA staff are convinced that the 'raid' had something to do with Andanson and believe French spooks carried out the seizure of property at gunpoint.

There is also talk that the 'raiders' many have been British SAS troopers, from the MI6's disposal team *The Increment*, who are also alleged to have been involved in the crash at the tunnel. Contacts I have spoken to in Paris, however, are adamant that the French DST were behind the armed 'robbery' and they were intent on removing the last damaging traces linking the DST and MI6 to the murders of Princess Diana, Dodi Fayed and Henri Paul. And I will NOT reveal my sources. As a journalist I have an obligation to protect sources of information.

The raid on the SIPA office was almost identical to the raids on the Big Pictures office in London and the home of Lionel Cherruault on the night after the crash. What exactly the French DST were looking for at the SIPA officer is not known. It is believed, though, that there was evidence in the office, put there by Andanson, of his involvement in the crash and that he was at the tunnel. If Diana's death was an 'accident', according to the theories of the British and French authorities, why were any of these raids necessary? By definition, 'accidents' do not need to be covered up because they are caused by chance events.

And suicidal people, usually acting impulsively, do not make intricate plans to burn themselves to death, locking the doors from the outside and losing the keys to the car. James Andanson, was murdered by the French DST to prevent him from destroying the 'great accident theory' and the DST were also behind the raid on the SIPA office to eliminate the last traces of evidence. They must have thought it was the end of the story, how very wrong they were! Mohamed Al Fayed and John McNamara stuck to the case and would not give up the fight for the truth. But irrespective of the brave and expensive campaign waged by the Al Fayed camp, it was without doubt that the quasi-inquest would never allow a murder verdict to be arrived at by a jury - why? Quite simply, the Monarchy would have collapsed....

Chapter 9

The Queen's Emissary

(Eliza Manningham-Buller, former Director General MI5)

To serious students of the international intelligence community, the May 2002 appointment of Eliza Manningham- Buller to Director General of MI5 (The Security Service) was no surprise, it was predicted in the first quarter of 1999. On the same day Manningham-Buller was promoted to head MI5, the Queen hosted a Downing Street reception for her former Prime Ministers. The Windsors certainly approve of Manningham-Buller's appointment and indeed sanctioned her appointment.

Manningham-Buller is of blood-blooded aristocratic lineage, a safe pair to trust with the ship of state, and to prop-up the British Establishment in the fall-out from the murder of Princess Diana. Manningham-Buller is the daughter of Viscount Dilhorne, a former Tory Lord Chancellor. She joined MI5 in 1974 after teaching English at a private school for girls and quickly climbed through the ranks of MI5. In 1984 (no pun intended on Orwell's great novel) she was heading MI5's anti-Soviet affairs section as the "Evil Empire" bordered on imminent collapse.

By 1988, she was leading MI5's Middle East section and in 1991 she became MI5's Washington liaison officer. A year later she left the US to lead all of MI5's anti-IRA operations on the mainland. The Metropolitan Police Special Branch (MPSB) had just lost the 'franchise' and now submitted to MI5 primacy amid considerable acrimony. By late July 1997, Manningham-Buller had risen to become Deputy Director General of MI5. She had made a 'startling' rise through the ranks, no doubt because of family connections to 'The Firm' as the royals call themselves.

Of equal interest, is the fact that Manningham-Buller, by July 1997, in her position as Deputy Director General of MI5 was privy to top-level operations of the nature of the surveillance operation carried out against Princess Diana and her 'contacts'. A month later, on 31 August 1997, Manningham-Buller was in a position to exert considerable operational influence over the Metropolitan Police Special Branch; alleged to be behind the raids on Lionel Cherruault's home and Big Pictures photo agency in London.

Going back a few years, interesting and entirely relevant details are to be found in Manningham-Buller's immediate ancestry on her mother's side. Her mother was Lady Mary Lilian Lindsay, 4th daughter of the 27th Earl of Crawford. The Earls of Crawford, hold the post of Premier Earl of Scotland, vying for pivotal position with the Lords High Constable of Scotland.

Manningham-Buller's brother in law Sir John Parsons is the former Deputy Keeper of the Queen's Privy Purse also known as the 'royal slush fund'. Her cousin Robert Alexander Lindsay, the Earl of Crawford later served as the Queen Mother's Lord Chamberlain, appointed in 1992, at the same time his cousin Eliza was heading back to Britain to take over MI5's operations against the IRA. Jobs for the boys and girls, one might argue and convincingly so.

The Queen Mother had shown inexplicable kindness to the MI5 traitor Anthony Blunt, who many said should have been hung, comrade of the Soviet Union. Not since Blunt has there been such close family connections between MI5 and the Royal Household. It is no 'accident' that Eliza Manningham-Buller was appointed to Director General of MI5. The public clamour for an 'inquest' or British-led investigation into the murky death of Princess Diana was becoming deafening.

The majority of the Queen's subjects do not believe the princess's death was an accident but that is not to say that the

Queen ordered the hit on Diana. The spooks have carte blanche to act as they please without royal commission. Former royal butler Paul Burrell is completely right to say that the Queen does not know about the 'secret work' undertaken by MI5 and MI6. The spooks have carte blanche to defend their stranglehold on power and that includes propping up the Monarchy and State by whatever means necessary.

It is not known exactly how influential the royals are in the selection process for senior intelligence officers but the views of the Monarch are taken on board and are part of the selection process. The Queen favoured Manningham-Buller because of her ancestral links to the royal household and the fact the Eliza could be 'trusted' to keep any embarrassing secrets about the royals from leaking into the public domain. But Eliza did not succeed entirely.

The issue, actually came to a head with the arrest and prosecution of Paul Burrell and the whole strategy eventually backfired in spectacular fashion. The strategy to cover up the secrets of Diana's little box, worked in reverse and ensured that many of the princess's secrets seeped into the public domain, causing the House of Windsor and associated hangers-on, considerable distress, fundamentally damaging the public's perception of the monarchy forever.

The Republican movement has never had it so good. Diana, certainly, would have let off a few chortles, probably vindictive ones. I am reminded of Christopher Hitchens famous line to Diana at the Serpentine: **"You have done more to bring about a Republic without trying than I have by trying."** And this reason more than anything, even the anti-landmines campaign, was why the Establishment needed to neutralise the Diana Threat. Jobs for the boys, no more if the monarchy collapsed....

And British Intelligence have for centuries cleared up after the royals. Even before MI5 and MI6 were formed, their predecessors were employed both secretly and directly by Parliament and part of their remit was to uphold the monarchy at any cost and that included eliminating troublesome individuals. Some people even refer to MI6 as the Monarch's private security firm but the spooks do have other tasks to perform as well as cleaning up after royal faux pas.

Eliza Manningham-Buller was the perfect choice for Director General of MI5 in the eyes of the Monarch and little Eliza, unbeknown to her at the time, was stalked as a potential MI5 officer from the age of 13. Her rise through MI5 has been startling, particularly given the fact that her record on combating 'terrorism' has been poor. One must remember her infamous instruction to Parliament the day before the 7/7 London bombings: **"There is no group with the willingness or capability to carry out terrorist attacks in Britain at this time."**

Indeed, Eliza leapfrogged all of the competition for the post of Director General, and in the opinions of many commentators, the competition was better qualified to lead MI5 and combat 'genuine' terrorist threats to the UK. One such candidate was former Assistant Commissioner of Metropolitan Police, David Veness, who was seen as the ideal choice because of his role as Anti-Terrorist Squad Chief at the Met. But his chances of becoming DG were seriously afflicted by a very unsavoury affair in the English Channel on 21 December 2001, just weeks after 9/11.

The cargo ship MV Nisha had been chartered, we were led to believe, by Al Qaeda to carry a huge amount of explosives into the UK. When the ship was boarded in the English Channel, with the rapacious media watching everything that happened, no explosives were found. **One might add that this was the same Al Qaeda, to which MI6 paid £100,000 of taxpayers' money to fund an assassination attempt against Colonel Gaddaffi, the Libyan leader.** The attack failed but what this incident proved is that MI6 will go to any lengths to get a troublesome individual off the scene permanently,

The fall out from the MV Nisha affair, although it achieved exactly what MI5 wanted it to achieve; the terrorisation of the public in the so-called 'war on terror', also put the post of DG out of the reach of the hapless Veness. But he should not have been blamed for the faux pas. Veness was tipped off about the MV Nisha by 'MI5' and many intelligence analysts claim that he was set up for a fall to discredit him, thus ensuring he did not become DG of MI5.

The then Home Secretary David Blunkett was opposed to the rise of Eliza Manningham-Buller, seeing her as 'old school', and preferred Veness to take the lead at MI5. But the media coverage after the MV Nisha calamity was so damaging, New Labour had to distance the affair and Veness was seen as soiled goods. He could not in these circumstances, and did not become DG of MI5. And there was much opposition to Veness from within the Manningham-Buller faction inside MI5.

The MI5 faction did not like the idea of a 'copper or plod' leading them and sharing their 'dirty secrets', which are almost always out of bounds for the police, who simply do as they are told by the spooks. But the MV Nisha affair alone was not enough to deselect David Veness. Sir Stephan Lander, former DG, made a personal recommendation that Eliza should get the top job.

This is the same Stephan Lander who told Daily Mirror editor Piers Morgan, **"I could read all of your emails this afternoon if I wanted to Piers."** The lapdog editor replied by stating that he 'felt much safer knowing that such an intelligent man was protecting us from terrorism'. Would that be the terrorism of the press and their annoying questions? But journalists are seldom brave and the courage factor diminishes still further in the post of editor.

Eliza it was who got the 'top job', to coin Diana's phrase in the famous Panorama interview, and the opposition fell on their swords, most notably due to MI5's atrocious or planted 'intelligence' regarding the non-existent threat posed by the MV Nisha. Eliza won through, backed to the hilt by the Queen, MI5 and the 'sudden failure' of her opponents. Her record on combating terror has been woeful but on upholding the finest 'traditions' of the British Establishment, she has excelled, propping up a crumbling monarchy, which is one of MI5's primary functions, if not the primary function. It is oft said that if MI5 were disbanded, the monarchy would collapse – over to the Republican movement on that one.

And part of Eliza's role of upholding the Establishment, no matter what foul deeds have been done to achieve this end, was overseeing the police 'investigation' into 'allegations' of 'theft' against Paul Burrell. It is pertinent to remind readers of the Queen's assignation with Burrell in December 1997: **"Be careful, Paul. No one has been as close to a member of my family as you have. There are 'powers' at work in this country about which we have no knowledge,"** and those powers most definitely include MI5!

The 'Squidgygate' tapes of Diana's intimate telephone conversations with 'friend' James Gilbey did not publicly surface until 24 August 1992. They were placed on the airwaves in 1989 and the Sun newspaper was sold a copy of the recording but decided not to publish the material because it was deemed highly sensitive. MI5 are believed to be behind the plot to discredit Diana by recording the 'private' telephone call and then rebroadcasting it on civilian band radio to make it look like the call was intercepted by an 'enthusiast'.

Diana's former royal protection officer, Ken Wharfe opines that the release of the recording is "credible evidence" that the Establishment were out to "destroy" his former boss. Ken Wharfe, ever the loyal plod, also blames the Al Fayed bodyguards for the crash in the Alma Tunnel, suggesting it was their "incompetence" that created the scenario for the 'accident' to happen. It should also be noted that Diana did not trust anything to do with the State and that included Wharfe. Diana dispensed with royal 'protection' because she was convinced they were spying on her and reporting back to their masters - MI5 and from there to the royal household.

Part of Eliza Manningham-Buller's role in the aftermath of Diana's death, was the suppression of photographs of the crash but in this she failed also. But more importantly, her remit was to neutralise the damage that could be caused by the release of the contents of Pandora's box of tricks, which included a tape she made as 'insurance' against assassination, and the tape recording she made of the allegations made by royal valet George Smith.

In 1996, as the princess's arranged marriage to Prince Charles drew to a very public end, she befriended George Smith and made a tape recording of his astonishing allegations: first, he was raped by an aide of Prince Charles and second, he once saw a 'male royal' engaging in a homosexual act with a male employee. The *Mail on Sunday* would later suggest the 'male royal' was Prince Charles but the truth remains unclear. Paul Burrell claims he last saw this explosive tape in the company of Diana's sister, and Lady-in-Waiting to the Queen, Lady Sarah McCorquodale.

Diana saw the tape as so damaging to the royals that she kept it under lock and key, for a rainy day, one might presume. And Burrell also claims that the Spencer family shredded most if not all of Diana's personal correspondence in the days after the funeral, again presumably to conceal family secrets and protect the Monarchy's **'right to rule'**.

On page 378 of *A Royal Duty*, Burrell wrote: -

The full picture emerged with the judge's approval. Scotland Yard was looking for a signet ring given to the princess by Major James Hewitt; a resignation letter from her private secretary

Patrick Jephson; letters from Prince Philip to the princess; and a tape, which became known after the trial as the Rape Tape. It was a recording made by the princess in 1996 when she informally interviewed former KP orderly and ex-Welsh Guardsman George Smith. He had alleged that after a night of heavy drinking he had been raped in 1989 by a male member of staff who worked for Prince Charles. It all came to a head because George who had worked at Highgrove, St James's Palace and KP, had been suffering nightmares, was drinking heavily, and his marriage was falling apart. He blamed it all on an incident that he said he was bottling up.

And again on page 379, he wrote: -

The princess knew the member of staff in question. From that moment on she loathed him. 'I know what that evil bugger did. I know what he did to George, and I will never forgive him for that,' she seethed, after her futile attempts to bring about justice. He [George Smith] never returned to work, and accepted a settlement [Lawyer, Fiona Shackleton] at the end of his employment of around £40,000.

The princess ensured that the tape never saw the light of day. But the mystery of its whereabouts, and the threat its contents posed, emerged during the police investigation of my case. Lady Sarah McCorquodale had asked that Scotland Yard 'ascertain' the contents of the box. In court, DS Milburn said: "I was looking for the contents of that box. All of a sudden, the undertones behind the raid on my home became clear....

The Spencer family alleged that Burrell "retained the material up until the beginning of his trial," and as part of a deal with the royals to collapse it, he handed over the tape. The police did not find the tape when they raided Burrell's home. And this was not the first time the police had shown interest in the tape. Scotland Yard's Organised Crime Group, allegedly at the behest of Prince Charles, covertly filmed Diana's visits to Smith. What 'organised crime' the Organised Crime Group thought may be going on is beyond rationale. Perhaps they should have investigated more thoroughly the fire bomb attack on Burrell's flower shop....

Keith Perry, writing in the *Sunday Express* on 17th November 2002, stated that in the run up to the collapse of Burrell's trial, the Crown Prosecution Service and Eliza Manningham-Buller viewed the tapes, possibly 16 to 18 in number, although Burrell claims he only ever had 6 of them. It is interesting that the tapes did not play a part in Burrell's trial, at least not officially, so why were the CPS and Manningham-Buller viewing the tapes, which apparently did not substantiate the 'Crown's' case against Burrell?

Piers Morgan summed it up succinctly in *The Insider:* 'This will go on for weeks, and can only be damaging to the Royal Family. They must be mad allowing Burrell to potentially take the stand. Cornered and desperate, he might say anything, and he knows the lot because he was there.' And suddenly, the Queen remembered her discussion with Burrell at Buckingham Palace in December 1997 and was certain that Burrell told her that he was taking some of Diana's belongings into his possession for safekeeping. Burrell also took six of the tapes, what happened to the rest?

There have been selective leaks of the tapes and the probably reason for this is that Scotland Yard took the blame, again, for the whole fiasco that was the Burrell trial. Others suggest that leaks were made in a flurry in March 2003, to prevent Charles speaking out against the Iraq war. Whatever, the truth, it is clear that no proper investigation was made into George Smith's allegations that he was raped and that he saw a 'male royal' engage in homosexual acts with a member of staff.

The Peat Report established no wrongdoing in the Royal Household and achieved the primary objective of "restoring order" to the Prince's Household. All nice and neat and tidy, yet again. It never ceases to amaze me that any member of the Establishment accused of wrongdoing is eventually exonerated and much the same can be said of Parliament under the corrupt regime of Tony Blair.

The tapes, leaked in a controlled fashion, did far less damage than they might have done if released in their entirety without being doctored first. And imagine the disaster that would have ensued if the tapes had been released, driven by the impetus of Princess Diana, an icon across the world! Such a scenario would likely have brought down the House of Windsor or at the very least, prevented Charles from inheriting the throne and supplanting Prince William as the heir apparent. The decision, with great foresight, was made to eliminate the Diana question and it was, well almost.

Just before midnight on 30th August 1997 and even before the Mercedes S280 pulled off from the rue Cambon on the journey that would enter the annals of history, the British Establishment signalled its intention to resolve the Diana question once and for all. The very public attack on Mohamed Al Fayed in the Sunday Mirror was the opening shot of the night's events. MI6, tasked by Prince Philip, who Al Fayed accuses of ordering the hit on Diana and Dodi, had instructed the spooks to draw up a damning dossier against the Al Fayeds.

This was not mere brinkmanship, both sides, particularly the Windsors meant business and one side or the other would not survive the battle for survival. As far as the Windsors were concerned it was them or the Al Fayeds and that also included Diana who had left the royal clique behind and become the greatest threat to the monarchy since Wallis-Simpson. The Queen Mother believed Diana was a far greater threat to the House of Windsor than Wallis-Simpson.

With these great threats, not to national security or the public, only to the House of Windsor and its small army of hangers on, a safe pair of hands was needed at MI5 to ensure the tapes were kept out of the public domain or at the very least, if they leaked, the damage minimised. Eliza Manningham-Buller has fulfilled her role to the Monarch and ensured that the damage was minimised. In this regard, her time in office as DG can be regarded as a success but in the war on terror, she has been an abysmal failure.

No one can forget the cock up, Eliza made of the report to Parliament, the day before the 7/7 attacks on London. But of even greater concern to the whole nation, is that just fourteen months later, Eliza is on autocue again to tell the nation, as part of MI5's terror fantasy, that thousands of would-be terrorists are on the loose in Britain and that the poor old spooks need yet more millions to protect us or merely to waste on cover ups or plotting yet more illegal wars in Iraq or Iran. What changed during those fourteen months to create such a colossal increase in the 'terror threat'?

On 6th July 2005, Manningham-Buller told Parliament there was no threat to the nation from any group – the next day over 50 people were murdered on the streets and subways of London. And fourteen months later, suddenly from having no credible threats to the nation, thousands have sprung up, in the dark like mushrooms to threat our very existence on the planet. As a trainee journalist, I was taught a rudimentary lesson about the relationship between government and the governed: **"Treat them like mushrooms: keep them in the dark and feed them on bullshit!"**

(Paul Burrell, covertly recorded on camera in a New York hotel room at the height of the quasi-inquest. He admitted lying at the 'inquest' – perjury – as a 'favour to the Queen'. He laughed off his dishonesty by explaining, "well, she's the Queen." But the damning proof of his collusion with the Establishment came when Lord 'Justice' Scott-Baker ruled he should NOT be prosecuted for breaking the 'law')

Eliza Manningham-Buller was appointed just before the arrest and prosecution of Paul Burrell; the objective of which was designed to neutralise the threat the tapes posed to the House of Windsor. In short order the Paget Investigation was ordered into the deaths of Princess Diana and Dodi Fayed, with Eliza at the helm again. And with the Paget whitewash concluded and the 'secrets' of Diana's box hidden away, the Queen's Emissary at MI5, retired from the service in April 2007 to be replaced by Jonathan Evans who has proved to be even more Stalinist than his predecessor.

Chapter 10

Whitewashed

('Sir' John Stevens, former Metropolitan Police Commissioner)

Lord Stevens could have been reading from the pages of a gripping, fast paced thriller. This was a story of historic proportions and it had everything: the mysterious death of a princess adored by millions, an exotic Egyptian lover, son of a billionaire, the sinister shadow of the secret services, an alleged high-speed chase through the most romantic city in the world, and the devastating crash into the thirteenth pillar of an underground tunnel, and the faithful plod delivered his report with the clinical detachment of a penny-pinching funeral director.

Maybe he thought his boorish tone would put us all to sleep and consequently we would miss all the important points of his so-called 'investigation' into the deaths of Princess Diana and Dodi Fayed. But a great many of us were gripped nonetheless, wide awake and not likely to be 'kept in the dark and fed on bullshit'. Instead of being treated like mushrooms, the public delivered a devastating verdict on his Paget Report.

In national newspaper polls conducted on 15th December 2006, close to 90 per cent of the public said they believed Stevens had whitewashed the 'investigation' and he disappeared again into the wilderness from whence he came. It was a damning result, 'not for the fainthearted' to coin the title of his book, which interestingly was ghost-written for him. If Stevens could not even write 'his own' book, and needed to employ a ghost-writer to make him look good, just who on earth wrote the Paget Report?

After the Surrey coroner, Michael Burgess, was pushed aside and the retired Judge, Dame Elizabeth Butler-Sloss with connections to the Royal Household, was parachuted in to conduct the inquests, the Stevens investigation was suddenly and prematurely closed down. Speaking on 14th December 2006, Al Fayed said: "I will never accept this cover up of what really happened. For nine years I have fought against overwhelming odds and monstrous official obstructions. I will not stop now in my quest for the truth. It is the only thing I can do for those two wonderful people who lost their lives. I shall keep searching for the truth, no matter what."

On page 4 of the Paget Report, Stevens' wrote: 'Detailed consideration of the conspiracy allegation made by Mohamed Al Fayed led the MPS to determine that a criminal investigation should be conducted. Although the crash and the deaths occurred within French jurisdiction, any alleged offence of conspiracy was primarily based in the United Kingdom and the allegation came under that jurisdiction.

'The French authorities agreed to support the Coroner by allowing special operating procedures in relation to International Letters of Request (ILoR) due to the volume of enquiries anticipated.' And again on page 5: 'Mohamed Al Fayed has made a principal crime allegation, supplemented by numerous linked claims and assertions. In essence Mohamed Al Fayed's allegation is that the 'Security Services' (unless otherwise specified, this is taken to be the Secret Intelligence Service (SIS) - commonly known as MI6) acting at the behest of HRH Prince Philip, arranged for or carried out the murder of Dodi Al Fayed and the Princess of Wales.

'The alleged motive was that the Princess of Wales was pregnant with Dodi Al Fayed's child and there was to be an imminent announcement of their engagement. It is suggested by

Mohamed Al Fayed that the Royal Family 'could not accept that an Egyptian Muslim could eventually be the stepfather of the future King of England'.

'It is alleged that the Security Services of the United Kingdom covertly obtained the information concerning pregnancy and engagement, with or without the co-operation of overseas agencies, precipitating the need to put into operation a plan to murder them. Mohamed Al Fayed further alleges there was a cover-up by the 'Establishment' to prevent the conspiracy and murders from coming to light.

Not unsurprisingly, Mohamed Al Fayed has never been believed by British authorities, that anything other than an 'accident' took place in the Alma Tunnel on 31st August 2007. This is entirely in keeping with the original decision of French and British authorities, just an hour after the crash, to promote the 'accident theory' and in the ten years that has elapsed since, the British and French have stuck to their initial, and later 'investigated' verdict. Any version of events that did not confirm their accident theory, was overlooked or blocked completely.

And again, I reiterate, by definition 'accidents' do not need to be covered up. Accidents are caused by chance, random events beyond anyone's control but the crash in the Alma Tunnel was caused by a combination of orchestrated events and the evidence to prove that the crash was not an accident, has been suppressed by "monstrous official obstruction". The accident theory arguments can be torn apart with just elementary logic and rationale. But not so, if we are to believe Stevens and the Paget Report.

On page 40 of the report, Stevens asked Claude Roulet if he was aware of the planned engagement between Dodi Al Fayed and Diana Frances Spencer-Windsor. Roulet said: ""I was never told that directly, but a few days before their arrival in Paris Dodi asked me to go to Repossi's [sic], a jeweller's in the place Vendôme, and see a certain ring that Diana had seen in the window at Repossi's in Monte Carlo."

"Previously in 1997 we had both been to Dubail's, which was also a jeweller's in the place Vendôme, to see a watch that Dodi wanted to offer Diana, but after the Monte Carlo episode he wanted in fact to offer her this ring which they had not been able to find at Repossi's in Paris."

Alberto Repossi was so outraged by his ordeal at the hands of British investigators that he sent a detailed letter of protest to

Lord Stevens. In a damning attack on the tactics used during his encounters with the inquiry team, Mr Repossi said: "My real concern is that attempts were certainly made to get me to change what I knew to be the truth. I believe they were doing this in order to support theories or conclusions that they had already arrived at or decided upon long before they saw me and my wife, Angela. They only seemed interested in trying to show we were lying."

Alberto Repossi claims that he was threatened by the Paget Inquiry's detectives, who said that he could be imprisoned if he knowingly misled the investigation. Repossi is certain that the detectives wanted him to change his story and say that Diana and Dodi had not visited his jewellery boutiques in Monte Carlo and Paris to purchase an engagement ring, see pages 18, 25. Mr Repossi has offered to testify at the Inquest in October 2007.

"They warned me that if anyone lied to Lord Stevens – and anyone could include the Prime Minister or even the Secret Service – then he had the power to get people sent to prison. I told them I'd told the truth and if other people had changed their stories perhaps it was because the police had persuaded them, in the same way they were trying to persuade me to change my story. They kept repeating the warnings of the risk to my reputation and the bad press coverage I would get. But despite all this, I was not prepared to change what I'd said before because it was the truth."

Mr Repossi claimed officers had told him the final interview would be an informal chat to bring him up to date with the inquiry's progress, but he is convinced the meeting was tape-recorded in the hope he would make an unguarded admission. He said: "I spent hours and hours of what I can only describe as interrogation. My wife and I were separated and the officers often left the room to confer with colleagues interrogating my wife, and came back to trick me." When the jeweller asked for copies of the interview tapes, two of the five cassettes he was sent were blank, he claims. The Yard blamed technical problems. "This is very unprofessional if this is the case," Mr Repossi said.

He also complained that investigators used inconsistencies in his recollection of events in 1997 to suggest he was telling lies. "I wasn't seen or interviewed about any of this by the French police or the original investigating judge. The first time I was asked to talk about exactly what happened was eight years after the crash, so it's hardly surprising I've forgotten or become confused about some of the details. I feel that the investigators took me by surprise with the details they were trying to get me to remember after eight years, and causing confusion which in the last meeting I had they used to imply that I was a liar," he said.

Mr Repossi said he was also infuriated by claims made by bodyguard Trevor Rees-Jones, the only survivor of the crash, who cashed in on the controversy by publishing a book in 2000 completely rejecting the assertion that Dodi had bought an engagement ring in Monte Carlo. He said: "I realised I had to speak up after I saw the book by Rees-Jones, because he was telling such outrageous lies. My intention has always been to help get to the truth of what actually happened."

Repossi's testimony - backed up by receipts and CCTV footage - reveals Dodi and Diana picked a $305,000 emerald and diamond ring from a range of engagement bands called "Did Moi Oui" which means "Tell Me Yes" at his Monte Carlo jewellery store in August 1997. It is clear that Lord Stevens wanted Repossi to change his story and say the couple had never visited his boutique but the hard evidence proves they did.

And René Delorm, with regard to the visit to the Monte Carlo branch of Repossi, stated to the Paget Inquiry: "I have been asked about the trip to Monaco and whether I was always with them. I was with them all the time. Dodi told me to stay in front of them and the bodyguard, John was behind. We were never separated. At one moment they went into a jewellery store but I didn't go with them. I have been asked if they went to Repossi. Yes, they went in there or at least I assume it was Repossi - they were inside for about 15 minutes, we waited outside."

And yet, bodyguard John Johnson, told Paget: "I have been asked if I have any knowledge of a jewellery store named

'Repossi'. I have never heard of it. As I have said, when Dodi and the Princess walked around Monaco, they walked briefly into a flower shop and a CD shop and that was it. I do not recall them stopping and looking into a jewellers window. We must have passed half a dozen or so jewellers during the walk but I don't recall stopping outside any of them for any period of time. It is possible that they stopped outside a jeweller's shop, but they certainly did not go into one."

It should be noted that Johnson and Rees-Jones became estranged from Mohamed Al Fayed after the crash in 1997 and Rees-Jones can only remember those matters he wants to remember. It is also rumoured that Rees-Jones has been threatened by British Intelligence and as a former soldier he knows only too well what could happen to him if he does not play ball.

But threats aside, real or alleged, Alberto Repossi insists he was threatened by detectives from Scotland Yard. He claimed the detectives wanted him to change his story and to say that he had not sold Dodi Fayed an engagement ring and that he had not visited his store to collect any such ring. The detectives also threatened him with imprisonment if he lied. Repossi stuck to his version of events and the threats of the detectives, having had their bluff called, proved to be worthless.

Every witness who has come forward to say the crash was not accident has been ignored by the French and British police. And people who confirm that Diana and Dodi were planning to get engaged or were in fact already engaged, have been threatened. And Richard Tomlinson, former MI6 officer, has been raided, beaten, threatened and harassed from Britain to New Zealand and back again.

Indeed, on 5th March 2007, the day of the pre-Inquest hearing at the High Court in London, the French authorities moved against Tomlinson to try and silence him on the instructions of MI6. Tomlinson wrote on his blogspot: "MI6 have started proceedings against me in France to execute Lord Justice Parks order of 1999 against me. This order, if executed against me in France, will prevent me talking about all and any aspect of my work in MI6. If the French do execute it against me, then it will also prevent me giving video evidence (if I am asked to do so) to the Butler-Sloss chaired inquiry into the death of Princess Diana. It does strike me as odd that MI6 have not attempted to execute this order against me in France for the past eight years but have now decided to do so."

I emailed Tomlinson the same day to offer my advice on a possible remedy. I told him to send a video recording of his proposed testimony to Mohamed Al Fayed and Michael Mansfield QC, so as to circumvent the imminent gagging order. If Butler-Sloss refused to admit the video evidence, it could be taken as a sign of further cover-up and deliberate blocking of evidence that would only benefit Al Fayed's campaign.

The fact that MI6 ordered Tomlinson to be silenced on the very same day of the pre-Inquest hearing in London, shows desperation on the part of the spooks to suppress, by force if necessary, all damaging information and evidence to prove their role in the murders of Princess Diana, Dodi Fayed and Henri Paul. After all, we are told time and again, that the crash was an 'accident', so why resort to threats and intimidation? Accidents, by definition, do not to be covered up. By 8th March 2007, Tomlinson's blogs on which I had posted several messages offering support and advice, was taken down by MI6. Tomlinson was in serious trouble.

And the same is also true of the loaded, prejudicial Paget Inquiry. Lord Stevens of Kirkwhelpington, a life-peerage of the Royal Household, claims to be 'impartial'. Indeed his fairness and balance extended so far as to ignore the vital 18 witnesses to the events immediately prior to and after the crash. In fact, Stevens says there are only 13 witnesses not 18. But even those 13 witnesses have effectively been ignored. A key witness to the crash has broken his silence to tell how he saw a dozen "shady figures" at the scene moments before her death. Record producer Jacques Morel, 59, is convinced they expected to see her Mercedes brought to a halt by another car.

Paget Inquiry Detectives interviewed Mr Morel for three days in London. He was driving home with his wife Moufida in Paris on the night of August 31st, 1997, he said: "As we entered the Alma tunnel I looked to my left and saw about a dozen shady figures on a tiny pavement by the side of the opposite carriageway. They were all standing in a long line. The sight was unforgettable. The pavement is less than 30cm (12in) wide and next to fast traffic. They would have been breathing in petrol fumes and it was very dirty down there. It was certainly not a sensible place to stand around."

Mr Morel, who now lives in Tunisia, said: "There was an almighty bang and a great big flash of light. Immediately my wife and I realised there had been a crash. My first thought was that those inside the tunnel were connected with what had happened. This thought has never left me. We could see a car coming from the opposite direction had gone straight into a pillar. All of the other drivers stopped, so I did too. There was a symphony of car horns and then white smoke filled the tunnel. I got out of my car and rushed towards the crash scene."

"I was devastated when I saw the Princess in her white trousers in the back of the car. She was easily recognisable. She looked so serene and peaceful, but it was the end. It was one of the most heartbreaking scenes of my life. I will never forget seeing her face. Others were lying around Diana and I remember the driver looking as though he had his head in his hands. **It was then that I also saw a white Fiat Uno being driven away.**" But despite his crucial evidence of what happened, Lord Stevens glossed over his testimony and again the white Fiat Uno was irrelevant.

Lord Stevens also interviewed an unnamed security officer on Tony Blair's team, who claimed that whilst idly chatting to the co-pilot of the Prime Minister's flight, he was told something very bizarre. The co-pilot, according to information with the Paget Inquiry, asked him: "What's really going on? We've been on standby in Scotland since 5pm on Friday waiting to make this flight to Northolt with the Prime Minister."

It was one of the first weekends the recently elected Prime Minister had spent at his Sedgefield constituency with his family since his election victory in May 1997. When news arrived overnight that Diana was dead, Mr Blair's weekend, which had been largely free of public engagements, was thrown into disarray. After delivering his 'People's Princess' tribute, he returned to London to receive Diana's body at Northolt airport at 5pm on the Sunday.

The Prime Minister's wife and their three children were put on a scheduled British Midland flight from Teesside airport at tea-time for them to return to Downing Street. Normally, the Prime Minister would have travelled with them. But instead, he boarded an RAF plane piloted by a crew based in Scotland which had flown to Teesside. Waiting on the tarmac for Mr Blair was the unnamed security officer and if true, his statement is shocking in that it shows an 'incident' was expected. Why reason does a security officer on Blair's security team have to lie?

And former MI6 officer Richard Tomlinson was disgusted with the Paget Report. On his Internet blogspot, before it was banned on 8th March 2007, he wrote: 'First, to clarify some of the errors in the Paget report, the assassination plot was definitely aimed at President Slobodan Milosevic, and not some other "extreme nationalist leader" as the Paget report claimed.

'Second, the plan was definitely written in the form of a "minute", complete with a numbered yellow minute board, which in SIS is an accountable document that is considered a "hanging offence" to destroy. I find it very hard to believe that this document has been destroyed - more likely SIS have hidden it from the police, in order to reduce the risk of a prosecution against Nicholas Fishwick, the author of the minute.

'I have nothing against Fishwick - indeed I quite liked him personally. But the fact that the Attorney General has declined to prosecute him illustrates perfectly the double-standards of the current and former Attorney Generals when faced with prosecution decisions involving SIS. Leaving aside any moral views on the value of assassinating Slobodan Milosevic, it is illegal in the UK to incite to murder.

'When I was locked up in HMP Belmarsh, there were other inmates serving lengthy sentences for threatening murder. According to the Express article, the Attorney General was presented by the police with irrefutable evidence that Fishwick had incited a murder, yet he has taken no action. Why?

'Because SIS would have asked him not to - just as in 1998 when Hong Kong Governor Chris Patten leaked raw CX reports to his biographer Richard Dimbleby in order to spice up his book sales yet escaped prosecution on the recommendation of SIS, or just as in the case of "fourth man" Anthony Blunt, who escaped prosecution whereas Philby, Burgess and MacLean were extensively prosecuted.

'Of course, the Attorney General would claim that the decision to prosecute or not is "impartial", and he does not have to abide by the recommendation of SIS. But I would bet a lot of money that there is no example in recent history where this or any other Attorney General has not followed the advice of SIS in a prosecution decision.' Tomlinson clearly accused Lord Stevens of altering the testimony given to him by the former MI6 officer.

He concludes: 'Essentially, if SIS want to take it out on somebody, they have the power and influence to do so - illustrated perfectly by the 1998 prosecution against myself for showing an innocuous book synopsis to Shona Martyn of Harper Collins in Australia, for which I received a twelve month prison sentence, or by the disproportionate actions against me currently for drafting a fictitious novel on my computer.' Tomlinson's computers were seized by police and returned to him destroyed and unusable; he has suffered a great deal of harassment from the British and French authorities.

But there is little point in reprinting vast swathes of the Paget Report here, I have not the space and as there is relatively little that is new in its 'findings' and Stevens has pretty much reiterated the French 'investigation' and overlooked every piece of evidence to prove the crash was no accident. The Paget Report can be downloaded from the Internet at www.sky.com/news

It is certainly worth studying, all 831 pages of it, if only as light entertainment in the continuing theatre of the 'Great Accident Theory', showing at every Government Department in Britain, including the Inquest in Court 73 of the 'Royal' Courts of Justice on the Strand, London.

Chapter 11

Open Verdict?

The 2nd March 2007, witnessed Harrod's boss Mohamed Al Fayed win an extraordinary victory at the High Court over the way the inquests into the deaths of the Princess of Wales and his son Dodi would be conducted. The Deputy Royal Coroner, Baroness Butler-Sloss had previously ruled that the joint inquest would be held without a jury and that she alone, would rule on the verdict. Immediately, accusations of cronyism were thrown at the Baroness, a life-long friend of the Establishment.

It was perfectly clear that the public's perception of the loaded process of the inquest was to cover up the original cover up and rule that the deaths of Diana and Dodi were accidental. The Queen had said that she thought the inquest should be held before a jury to preclude the perception that there had been a cover up. But Butler-Sloss was adamant and she attempted to proceed alone as judge, jury and executioner, as it were, until she was stopped by Al Fayed at the High Court.

The panel of three senior judges, Lady Justice Smith, Mr Justice Collins and Mr Justice Silber said: "We quash the decisions to conduct the inquests as deputy coroner for the Queen's Household and without summoning a jury." And ordered that Butler-Sloss would hear the inquest with a jury. The judges went on to say: "The Coroner shall reconsider the district in which the inquest shall be conducted in the light of the judgment." The judges also gave advice as to the location of the hearings. The Westminster Coroner immediately accepted the inquest into his jurisdiction to enable the hearings to be held at the High Court in May 2007.

Neutral Citation Number: [2007] EWHC 408

(Admin) Case No: CO/675/2007
Case No : CO/685/2007

IN THE HIGH COURT OF JUSTICE
QUEEN'S BENCH DIVISION
ADMINISTRATIVE COURT
Royal Courts of Justice Strand,

London, WC2A 2LL

Date: 02/03/2007 Before :

LADY JUSTICE SMITH
MR JUSTICE COLLINS
MR JUSTICE SILBER

Between :

Jean Paul and Gisele Paul and The Ritz Hotel Limited

Claimant

- and -

Deputy Coroner of the Queen's Household and Assistant Deputy Coroner
for Surrey (Baroness Elizabeth Butler-Sloss)

Defendant

Mohamed Al Fayed

Claimant

- and -

Deputy Coroner of the Queen's Household and Assistant Deputy Coroner
for Surrey (Baroness Elizabeth Butler-Sloss)

Defendant

Mr Richard Keen QC, Mr Thomas De la Mare and Ms Victoria Windle
(instructed by Stuart Benson & Co) for M. and Mme Paul

Mr Michael Beloff QC, Mr Thomas de la Mare and Ms Victoria Windle
(instructed by Barlow Lyde & Gilbert) for
The Ritz Hotel Limited

Mr Michael Mansfield QC, Ms Henrietta Hill and Mr Navtej Singh
Ahluwalia (instructed by Lewis Silkin LLP) for
Mr Mohamed Al Fayed

Mr Ian Burnett QC and Mr Jonathan Hough (instructed by Mr Michael
Burgess, solicitor) for Lady Butler-Sloss Mr Edmund Lawson QC
(instructed by Naz Saleh) for The Commissioner
of the Police of the Metropolis

Judgment Approved by the court for handing down

Al Fayed & Ors v Butler-Sloss

Lady Justice Smith : This is the judgment of the Court

Introduction

1. This is a claim for judicial review of certain rulings made on
    8th January 2007 by the Rt Hon Baroness Butler-Sloss, sitting as
    Deputy Coroner of the Queen's Household and as Assistant
    Deputy Coroner for Surrey. The application is brought by
    interested persons to the forthcoming inquests into the deaths
    of Diana, Princess of Wales and Mr Emad El-Din Mohamed Abdel
    Moneim Fayed, to whom we shall refer as Dodi Al Fayed. The
    claimants are Mr Mohamed Al Fayed, father of Dodi Al Fayed, M
    and Mme Paul, the parents of Henri Paul, and the President of
    the Ritz Hotel.   At the commencement of the hearing, having
    read the papers, we granted permission to bring the claim.

2.   As is well known, Diana Princess of Wales and Dodi Al Fayed
    died on 31st August 1997, when the Mercedes motor car in
    which they were being driven by Henri Paul collided with a
    pillar in the underpass of the Pont D'Alma in Paris. Their
    bodies were repatriated later that day. The body of Dodi Al
    Fayed was brought into Battersea Heliport, from where it was
    taken to a mortuary in Fulham, in the coronial district of West
    London. The coroner for West London, Dr Burton, was
    informed of the presence of the body and became seized of
    jurisdiction to inquire into his death. The Princess's body was
    brought into Northolt Airport, which also lies in the coronial
    district of West London. Dr Burton became aware of the arrival
    of her body in his district and was seized of jurisdiction to
    inquire into her death.

3. Following Home Office guidance for coroners in relation to
    bodies repatriated from abroad, Dr Burton made enquiries as to
    where the Princess and Dodi Al Fayed were likely to be buried.
    This guidance was given in recognition of the fact that the
    family of a deceased person who dies abroad is unlikely to have
    any connection with the district within which the port of entry
    lies; it will usually be more convenient for the family if any
    inquest is conducted in the district in which the funeral is to
    take place. Enquiries of the Al Fayed family suggested that
    Dodi Al Fayed would be buried within the coronial district of
    Surrey, as in the event he was. On the basis of that
    information and acting under his powers under section 14 of

the Coroners Act 1988 (the 1988 Act), Dr Burton transferred jurisdiction over Dodi Al Fayed's death to the coroner for Surrey. Dr Burton's enquiries at Buckingham Palace suggested that the Princess would probably be buried at Windsor, within the precincts of the Castle. In fact, she was buried at Althorp, her family home. However, acting on the information he had been given, Dr Burton transferred jurisdiction over the Princess's death to the coroner of the Queen's household. In fact, as it happened, Dr Burton was, at that time, the coroner of the Queen's household, so the transfer was a formality; he transferred jurisdiction from himself as coroner for West London to himself as coroner of the Queen's household. One of the questions which this court will have to decide is whether section 14 of the 1988 Act empowered Dr Burton to transfer jurisdiction in respect of the Princess's death to the coroner of the Queen's household.

4.   Soon after the death, Mr Mohamed Al Fayed publicly raised allegations that the collision in the underpass had been engineered by persons who wished to dispose of the Princess and his son. His belief was that there had been a conspiracy between HRH Prince Philip, Duke of Edinburgh and the UK Security Services. These allegations were widely reported in the media. The French authorities carried out an investigation into the circumstances of the deaths and concluded that the car crash had been a tragic accident. During this time, no inquest was opened into the deaths. However, in 2003, no doubt on account of the continuing public concern about Mr Al Fayed's allegations, it was decided that inquests should be opened. By this time, Dr Burton's place as coroner of the Queen's household had been taken by Mr Michael Burgess, who was also the coroner for Surrey.

5.   In January 2004, Mr Burgess opened inquests into both deaths and announced that they would stand adjourned pending an investigation into the deaths and the allegations of conspiracy to murder. This investigation was to be carried out by the Metropolitan Police under the personal direction of the then Commissioner, Sir John Stevens, now Lord Stevens. That investigation, known as Operation Paget, was completed in late 2006. Meanwhile, Mr Burgess had announced that his conduct of these two inquests, which were plainly likely to last for a considerable time, was incompatible with his regular duties as coroner for Surrey and, in August 2006, Lady Butler-Sloss, a retired judge and former President of the Family Division, was appointed as deputy coroner of the Queen's household and as assistant deputy coroner for Surrey. These appointments were

made to enable her to conduct both inquests.

6. The Metropolitan Police decided that it would be appropriate to publish the report of their investigation. It is properly to be called 'The Operation Paget Crime Report' although it has been colloquially referred to in court and by Lady Butler-Sloss in her rulings as 'The Stevens Report'. We will do likewise. The report concluded that there was no evidence to support the allegations of conspiracy to murder. There was therefore no reason why the case should be referred to the Director of Public Prosecutions and the way was open for the inquests to proceed. The decision to publish the Stevens Report was taken by the Metropolitan Police but Lady Butler-Sloss was consulted before the decision was taken. She had no objection to publication; indeed, she supported it.

7. On 8th January 2007, Lady Butler-Sloss convened a pre-inquest hearing at which four issues fell to be determined. These were:
    (i) the identity of those persons properly interested in the two inquests;
    (ii) whether two separate inquests were to be held or concurrent inquests;
    (iii) whether two separate inquests were to be held or concurrent inquests; of the Queen's household;
    (iv) whether Lady Butler-Sloss should hold the inquests with or without a jury.

8. The first two issues did not give rise to dispute. The interested persons were identified. The interested persons in respect of the Princess's inquest are HRH Prince William and HRH Prince Harry, Lady Sarah McCorquodale (the Princess's sister and executrix), Mr Al Fayed, the President of the Ritz Hotel, the parents of M. Henri Paul, Mr Trevor Rees and the Commissioner of Police of the Metropolis. In respect of the inquest of Dodi Al Fayed, the interested persons are Mr Al Fayed, the President of the Ritz Hotel, the parents of M. Henri Paul, Mr Trevor Rees and the Commissioner of Police of the Metropolis. Not all were represented at the hearing. All those who were represented were agreed in respect of the second issue, namely that the inquests must be held concurrently.

9. On the third issue, on which a dispute arose, Lady Butler-Sloss held that she had jurisdiction to act as deputy coroner of the Queen's household. We will return to that issue in due course. On the fourth issue, which was also disputed, she decided that she would conduct the inquests without a jury. That decision is

also challenged in these proceedings. A further issue then arose for determination. As Lady Butler-Sloss had decided that the inquests should be held concurrently, she had to decide whether to act as deputy coroner of the Queen's household or as assistant deputy coroner for Surrey. Either the Princess's inquest had to be transferred to the coroner for Surrey or Dodi Al Fayed's inquest had to be transferred to the coroner of the Queen's household. This issue was also disputed. Lady Butler-Sloss decided to transfer the inquest of Dodi Al Fayed into the jurisdiction of the coroner of the Queen's household. However, realising that there might be a challenge to this ruling among others, she decided that she would not give effect to that decision until 5th March, at which time she intended to hold another hearing, to consider the scope of the inquests.

10. It is in respect of these three disputed decisions that these proceedings for judicial review are now brought. A fourth issue also arises, namely whether by supporting publication of the Stevens Report, Lady Butler-Sloss has compromised her independence and impartiality.

11. At the hearing before Lady Butler-Sloss, it was not suggested that Dr Burton's use of section 14 of the 1988 Act to transfer jurisdiction over the Princess's death was impermissible because section 14 did not confer the necessary power. It was, however, submitted that he had had no proper factual basis to make the transfer. He was acting in the belief that the Princess was to be buried at Windsor and, in the course of the hearing, it became clear that there was material which supported that belief. Accordingly, the basis upon which jurisdiction was challenged before Lady Butler-Sloss has not been relied on before us.

12. The submission made by the claimants is that, on their true construction, the relevant provisions in the 1988 Act show that the power in section 14 does not enable transfers to be made either to or from the coroner of the Queen's household. A deputy or assistant deputy coroner has the same powers and is subject to the same obligations under the 1988 Act as the coroner. If that submission is correct, Lady Butler-Sloss has never had jurisdiction to hold an inquest into the death of the Princess and so cannot act as deputy coroner of the Queen's household in holding the inquests as she has proposed.

13. The submission is given some apparent support from the wording of the 1988 Act coupled with the anomalous and

anachronistic existence of the post of coroner of the Queen's household. For the purpose of the exercise of coronial jurisdiction, the country is divided into districts which are specified in orders made either under section 4 of the 1988 Act or under provisions in the Local Government Act 1985. Prior to local government reorganisation in 1972, coroners were appointed for either counties or boroughs. Most counties were divided into coronial districts under powers conferred by section 12 of the Coroners (Amendment) Act 1926. The jurisdiction of a coroner is in general limited to consideration of dead bodies lying within his district.

14. The coroner of the Queen's household is a special case. His obligation to inquire into deaths caused in a royal palace or a house where the King was abiding was established by an Act of 1541 (33 Hen.8 CAP XII), which was entitled:

"An Acte for murther and malicious bloodshed within the Courte."

The purpose behind the Act was to enable acts of violence at Court to be tried by a jury before the Lord Steward or another specified officer of the Court. The coroner to the household would, in the case of a death, hold the necessary inquest which would result in what would in recent years be termed a committal for trial. It is to be noted that the office of coroner to the royal house had existed before the Act of 1541, since section 22 of that Act records:

"And forasmuch as before His Time one Richard Staverton of Lincoln's Inn, Gentleman, was commanded and appointed by the King's Majesty to occupy the Office of the Coroner to his said House, by Force whereof he hath continued Officer in the same by the Space of sixteen years or more, Be it enacted ... that the said Richard Staverton shall have, occupy and enjoy the said Office of Coroner during his Life ..."

Thus it is clear that the Act was concerned to put the office on a statutory basis so that there would be a coroner available at all times to ensure that violent death within the Court could be properly investigated and those responsible brought to a speedy form of justice.

15. The position of the coroner of the Queen's household is now dealt with in section 29 of the 1988 Act. This provides:

"29. Coroner of the Queen's household.

(1) The coroner of the Queen's household shall continue to be appointed by the Lord Steward for the time being of the Queen's household.

(2) The coroner of the Queen's household shall have exclusive jurisdiction in respect of inquests into the deaths of persons whose bodies are lying –

(a) within the limits of the Queen's palaces; or

(b) within the limits of any other house where Her Majesty is then residing.

(3) The limits of any such palace or house shall be deemed to extend to any courts, gardens or other places within the curtilage of the palace or house but not further; and where a body is lying in any place beyond those limits, the coroner within whose district the body is lying, and not the coroner for the Queen's household, shall have jurisdiction to hold an inquest into the death.

(4) The jurors on an inquest held by the coroner of the Queen's household shall consist of officers of that household, to be returned by such officer of the Queen's household as may be directed to summon the jurors by the warrant of the coroner.

(5) All inquisitions, depositions and recognizances shall be delivered to the Lord Steward of the Queen's household to be filed among the records of his office.

(6) The coroner of the Queen's household –

(a) shall make his declaration of office before the Lord Steward of the Queen's household; and

(b) shall reside in one of the Queen's palaces or in such other convenient place as may from time to time be allowed by the Lord Steward of the Queen's household.

(7) The provisions of Schedule 2 to this Act shall have effect with respect to the application of this Act and the law relating to coroners to the coroner of the Queen's household."

Schedule 2 disapplies the provisions of the Act which cover the appointment of other coroners. In addition section 5 which deals with the jurisdiction of coroners is excluded. It provides:

"(1) Subject to subsection (3) [which gives powers to act for another coroner in a district within the same administrative area where that other coroner is ill, incapacitated, or absent or there is a vacancy] and section 7 [which deals with deputies] and 13 to 15 below, an inquest into a death shall be held only by the coroner within whose district the body lies.

(2) ... a coroner shall hold an inquest only within his district."

In addition, the powers to appoint deputies and their functions are to have the necessary modifications required by the terms of section 29. Provisions relating to juries are excluded following section 29(4). Paragraph 5 is important. It reads:

"Subject to the provisions of this Schedule and Section 29 of this Act, the coroner of the Queen's household shall, within the limits laid down in subsection (3) of that section –
(a) have the same jurisdiction and powers; and
(b) be subject to the same obligations, liabilities and disqualifications; and
(c) generally be subject to the provisions of this Act and the law relating to coroners in the same manner as any other coroner."

16. Section 14 is not specifically disapplied in Schedule 2. It provides, so far as material:

"(1) if it appears to a coroner that, in the case of a body lying within his district, an inquest ought to be held into the death but it is expedient that the inquest should be held by some other coroner, he may request that coroner to assume jurisdiction to hold the inquest, and if that coroner agrees he, and not the coroner within whose district the body is lying, shall have jurisdiction to hold the inquest.

(4) Where jurisdiction to hold an inquest is assumed under this section, it shall not be necessary to remove the body into the district of the coroner who is to hold the inquest.
(7) On the assumption by a coroner of jurisdiction to hold an inquest under this section, the coroner –
(a) shall also assume, in relation to the body and the inquest, all the powers and duties which would belong to him if the body were lying within his district ... and
(b) may exercise those powers notwithstanding that the body remains outside his district or, having been removed into it, is removed out of it by virtue of any order of his for its examination or burial."

Subsection (7) enables a coroner to whom jurisdiction has been transferred under section 14 to use that section to make a further transfer if that is considered expedient.

17. It is apparent that the purpose behind section 14 is to enable inquests to be held at places which are more convenient to those interested, in particular the family of the deceased. That this will usually be the case in respect of bodies returned

to this country following deaths abroad is obvious and this led to the Home Office guidance to which we have already referred.

18. The submission that section 14 does not apply to the coroner of the Queen's household is based on the limits to his jurisdiction expressed in section 29(3) coupled with the reference in section 14 to the need that the body to be transferred or to be received is within the coroner's district (see section 14(1) and (4)). The coroner of the Queen's household does not have a district: indeed, he is not a district coroner, which is the description applied in, for example, Jervis on Coroners (see 12th Edition Paras: 2-12). Section 5(1), which has been disapplied by Schedule 2 Paragraph 1, limits the jurisdiction of a coroner to his district, subject to, inter alia, section 14. Section 13 deals with orders of the High Court to hold an inquest where the coroner has failed to hold one when he should have done or there have been defects in the inquest that has been held. Section 15 gives power to the Secretary of State to direct an inquest where he receives a report from a coroner that 'a death has occurred in or near his district' which requires an inquest but 'owing to the destruction of the body by fire or otherwise, or to the fact that the body is lying in a place from which it cannot be recovered, an inquest cannot be held except in pursuance of this section.'

19. Section 29(2)(b) means that the jurisdiction of the coroner of the Queen's household is moveable in that it depends upon where Her Majesty may happen to be residing if not in one of her palaces. Thus, it is submitted that even if, by a stretch of language, a royal palace could be regarded as a district, a place where Her Majesty might from time to time be could not. Furthermore, it is clear from the Act that coroners are to be appointed 'for each coroner's district' (section 1(1)) and that the districts are to be identified by the Secretary of State (section 4). Accordingly, the word 'district' when used in the Act must, it is said, refer only to the districts to which ordinary coroners are appointed and cannot be extended to include the palaces or houses within s.29(2). Mr Keen QC (who appeared for the parents of Henri Paul) submitted that, as he put it, the gateway to section 14 was contained in section 5(1) and that that section's exclusion by virtue of Paragraph 1 of Schedule 2 meant that section 14 could not apply to the coroner of the Queen's household.

20. The result, if the claimants' submissions are correct, is indeed strange. It is to be noted that many of the sections of the Act

which concern the powers of a coroner are related to bodies lying within that coroner's district. Thus section 19 enables a coroner to direct a post-mortem if he considers that such an examination may prove an inquest to be unnecessary. Section 22 enables a coroner to direct removal of a body for a post-mortem examination 'to any place ... either within his district or within an adjoining district of another coroner'. The absence of such a power for the coroner of the Queen's household would produce an obvious difficulty, since presumably any post-mortem examination would have to be held in the palace or house concerned.

21. In addition, the section which establishes the duty to hold an inquest is section 8. Section 8(1) provides:

"Where a coroner is informed that the body of a person (the deceased) is lying within his district and there is reasonable cause to suspect that the deceased –

(a) has died a violent or an unnatural death;
(b) has died a sudden death of which the cause is unknown; or
(c) has died in prison or in such a place or in such circumstances as to require an inquest under any other Act, then, whether the cause of death arose within the district or not, the coroner shall as soon as practicable hold an inquest into the death of the deceased with or, subject to subsection (3) below, without a jury."

If, by virtue of the limitation to a body lying within his district, that duty cannot be said to apply to the coroner of the Queen's household, there is precious little left of the obligations, jurisdiction or powers or any provisions of the Act which could apply in accordance with Paragraph 5 of Schedule 2.   It seems to us that to adopt such a narrow construction of the reference to district would be contrary to the intention of Parliament. It was, in our view, contemplated that, subject to the express exclusions, the provisions of the Act which laid down the powers and the obligations of coroners should apply equally to the coroner of the Queen's household. While we recognise that the word 'district' does not easily, in its natural meaning, fit in with what was referred to before us as the topographical limit to the jurisdiction of the coroner of the Queen's household, to construe it as the claimants would wish would be to produce an absurd situation. We were not impressed with the submission of Mr Beloff QC (who appeared for the President of the Ritz Hotel), that, since the office of coroner of the Queen's household itself was an anomaly and there were very few calls on him, the administrative difficulties were not of any real significance.

22. If the argument is refined to submit that it is only sections 13 to 15 which do not apply because of the reference to them in section 5(1), in our view it fares no better. Section 15 contains a necessary power to deal with a situation where a body is destroyed. Section 29(2) gives the coroner of the Queen's household exclusive jurisdiction in relation to inquests into the death of persons "whose bodies are lying" within the limits of a palace or house. If, for example, the body of the unfortunate lady who was killed in the fire at Hampton Court in 1983 had been destroyed, the coroner of the Queen's household would not have been able to act. It may be argued that, in such circumstances, the coroner for the adjoining district could use section 15 and the Secretary of State could direct the coroner of the Queen's household to hold the inquest. While that might provide a possible solution, it is an unsatisfactory situation since it is clearly anticipated that the coroner of the Queen's household is to concern himself with deaths in royal palaces, albeit the reference to a 'body lying' is not limited to a 'body dying'.

23. In any event, it is obviously desirable that the coroner of the Queen's household should be able to make use of section 14. While we recognise that it will be exceptional for it to be expedient for him to assume jurisdiction over a body lying elsewhere, the same cannot be said in relation to transfer out of his jurisdiction. If, for example, a visitor to a royal palace were to be killed in an accident, it would almost certainly be more convenient for any inquest to take place where he lived or was to be buried. Furthermore, it might well be desirable to be able to avoid the holding of an inquest altogether by use of the powers conferred by section 19 and it might be far more convenient for those powers to be exercised by the coroner who otherwise would be holding the inquest.

24. While the claimants submitted that the natural meaning of the sections in the Act led to the conclusion they espoused, they accepted that, if we were of the view that the provisions were ambiguous, it might assist us to look at the their history. At one stage of the argument we were of that view and we agreed to examine the history.

25. The 1988 Act was a consolidating Act with amendments to give effect to recommendations of the Law Commission. The only relevant recommendation was to make clear in section 29 that

the jurisdiction of the coroner of the Queen's household applied to palaces generally and in addition to houses at which Her Majesty was residing. Section 29(2) of the Coroners Act 1887 provided:

"The coroner of the Queen's household shall have exclusive jurisdiction in respect of inquests on persons whose bodies are lying within the limits of any of the Queen's palaces or within the limits of any other house where Her Majesty is then demurrant and abiding in her own royal person, notwithstanding the subsequent removal of Her Majesty from such palace or house."

This could be construed to mean that the jurisdiction only applied to a palace or house in which at the material time Her Majesty was 'demurrant and abiding'. This gave rise to some concern whether the coroner of the Queen's household ought to have assumed jurisdiction to deal with the death resulting from the fire at Hampton Court (at which Her Majesty was not then nor has ever been 'demurrant and abiding'). The terms of section 29(2) of the 1988 Act clear up that ambiguity.

26. Since the 1988 Act is otherwise a consolidating Act, it is to be assumed that it did not change the meaning of the Acts which it consolidated. Thus it can assist us in determining the true construction of the 1988 Act to look at its predecessors. The main Act was that of 1887, itself a consolidation of a number of exceedingly ancient Acts mainly passed in the reigns of Edward I, Edward III and Henry VIII. Section 3(1) of the 1887 Act (now section 8(1) of the 1988 Act) commenced as follows:

"When a coroner is informed that the dead body of a person is lying within his jurisdiction ..."

Section 6 (now section 13 of the 1988 Act) provided by subsection (2) that the court might order that the inquest it directed should be held 'either by the said coroner, or if the said coroner is a coroner for a county, by any other coroner for the county, or if he is a coroner for a borough or for a franchise then by a coroner for the county in which such borough or franchise is situated, or for a county to which it adjoins ...'

The coroner of the Queen's household was a coroner for a franchise – see section 29(8) and section 42. Section 42 also stated:

"the expression 'franchise' means the area within which the

franchise coroner exercises jurisdiction."

27. There can therefore be no doubt that, under the 1887 Act, the coroner for the Queen's household was subject to all the general duties imposed and had all the general powers granted by the Act. Furthermore, since he was a franchise coroner, the area in which he exercised his jurisdiction was and could only have been the palaces or houses where Her Majesty was demurrant and abiding or, to use more modern terminology, residing.

28. Section 16 of the Coroners (Amendment) Act 1926 introduced a power to enable a coroner to allow a body lying within his jurisdiction to be removed to the jurisdiction of another coroner if that other coroner agreed. This was the precursor for what has become section 14 of the 1988 Act, but removal of the body was required. It is to be noted that it refers, in accordance with the 1887 Act, to the jurisdictions of the respective coroners. This power was extended by section 2 of the Coroners Act 1980 to comprehend powers which are now contained in section 14 of the 1988 Act. Section 2(1) commenced as follows:

"If it appears to a coroner that an inquest ought to be held on a body lying within his area ...."

Section 3(4) of the Act, reads:

"At the beginning of section 7(1) of the Coroners Act 1887 (jurisdiction of a coroner dependent on the presence of the body in his area) there shall be inserted ... [some words which are not material]."

Section 7(1) of the 1887 Act in fact uses the word 'jurisdiction', not area, but the draftsman of the 1980 Act clearly thought that there was no difference, since the jurisdiction was limited to an area, whether of a franchise or a county or a borough.

29. It is in our view clear that, before 1988, the coroner of the Queen's household was able to make use of the powers contained in the 1980 Act which were foreshadowed in the 1926 Act as well as all other powers which were given to coroners generally. Parliament in a consolidating Act could not have intended to change that. The use of the word 'district' was, it seems, regarded as a satisfactory synonym to 'area' since it was to do no more than identify the area which defined a particular coroner's jurisdiction. The history of the

provisions relating to the coroner of the Queen's household confirm beyond any doubt that the sensible construction is the correct one and that accordingly Dr Burton had jurisdiction to transfer the Princess's inquest to himself as coroner of the Queen's household and Lady Butler-Sloss has jurisdiction to transfer it away from herself to any other coroner who is agreeable if to do so is considered expedient.

30. The claimants submitted that Lady Butler-Sloss should sit with a jury and had erred by refusing to do so. It was submitted that she should have considered whether she was obliged to sit with a jury by reason of the provisions of section 8(3)(d) of the 1998 Act and, if she had done so, she would have concluded that she was required to sit with a jury. At the preliminary hearing, her attention was not drawn to this provision; indeed, all counsel submitted that the mandatory provisions of section 8(3) did not apply in the instant case.

31. Section 8(3) of the Act provides four sets of circumstances in which a coroner is obliged to conduct an inquest with a jury. In so far as material, the section provides:

"(3) If it appears to a coroner, either before he proceeds to hold an inquest or in the course of an inquest begun without a jury, that there is reason to suspect -....;

(d) that the death occurred in circumstances the continuance or possible recurrence of which is prejudicial to the health or safety of the public or any section of the public,

he shall proceed to summon a jury..."

32. We are uncertain of the reasons or justification for this provision but our task is to apply it. A number of points may be made about this mandatory provision. It applies to deaths that have occurred abroad (Re Neal [1995] 37 BMLR 164). For the provision to apply, the circumstances need not "cause the death" (see Jervis 10-27). The prospect of recurrence required for the section to be applicable is low; it is the possibility of recurrence and not any higher chance. For the provision to apply, only a section of the public needs to be at risk from recurrence.

33. Mr. Burnett QC, who was instructed by Lady Butler-Sloss but was asked to adopt a role similar to that of amicus and not to take an adversarial stance, submitted that it was unnecessary for Lady Butler-Sloss to have considered this provision as the

circumstances of the deaths of the Princess and Dodi Al Fayed did not require it. He drew attention to the reasoning of the Court of Appeal in R v HM Coroner at Hammersmith ex parte Peach (No 1 and 2) [1980] 1 QB 211 in which it was held that a coroner was obliged to sit with a jury under the section 13(2) of the Coroners (Amendment) Act 1926, as amended, where the deceased, who was watching a demonstration, was struck a violent blow on the back of his head from which he died.

34. According to Mr. Burnett, the reasoning of the Court in Peach shows that if Lady Butler-Sloss had considered this provision, she would not have decided that she should sit with a jury. So, he said, her decision to sit without a jury should not be quashed on that ground. In support of this submission, he attached importance to the statements in the Peach case of:

(a) Lord Denning MR, which was that a jury must be summoned when "the circumstances are such that similar fatalities may possibly occur in the future, and it is reasonable to expect that some action should be taken to prevent their recurrence" (page 226);

(b) Bridge LJ, who said that the recurrence of the circumstances referred to are those which

"may reasonably and ought properly to be avoided by the taking of appropriate steps which it is in the power of some responsible body to take" (page 227);

and

(c) Sir David Cairns, who explained that "The difficulty is to find a meaning which does not do violence to the words of the Act and which gives effect to what may be taken to have been the intention of Parliament. The reference to 'continuance or possible recurrence' indicates to my mind that the provision was intended to apply only to circumstances the continuance or recurrence of which was preventable or to some extent controllable. Moreover, since it is prejudice to the health or safety of the public or a section of the public that is referred to, what is envisaged must I think be something which might be prevented or safeguarded by a public authority or some other person or body whose activities can be said to affect a substantial section of the public. I cannot find any justification for any further limitation of the meaning of the paragraph in question." (page 228)

We do not understand the basis for the statement that the activities must affect 'a substantial section of the public' as the statute does not include that requirement.

35. Mr. Burnett submitted that we should apply the test suggested by Sir David Cairns, which sets the highest threshold for invoking the subsection and we will assume that this is the appropriate test. He then contended that the deaths in this case were caused, according to the issues raised, either by speeding coupled with the consumption of alcohol or as the result of a conspiracy to murder. In either event, the existing criminal law covered the situation with the consequence that, even if Lady Butler-Sloss had considered the subsection, she would not have used it to summon a jury. He cited, as an analogy, the decision of this Court in R. v HM Coroner for the Eastern District of the Metropolitan County of West Yorkshire ex parte National Union of Mineworkers [1985] 150 JP 58 in which it was held that the coroner was correct not to summon a jury pursuant to the predecessor section of section 8(3)(d).

36. In that case, a picket had been knocked down by a lorry and it was considered of crucial importance that the facts of that case did not have

"any particular feature which distinguishes it from any other kind of road accident to the circumstances of which courts, time and time again, have to listen in order to reach a determination be it in criminal or civil proceedings." (per Watkins LJ at page 62).

37. It is true that the deaths with which these present inquests are concerned occurred as a result of a collision on a road. However, the circumstances leading up to this collision were very unusual and had additional features to those found in a more usual type of road accident. As appears from the Stevens Report, the car carrying the Princess of Wales and Mr Al Fayed was being pursued by the paparazzi moments before the fatal crash. One eye witness, Didier Gamblin, a fire safety officer at the Ritz Hotel, explained that:

"The couple came out at about 9.45 in the evening. Although we had come to an agreement with the paparazzi they did not do what we had asked them. They came closer to the car than expected, although they did not rush forward as they had done when the couple arrived. But when the couple's car drove off they went completely crazy. They called their motor bikes and set off like lunatics to follow the car. They could have knocked pedestrians over on the pavement. People had to press themselves against the wall to let the paparazzi's motor bikes past, they were driving on the pavement...."

38. There was other evidence to the same effect and it is clear that it is at least arguable that the fatal accident was caused or contributed to by the pursuing paparazzi. Indeed, as we have explained, it is not a condition for invoking this sub-section that the circumstances which might possibly recur actually caused the deaths in question. In our view, there is a real likelihood of people in the public eye being pursued by the paparazzi in the future. It is well known that people in the public eye (including by way of a recent example, Miss Kate Middleton, Prince William's friend) are often stalked by photographers. During the hearing we were shown letters written to the press by Sir John Major and Sir Christopher Meyer, Chairman of the Press Complaints Council, expressing concern about the harassment of Miss Middleton and pointing out the similarity between her treatment and that suffered by the Princess of Wales. They drew attention to the dangers of such behaviour and called for new sanctions against the paparazzi.

39. It is likely that there will be a recurrence of the type of event in which the paparazzi on wheels pursued the Princess and Dodi Al Fayed. It is not only members of the Royal Family and their friends who receive this unwelcome attention; any celebrity is vulnerable. Not only is the safety of the person pursued potentially put at risk but there may well be a risk to bystanders. In our view, occurrences such as this are prejudicial to the safety of a section of the public. It is possible that this danger could be prevented by legislation or other means.

40. There are a number of ways in which these events could, in the words of Sir David Cairns in Peach, be 'preventable or controllable' whether by rules preventing newspapers from using material obtained by the paparazzi in this way or making the pursuit of people in the way described by Didier Gamblin an aggravated form of dangerous driving or speeding. Accordingly, it is our view that, as a matter of law, Lady Butler-Sloss's decision not to summon a jury was wrong and must be quashed. It is most unfortunate that the applicability of section 8(3)(d) was not argued at the hearing, as, if it had been, this application might have been avoided.

41. In the light of our conclusion on section 8(3)(d), it is not strictly necessary for us to deal with the submissions seeking to challenge the coroner's exercise of discretion under section 8(4) not to summon a jury. However, we wish to make three observations on this issue.

42. First, Lady Butler-Sloss made her decision under section 8(4) before she had considered the scope of the inquest. In our view, the logical approach is for a coroner first to determine the scope of the inquest and only then to make a decision on the relevance and applicability of sections 8(3) and (4). Here it can properly be said, as was urged by Mr Burnett, that although Lady Butler-Sloss had not yet made decisions on the scope of the inquests, she knew a great deal about the likely scope from reading the Stevens Report. We accept that that is so, but we are of the view that, as a matter of principle, the right course is to determine the scope of the inquest before considering whether to summon a jury.

43. Our second observation is that, in reaching her discretionary decision under section 8(4), it appears to us that Lady Butler-Sloss did not some relevant matters into account. She mentioned a number of factors relevant to the issue but the dispositive reason for her decision to sit without a jury was that she, sitting alone, would be able to provide a reasoned explanation for her conclusions whereas a jury would not; it would be able to provide only brief answers to a limited number of questions. It was in the public interest that a full explanation of the conclusions should be published. Although the validity of this reason was challenged, we do not accept the grounds of challenge; there is no need for us to explain why. In our view, the factors which Lady Butler-Sloss considered were properly taken into account.

44. However, it appears to us, from the arguments presented, that there were two additional factors relevant to the exercise of the coroner's discretion which ought to have been taken into consideration. First, it was the strongly expressed view of the family of Dodi Al Fayed that there should be a jury. That, of course, cannot be determinative but it is a relevant factor. This was recognised in the National Union of Miners case, and, in any event we believe that it is now regarded as good practice for coroners to consult the family of the deceased before making a discretionary decision under section 8(4). In this case, the sons and the sister of the Princess of Wales had indicated that they have no views on whether a jury should be summoned while Dodi Al Fayed's family felt that a jury would

be essential for a proper investigation into the deaths. We think the views of the Al Fayed family should have been taken into account.

45. Further, it appears to us that, when considering how to exercise the discretion under section 8(4) in a case to which the mandatory provisions of section 8(3) do not apply, it is appropriate to consider whether the facts of the instant case bear any resemblance to the types of situation covered by the mandatory provisions. By examining the policy considerations behind the mandatory provisions, it might be possible to find guidance as to the manner in which the discretion should be exercised. Lady Butler-Sloss did not undertake this exercise. Had she done so, we think that her decision might well have been different and she might well have concluded that she ought not to make any decision about whether or not to summon a jury until after she had determined the scope of the inquests.

46. Sections 8(3)(a) and (b) make it mandatory to summon a jury in cases where the death occurred in prison or while the deceased was in police custody or resulted from an injury caused by a police officer in the purported execution of his duty. The policy consideration behind these provisions is clear; in order that there should be public confidence in the outcome of the inquest, a jury should be summoned in cases where the state, by its agents, may have had some responsibility for the death. As we have said, in the present case, Mr Al Fayed has alleged that Duke of Edinburgh and the Security Services conspired to kill the Princess and Dodi Al Fayed. The allegation is that agents of the state have been involved in the deaths. If, when Lady Butler-Sloss determines the scope of the inquests, she decides that Mr Al Fayed's allegation must be inquired into, the possible role of state agents would be an important consideration material to her discretionary decision whether to summon a jury. Indeed, we think that that consideration might well be determinative in favour of summoning a jury. However, our decision to quash Lady Butler-Sloss's decision not to summon a jury is based on our conclusion that the mandatory provision in section 8(3)(d) applies in the circumstances of this case.

47. The claimants contended that, if, contrary to their first submission, Lady Butler-Sloss did have jurisdiction to hold the inquests as coroner to the Queen's household, she ought not to have chosen to do so. They advanced several reasons, not all of which had been fully ventilated before her at the hearing on

8th January. In the light of the conclusion we have already expressed, that these inquests must be heard by a coroner sitting with a jury, some of the submissions made cease to be of any great relevance. Others assume greater importance. We will deal with the points arising under this head, not in the order in which they were presented to us, but in the order in which it now appears to us to be convenient.

48. Lady Butler-Sloss's decision to transfer the inquest of Dodi Al Fayed to the coroner of the Queen's household was taken against the background of her decision that she would sit alone, without a jury. She clearly recognised that, if she had decided to summon a jury, she would have to transfer the Princess's inquest away from the Queen's household. That was because, under section 29(4), a jury summoned by the coroner of the Queen's household must comprise officers of the household. Lady Butler-Sloss accepted the submission made by Sir John Nutting QC, appearing on behalf of the Attorney General, that it would not be appropriate for her to sit with a jury drawn from the Queen's household. He did not doubt the capacity of such officers to reach a true verdict on the evidence but he submitted that it would be undesirable, even invidious, to ask such a jury to decide the questions that would arise. It was important, he said, to avoid any appearance of bias. Lady Butler-Sloss instantly agreed with him and no interested party expressed any dissent. It follows from that, that if the inquest is to be held with a jury, it cannot be held by the deputy coroner for the Queen's household. It follows that either the Princess's inquest would have to be transferred to Surrey or both inquests would have to be transferred to some other coronial district where it would be possible to summon a jury of 'ordinary people'. For that reason alone, it is now seen that the decision to sit as the deputy coroner for the Queen's household must be quashed.

49. However, other reasons were advanced why the decision cannot stand. It was submitted that the decision was flawed because it was based upon expediency. The basis of the Lady Butler-Sloss's decision was that, if she sat as assistant deputy coroner for Surrey, she would be compelled (by section 5(2)) to sit within the coronial district of Surrey. No suitably equipped venue could be found in that district. On the other hand, if she were to sit as deputy coroner of the Queen's household, (by virtue of paragraph 1 of Schedule 2 to the Act, which disapplies section 5(2)) she could choose where to sit. She knew that a suitably equipped court could be made available for her in the Royal Courts of Justice. So, in order to take advantage of that,

she chose to conduct both inquests as deputy coroner of the Queen's household. In our view, there is absolutely no reason why she should not have taken that reason of expediency into account. The provisions relating to transfer in section 14 of the Act are based on expediency.

50. However, a more important complaint was that Lady Butler-Sloss had failed to take other material matters into account. One of these was that, even assuming that the decision to sit without a jury was appropriate for the time being, Lady Butler-Sloss ought to have taken account of the need to keep open the opportunity to change her mind. Section 8, subsections (3) and (4) both envisage the need for a coroner to decide, even after the inquests have begun, that s/he ought to summon a jury. If this need were to arise for Lady Butler-Sloss, sitting as deputy coroner of the Queen's household, she would have to summon a jury of officers of the household and she had already decided that that would not be appropriate. So, she would then have put herself into the position whereby she would have to abandon the inquests entirely, transfer them to Surrey or elsewhere and start again with a jury drawn from the population of that district. Mr Burnett suggested that that would not be a problem; it would not inhibit the coroner from taking the decision to summon a jury if that became appropriate. Well, maybe not; but in our view, it would be better to avoid the problem in the first place.

51. Another point, taken in particular by Mr Beloff, was that Lady Butler-Sloss, sitting as coroner for the Queen's household did not appear to have the necessary qualities of independence and impartiality. Mr Beloff was at pains to disclaim any suggestion that Lady Butler-Sloss lacked the personal qualities of independence and impartiality. He acknowledged her standing and integrity. His expressed concerns related to the office itself.

52. Mr Beloff submitted that Lady Butler-Sloss's position as deputy coroner of the Queen's household lacked or appeared to lack independence and impartiality for structural reasons. The very name 'Coroner to the Queen's Household' gave the appearance of partiality in the context of inquests into the deaths of two people, one of whom was a member of the Royal Family and the other was not. Further, the two Princes were interested persons. Yet further, (a point emphasised particularly by Mr Mansfield QC on behalf of Mr Al Fayed) the inquests were concerned with a very grave allegation of conspiracy to murder in which it was said that HRH the Duke of Edinburgh was

complicit.

53. Mr Beloff drew attention to the fact that the Lord Steward of
the Queen's household appointed the coroner of the household
and, when the coroner appointed a deputy, the approval of the
Lord Steward had to be given. Thus, Lady Butler-Sloss's
appointment must have been subject to the Lord Steward's
approval. There was in fact no suggestion that she had been
chosen by the Lord Steward; indeed, the evidence was that,
when Mr Burgess told the Lord Chancellor that he did not feel
that, consistent with his duties as coroner for Surrey, he could
continue to take personal responsibility for these inquests, the
Lord Chancellor had suggested Lady Butler-Sloss as a suitable
person to act as his deputy. Nonetheless, submitted Mr Beloff,
there was an appearance of lack of independence in the
arrangements for appointment.

54. Mr Beloff showed us the declaration which the coroner of the
Queen's household makes on taking office. This includes an
undertaking to act 'for the good of the persons within the
household'. Mr Beloff accepted that Lady Butler-Sloss had not
been required to make that declaration but he submitted that,
as deputy, she must be subject to the same duties and
obligations as the coroner himself. The words of the
declaration suggested that the coroner had some special duty
towards the members of the Queen's household.

55. Mr Beloff also suggested, albeit somewhat faintly, that Lady
Butler-Sloss's position lacked independence because she did
not enjoy security of tenure. However, in argument, he had to
accept that her appointment was an ad hoc appointment for
the purpose of these inquests alone and that it was fanciful to
suggest that she could lack independence by reason of a fear of
removal or a desire to prolong her appointment.

56. Of greater merit was his submission in relation to the
acceptance by all parties that it would not be appropriate for
Lady Butler-Sloss to sit with a jury comprising officers of the
household. Why, asked Mr Beloff rhetorically, if it is clearly
unacceptable in this case to draw a jury from the officers of
the Queen's household, is it any more acceptable to have a
coroner who is the coroner to the Queen's household? There
is, he submitted, exactly the same appearance of bias.

57. Finally, he drew our attention to the fact that, in general,
inquests conducted by the coroner of the Queen's household

are funded by the Queen's household monies.

58. All the claimants submitted that it would appear to any fair-minded and informed bystander that there was a real risk that the coroner of the Queen's household would not appear to be impartial as between the interests and contentions of members of the Royal Family and those of the other interested persons.

59. In response to these submissions, Mr Burnett reminded us of the factual position that would become apparent to any fair-minded observer who informed himself of the facts. The Queen's household is in fact a department of state and is entirely distinct from the Royal Family. He explained the position of the Lord Steward. This official had no real power in respect of the appointment of Lady Butler-Sloss; nor could he have any influence over the way she conducted the inquests or bring about her removal. Mr Burnett accepted that, at first blush, the independence of the deputy coroner of the Queen's household might seem open to question, rather in the way in which the multiple functions of the Law Officers were thought by some to be open to question. However, he submitted that, on examination, they were found to be perfectly proper. The same was true of the position of deputy coroner to the Queen's household.

60. In our view, the point in issue here is not whether Lady Butler-Sloss ought to recuse herself on account of any personal lack of independence or appearance of partiality. The complaint is not about her but about the appearance of her position. The point in issue is whether, when choosing between the Surrey jurisdiction and the Queen's household jurisdiction, Lady Butler-Sloss should have taken account of the appearance of her title, Deputy Coroner of the Queen's Household. We think that there is much to be said for the suggestion that she should have considered the impression that the title might make on the world-wide public who will follow these inquests. They cannot be expected to understand the true nature of the Queen's household and the distinction between that and the Royal Family. It might look to them as though the coroner is on the side of the Royal Family. If this danger is taken into account, it would suggest that the right decision would be to sit in the Surrey jurisdiction where the problem would not arise. We are of the view that these matters should have been taken into account.

61. When these additional matters are taken into account, the expedience of sitting in the Royal Courts of Justice assumes

rather less significance. That is not to say that it is not important. But there was another way in which Lady Butler-Sloss could have achieved (and still could achieve) the desirable end of sitting in a suitable venue. She could have invited the coroner for Westminster (in whose district the Royal Courts lie) to accept jurisdiction over both inquests, pursuant to section 14. He could then have appointed her as an assistant deputy coroner for his district. In view of the fact that the Department of Constitutional Affairs has undertaken to fund much the greater part of the cost of these exceptionally expensive inquests, it is highly unlikely that the Westminster coroner would be uncooperative. Even if he were, the Secretary of State could direct him to assume jurisdiction.

62. When this broader view of the issues is taken, it is clear that the decision to opt for the jurisdiction of the Queen's household was flawed, even when taken against the background of the decision to sit without a jury. But if the coroner is to sit with a jury, it is clear that for the reasons we explained in paragraph 48 above, she cannot sit as deputy coroner of the Queen's household.

63. We can deal with the last issue quite briefly in view of the holdings we have already made and a concession made by Mr Mansfield towards the close of his submissions. All the claimants had submitted that Lady Butler-Sloss had compromised her personal impartiality by the way in which she had supported the publication of the Stevens Report. The report expresses a number of firm conclusions on many of the issues that will have to be determined during the inquests. The nub of the submissions was that, by supporting publication of the report, Lady Butler-Sloss had given the impression that she supported its conclusions. That was so, it was contended, despite the fact that Lord Stevens had said, at the publication Press Conference in December 2006, that it was not the role of the police report to prejudge those matters that would be heard in the coroner's court. That was all very well, submitted counsel, but it did not go far enough. Lady Butler-Sloss had not said anything herself at the time of publication. It was accepted that, in her ruling following the hearing on 8th January, Lady Butler-Sloss had said that, at the inquests, she would call and question all the witnesses whose evidence was relevant. But, submitted counsel, bearing in mind the way in which the contents of the Stevens Report had been reported in the media, Lady Butler-Sloss's remarks had not been enough to make it completely clear that all the issues remained open for

determination.

64. These submissions were advanced mainly by Mr Mansfield although Mr Keen associated himself with them. Counsel asserted that it was most unusual, probably unique, for a police report to be published before the opening of an inquest in the way that had occurred here. Mr Lawson QC, for the Commissioner of Police, explained that the decision to publish the report had been taken because there was a real risk that it would be leaked, probably selectively and possibly inaccurately. Completeness and accuracy were preferable. In any event, it was likely that the report would be discussed publicly before long; indeed it appears likely that it will be discussed at the next hearing, at which the scope of the inquests is to be determined. Mr Mansfield explained that the claimants' complaint was not so much that Lady Butler-Sloss had supported publication of the report; it was the fact that she had not clearly dissociated herself from its conclusions that gave rise to the impression that she accepted them. In the course of argument, Mr Mansfield accepted that, if Lady Butler-Sloss were now to make it clear that the conclusions of the report were entirely a matter for the police and that she would be approaching all issues with a completely open mind, any possibly misleading impression could be put right. Moreover, Lady Butler-Sloss could say that she would be giving the jury a direction to put all that they had read and heard in the media completely out of their minds. Mr Mansfield accepted that, if such statements were to be made and if Lady Butler-Sloss were to sit with a jury, there could be no further objection to her continuing as coroner on these inquests.

65. For our part, we do not think that there was anything of substance in these complaints. We do not think that Lady Butler-Sloss's support for the publication of the report could come anywhere to giving rise to a real possibility of bias in the eyes of the fair-minded and informed observer: see Porter v Magill [2002]1 AC 357. In any event, we consider that the function of the report was made adequately clear by Lord Stevens at the Press Conference and the process that she would follow was made sufficiently plain by Lady Butler-Sloss on 8th January. Now that the issue has been raised, no doubt she will make it even more clear that, so far as the inquest is concerned, nothing has been decided by the Stevens Report and that all issues are open for determination by the jury. In any event, a clear direction to the jury to put out of their minds what they have read and heard will be essential. It is our

view that, when the members of the jury have heard the evidence for themselves, they will find no difficulty in making their own minds up regardless of the conclusions of the Stevens Report. We repeat that, in our view, there is no reason at all why Lady Butler-Sloss should not continue to conduct these inquests.

66. **For these reasons, we grant the application for judicial review and quash the decisions to conduct the inquests as Deputy Coroner for the Queen's Household and without summoning a jury.**

Baroness Elizabeth Butler-Sloss was called to the Bar in 1955. She was appointed a Registrar, Principal Registry Family Division in 1970 and subsequently a High Court Judge, Family Division (1979-1988) and then to the Court of Appeal (1988–1999). From 1999 until her retirement in 2005 Lady Butler-Sloss was President of the Family Division. She was made Baroness Butler-Sloss of Marsh Green in 2006 and she has close connections to the Royal Household through her title.

Al Fayed had already highlighted her royal connections and had won an earlier appeal to ensure the pre-inquest hearings were held in public. Butler-Sloss had wanted to hold the pre-inquest hearings in private and thus deny both the public and the press any insight into the proceedings. This immediately provoked further accusations of a 'cover-up' and Al Fayed won the right to have the hearings held in public. Prior to the hearing at the High Court on 8th January 2007, Butler Sloss made some rather interesting observations: -

I propose to make some opening observations. I should first like to express my deepest sympathy to the relatives and friends of all those who died in the crash on the 31st August 1997.

The inquests into the deaths of Princess Diana and Mr Al Fayed were opened by Mr Michael Burgess as the Coroner of the Queen's Household and Coroner for Surrey on the 6th January 2004. He made an opening statement, which set out the position clearly and comprehensively and it is not necessary for me to repeat much of it.

I am however providing copies of his statement for the interested persons and it is being put on my website. Mr Burgess has appointed me deputy Coroner of the Queen's Household and assistant deputy Coroner for Surrey and has delegated to me responsibility for the two inquests.

There has been considerable delay in bringing these two inquests to a hearing but, as Mr Burgess explained in his statement, there have been an extremely lengthy French judicial investigation, which, together with the appeal process, has now almost come to an end. It was clearly necessary to have as much as possible of the French documentation and decisions to assist in these inquests. The French procedures did not allow us to use their documentation until the main investigations were complete.

As a result of serious allegations that the deaths of Princess Diana and Mr Al Fayed came about as a result of a conspiracy to murder them, Lord Stevens and a team from the Metropolitan Police, called Operation Paget, have investigated those allegations and their conclusions were made public in December 2006 in the Stevens Report. That Report is the property of the Metropolitan Police but Mr Burgess asked the Police to provide a separate report to assist the Coroner, the Coroner's Report, which I hope to receive shortly.

As soon as I receive the Coroner's Report, I expect to put in train arrangements for hearing the Inquests. I should like to underline certain points made by Mr Burgess about the hearing of an Inquest and the functions of the Coroner. In his statement Mr Burgess explained why it is necessary to hold these inquests. When a death occurs outside England and Wales, a coroner becomes involved if the body is brought into his district and he "has reason to suspect that the deceased has died a violent or unnatural death[or] has died a sudden death of which the cause is unknown."

An inquest is a fact finding inquiry, conducted by a coroner, with or without a jury, to establish reliable answers to four important but limited factual questions. The first relates to the identity of the deceased, the second to the place of his death, the third to the time of death. The fourth question relates to how the deceased came by his death. The authority of the coroner arises from the physical presence of the body in his district.

It is a much more limited function than that of a judge sitting in court. It is an inquisitorial and not an adversarial process and there are no parties to the proceedings. In due course it will be my function is to decide on the scope of the inquests and who *are the witnesses to be called. I shall hold all future meetings and hearings in public.   I shall give written decisions on contested issues raised today and in the future which will be provided to the interested persons and will be put on the website.*

Today, however is a preliminary meeting to consider legal issues of jurisdiction and procedure. No evidence will be called. It is being held in open court and the press and media are able to attend and report the proceedings. I would remind you that by the coroners rules of procedure, Coroners Rules 1984 (as amended) I am not able to receive any speeches as to the facts (r.40), though, obviously, I am able to consider matters of law with you.

I hope to deal with several issues, among which are:

- *Who are the interested persons;*

- *Do I have jurisdiction to sit as deputy Coroner of the Queen's Household;*

- *Should there be concurrent inquests or two separate inquests;*

- *Should I call a jury or juries?*

And so Al Fayed's victory at the High Court should not be seen as so much a triumph of 'justice', but rather a realistic recognition by the higher courts that the public mood was at boiling point on the issue of the jury. It was Tony Blair, never one to miss an opportunity for public attention, who labelled Diana the 'people's princess' and she remains so today, in the public's collective mindset, ten long years after she was killed at the Pont de l'Alma tunnel in Paris.

But Al Fayed, naturally was jubilant and the majority of the public shared his satisfaction at the ruling of the higher courts that the inquest would be held before a jury. He said: "This is not the end of the road, but an important step. The jury must now be allowed to hear the entirety of the evidence, but I fear there will be attempts to keep it from them. If so, that will be yet another battle I will have to fight." Al Fayed has promised to petition the higher courts for judicial review. The Harrods boss stunned reporters outside the High Court with a with vitriolic outburst against the royals and MI6, he said they are "gangsters and murderers and Nazi bastards."

On hearing of the appointment of Baroness Butler-Sloss to head the inquest, he said: **"It can truly be said that in this country the government chooses the judge it wants to get the verdict it wants. Just look at what happened with the Hutton Report and the Butler Report."** He was on the right note, both Hutton and Butler reports were loaded, farcical and the outcomes predetermined.

Butler-Sloss was parachuted in to replace the former Surrey Coroner Michael Burgess, who explained that he could not take the stress any longer. In short order, indeed, almost perfectly synchronised, the Paget Inquiry was wound up and a botched report published. Al Fayed was denied the right to comment on the report and make suggestions as to further lines of enquiry.

Lord Stevens had promised him prior access to the report but in the event prior access was limited to 'three hours' – not enough time to read the 831 pages of drivel, let alone comment on them. It was the classic tactical ambush and one that I have experienced many times in legal cases. When desperate stunts of this nature are pulled, it is clear that one has the enemy rattled. And Al Fayed, in his battle for the truth and justice, has rattled the British Establishment to the core.

The outcome of the judicial review at the High Court on 2nd March 2007, took everyone by surprise. After ten long years, and a campaign which has cost him £6 million, Al Fayed at last scored a victory. The newswires again went into overdrive, Diana's face appearing on every news channel and on the front-page of most national newspapers. As I watched the news bulletins, gripped be the fervour, it seemed for a moment that Diana was still alive. It was a surreal, perhaps macabre experience but shows just how interest there still is in the doyenne of the 20th Century.

In his judicial review application papers submitted to the High Court, Al Fayed again reiterated the prescient facts and I use the word prescient, because he knows only too well that his points will live on for as long as Diana lives on in the memories of those who lived to see the princess die.

Administrative Court between the Queen on the application of Mohamed Al Fayed versus Deputy Coroner of the Queen's household and Assistant Deputy Coroner for Surrey.

I, Mohamed Al Fayed, state as follows: -

1) I am the Claimant in this application, an Interested Person in the Inquests into the deaths of Diana, Princess of Wales and Dodi Al Fayed and the father of Dodi Al Fayed, deceased. I make this statement in support of my application for permission to apply for judicial review of the decision of Lady Butler Sloss, Deputy Coroner of the Queen's Household and Assistant Deputy Coroner for Surrey decisions to sit as the Deputy Coroner to the Queen's Household and her decision to do so, alone and without a jury, following a preliminary hearing into the Inquests heard on 8 January 2007.

2) I have been shown a copy of the Claim Form which is being filed in support of my application. I can confirm that the facts set out therein are, to the best of my knowledge and belief, true and accurate.

3) I have always made clear my absolute conviction that there should be a single hearing before a jury of ordinary members of the public empanelled to consider all the evidence relating to both Inquests concurrently. I have pressed for an effective, thorough, fearless and, above all, independent process where a jury of ordinary people is allowed to hear all the material evidence. Without all stages of this process being subject to full public scrutiny, there can be no accountability, still less, any confidence in the outcome.

4) Dr Burton originally excluded me from involvement in Princess Diana's inquest. Dr Burton, who was then the Coroner of the Queen's Household and Mr Burgess, the Coroner for Surrey, insisted that there should be separate inquests for Princess Diana and my son. Lady Butler-Sloss has at last agreed that I am entitled to participate in both inquests and that they should be held together.

5) However, I have been advised that the Deputy Coroner's appointment was made and approved by the Lord Steward of the Queen's household, Sir James Hamilton, 5th Duke of Abercorn, that the Deputy Coroner made a declaration of his office to the Lord Steward, that she may live in premises arranged by the Lord Steward of the Queen's Household and that even her salary

is paid by the Palace. If any of this is correct it is a highly unusual, indeed extraordinary, method for a judicial appointment. I simply do not believe that this is an appropriate way for these Inquests to be heard. I have no confidence in such a court. In any event, I do not believe that the public will be prepared to accept, nor should they accept, that an employee of the Queen, or at the very least a person whose very title indicates a close connection with the Royal Household should be allowed to hear and determine the outcome and findings of these Inquests.

6) I have full confidence in the abilities of a jury to be able to hear all the evidence impartially and reach a proper verdict on the circumstances surrounding their deaths. I am prepared to accept such a verdict, whatever decision they reach. Only a jury of ordinary citizens can deliver verdicts which will satisfy me and the public that there have been fair, transparent and most importantly, independent Inquests. The publication of the Report and findings of Lord Stevens, which was with the support and agreement of Lady Butler-Sloss, was, according to the Metropolitan Police, done for the purpose of "enhancing public debate" about events and issues in question. The only proper and indeed appropriate forum for this is at the Inquests where representatives of the public, sitting as a jury, can hear all the material evidence and reach decisions based upon that evidence

7) I am a grieving father who dearly misses his son. I cannot put into words my sense of loss. He and Princess Diana were two wonderful and loving people whose lives were cut brutally and tragically short. Were they in fact murdered? **That is my certain belief, shared with millions of others, that this is what happened.** I cannot accept that the truth will be revealed by someone who appears to be an employee of the Queen hearing and determining these inquests. If the British and French authorities are so confident in the evidence that they have amassed, I say that a jury of fair minded, honest, ordinary people should be given the task of hearing it for themselves and finally deciding the truth.

8) Lady Butler Sloss has stated that the next hearing will take place on or around 5th March 2007. In view of the very short time until that hearing, I ask for

that application to be expedited.

I believe that the facts stated in this statement are true.

Signed ....

Mohamed Al Fayed

When French judge Herve Stephan ruled that manslaughter charges against the paparazzi photographers following Diana and Dodi's car should be dismissed, Al Fayed launched an unsuccessful bid to get the ruling overturned. Outside France, he campaigned at the Court of Session in Edinburgh for a public inquiry to be held in Scotland. That strategy failed in 2004. One of the main strands of his campaign was to try to get the inquests into the deaths of Diana and Dodi held together.

Outside the High Court, in a bold mood after his success, he said: "Diana was the people's princess. The people must be allowed to hear all the evidence and then, and only then, decide how she died, why she died and who ordered her murder. I want Charles and Philip together in court. These are the people who ordered the murder." Lady Butler-Sloss, until her retirement Britain's most senior woman judge, decided in January that she would rule over the joint inquests alone in her capacity as deputy coroner of the Royal Household. She said it would be "an almost impossible task" for a jury.

On 5th March 2007 at the High Court, lawyers representing Mohamed Al Fayed applied for the case to be put back until October 1st, because of a "massive amount of work" still to be done. Michael Mansfield QC, representing Al Fayed, told Baroness Butler-Sloss that a delay of another six months would be "a pebble on the beach" compared with the 10-year wait for an inquest.

Mr Mansfield also called for the inquest to be heard at a venue other than the Royal Courts of Justice, which he said was too small. At a pre-inquest hearing at the Royal Courts of Justice, Lady Butler-Sloss said she intended to hear the inquests as assistant deputy coroner for inner west London but this development does not change the fact that she remains closely connected to the Royal Household.

On 2nd March, three senior judges ordered Butler-Sloss to

empanel a jury rather than hearing the case alone and directed her not to preside over the case in her capacity as deputy coroner for the Queen's Household. Lady Butler-Sloss told the court: "I am, of course, going to be sitting with a jury. I have no intention of ever appealing the decision of the administrative court." She was clearly stung by Al Fayed's successful judicial review application.

In detailed written submissions, Al Fayed's legal team called on Butler-Sloss to consider an adjournment. "She is invited to conclude that there is, frankly, a massive amount of work still to be done by the various experts before it would be appropriate to begin calling witnesses of fact."

The submissions added that the interested persons in the case, who include Mr Al Fayed, had only been able to begin a "phenomenal amount of work" following the release in December of a report on the case by former Metropolitan Police Commissioner Lord Stevens. "Bearing in mind the volume of issues and material in this case, a hearing date within six months of that publication seems, with respect, wholly unrealistic."

But Butler-Sloss told the court, aiming her words at the Princess's sister, Lady Sarah McCorquodale, and Major Jamie Lowther-Pinkerton, private secretary to Princes William and Harry: "I would be very sad if I was obliged to delay the start of the main proceedings for another six months. I feel that would be very, very hard on the families."

Mr Mansfield suggested as an alternative venue Westminster Central Hall, which was the venue for the Saville Inquiry into Bloody Sunday during its London sittings. But Butler-Sloss expressed the hope that Court 73 at the Royal Courts of Justice could be made suitable. Butler-Sloss has been accused of selecting a smaller courtroom to severely restrict the numbers of ordinary people, the general public, who could attend the hearings.

Pressing for a postponement of the inquest until next October, Mr Mansfield told the coroner: "All one is asking for at this stage, compared with the '10-year delay', is a short period of time within which to make proper preparations on behalf of Mr Al Fayed." The QC said he knew other parties involved in the inquest had similar points to make.

He said the inquest would have to inquire, among other things, into the Princess's alleged fears for her life, the suggestion that she was pregnant, and why her body was embalmed. The inquest should also have to inquire into the identity of the driver of a white Fiat Uno (James Andanson) at the crash scene and any cars which might have blocked the route of the Mercedes in which the Princess and Dodi died.

A central issue was the question of the samples taken from the Princess's chauffeur, Henri Paul, who also died in the crash. Mr Mansfield said there had been "a substantial change of position" in regard to the sampling and there could be missing samples, leaving "a great big question mark" over the alcohol levels in the chauffeur's blood.   But Butler-Sloss warned that she had no idea whether French medical witnesses were going to choose to give evidence. She said: "If they say they won't give evidence, there is nothing I can do about it." Butler-Sloss agreed that the issue was "central" to the inquest but was 'powerless' to do anything about it.

She said one doctor who had been approached, but whom she would not identify, had indicated he would be prepared to talk to her on the phone - "but not to give evidence". Further approaches were being made to the doctor. She said: "This is a serious matter, but these are French citizens with their own rights. I don't have power to require anyone to attend from France."

During one heated exchange Lady Butler-Sloss told Mr Mansfield that she had not been given "a shred of evidence" about any of the serious allegations Mr Al Fayed has made about the Princess's death. Following a call from Mr Mansfield to be given evidence gathered by Lord Stevens' team, Lady Butler-Sloss said: "There are a large number of serious allegations being made.

"It would be enormously helpful to me if I had some evidence from Mr Al Fayed's team to support the allegations that are being made because at the moment there is not a shred of evidence given to me about any of those allegations and for me to explore them, particularly for me to present them to the jury, I would need some evidence."

She said that if evidence were produced, she would allow the jury to consider Al Fayed's claims about the Princess's death but she added: "If there is no evidence to support them, I shall not present them to the jury because it would be my duty not to do so." Butler-Sloss has been accused of loading the process to ensure highly embarrassing evidence is not submitted to a jury, consisting of ordinary members of the public.

Mr Mansfield responded: "There is evidence."
Lady Butler-Sloss said: "I would like to see it."

Mr Mansfield answered: "You have it already."
Lady Butler-Sloss responded: "Ah."

Mr Mansfield said that Mr Al Fayed had co-operated fully with the Stevens investigation and had provided them with the evidence he had. He told the court: "A starting point which will undoubtedly come to light during the inquest is Princess Diana's premonitions or fears."

He added: "Mohamed Al Fayed gave a statement to the police about this and what he had been told by Princess Diana during the summer months, about her concerns, her fears and so on. He has already provided that." Mr Mansfield went on to say that Mr Al Fayed was aware that the Princess had confided in butler Paul Burrell.

The court was also told of a cache of letters from Prince Philip which led Princess Diana to fear for her life, has sensationally gone 'missing'. The letters, which are presumed to carry heavy threats against Diana, were seized during a police raid on the home of Diana's former butler Paul Burrell, who was entrusted to keep them as proof of the threat against her. Mr Mansfield QC said he wanted answers from the Royals about their dealings with the police and demanded to know the whereabouts of key letters written by and sent to Diana.

Replying to Mr Mansfield, Edmund Lawson, QC for the police said: "Regarding the allegations covering letters from the Duke of Edinburgh, despite the best efforts of the police to find any evidence or copies of them none have been." And he continued, "That's not to say none exist, but none has been found." The statement drew gasps of incredulity from the public gallery.

Mr Mansfield, acting for Mohamed Al Fayed, demanded to know why the letters Prince Philip wrote to his daughter-in-law led her to believe she would one day be murdered. Mr Mansfield also stated that he wanted Princes Charles to be called as a witness at the Inquest which is expected to last in the region of 8 months. He said: "There are two witnesses, in particular, we say are relevant to this matter."

"Prince of Wales, who was interviewed in the Operation Paget inquiry, but we don't know if notes were taken or a statement made because only a summary was given. And also the Duke of Edinburgh, who was responsible for letters sent to Diana and who refused to be interviewed. We would like to go beyond that and perhaps ask for a reason to be given." Mr Mansfield was responding to Butler-Sloss's demands for hard evidence.

Mr Mansfield then went on to say that he wanted to know the whereabouts of letters written by and sent to Diana. He said that he wanted the police to disclose any notes they had taken when interviewing Prince Charles and to reveal the reason Prince Philip had given for refusing to speak to detectives about the Princess's death. The packed courtroom heard that Mr Al Fayed had been told by Diana that "the secrets of her life" were held by Paul Burrell. Mr Mansfield told the tense hearing that the ex-butler may become a key figure.

The internationally renowned QC said he wanted to know where a letter written by the Princess for the attention of Paul Burrell was being held, and also the whereabouts of other letters "which undoubtedly exist" and had been penned to Diana by Prince Philip. The courtroom was in a state of shock by the time he had outlined his clear demands and the police's legal team were clearly rattled.

There can be little doubt that Butler-Sloss has repeatedly tried to block vital evidence and has pre-judged the evidence submitted as irrelevant. During the entire 10 years since the crash in the Alma Tunnel, both British and French 'investigations' have ignored the eighteen witnesses to the crash and blocked every piece of evidence which contradicts the 'accident theory'.

Butler-Sloss at first tried to hold the hearings in camera, precluding the press and public but was stopped by a determined Mohamed Al Fayed. Nose out of joint, the Deputy 'Royal' Coroner attempted to hold the Inquest without a jury so that she alone could decide on the matter. She was again stopped by Al Fayed at the High Court. Precisely why Butler-Sloss wanted a Soviet-style closed hearing in which the press and public played no part is not clear but certainly she was following instructions from the Lord Chancellor's Department to act like a dictator.

And the Butler-Sloss was thwarted by the Al Fayed legal team, she resorted to throwing her toys out of the pram and promptly quit. Her decision was seen as another delaying tactic but in truth, she did not want to be part of an open inquest that could result in the wrong verdict. Her named would have lived in infamy in the history books, not to mention the damage to her career as a tame servant of the Crown.

Chapter 12

20 Defining Issues

The burning question most people ask is: if there is nothing to hide, why attempt to keep out the press and public and hold the Inquest without a jury? Butler-Sloss has tried every trick in the book and some to load the process against Al Fayed and his legal team with the purpose to ensure that highly damaging evidence, which completely contradicts the 'accident theory' is not presented to a jury. The objective of which is to ensure the jury can only arrive at a verdict of 'accidental' death. Anyone who has serious experience of the British legal system, and I have, is not surprised by Butler-Sloss's predetermined blocking tactics.

Following a pre-Inquest hearing on 27th July 2007 at London's High Court, Lord Justice Scott-Baker ruled that 20 issues need to be determined at the full Inquest beginning in October. Scott-Baker claims to want to get at the truth but on 13th June at the pre-Inquest hearing, it was revealed that he intended to gag the media on an "ad hoc" basis when potentially embarrassing and highly damaging evidence is aired. The intervention of MI6 behind the scenes here is perfectly clear and Scott-Baker has simply caved-in to pressure.

The two stories conflict and it must be asked which is true? Scott-Baker cannot on one hand claim to want to get at the truth and then on the other hand, gag the press to preclude sensitive information from seeping into the public domain. This 'fair-minded' Judge had previously ruled that the Paget Report of Lord Stevens be removed from his website to ensure that the jury are not influenced by the report's discredited findings.

This must rank as one of the most stupid and illogical rulings ever laid down by a judge because millions of people have already downloaded and read the discredited Paget Report. But Scott-Baker's ruling was a recognition of reality: the Paget Report had been torn to pieces and discredited and he did not want the dodgy dossier to create further damage to the Inquest and the public's perception of it. He went on to outline twenty fundamental issues to be determined at the Inquest:

Lord Justice Scott Baker

Assistant Deputy Coroner of Inner West London

Pre-inquest hearing

Court 73, Royal Courts of Justice

27th July 2007

List of Likely Issues

1. Whether driver error on the part of Henri Paul caused or contributed to the cause of the collision

2. Whether Henri Paul's ability to drive was impaired through drink or drugs

3. Whether a Fiat Uno or any other vehicle caused or contributed to the collision

4. Whether the actions of the Paparazzi caused or contributed to the cause of the collision

5. Whether the road/tunnel layout and construction were inherently dangerous and if so whether this contributed to the collision

6. Whether any bright/flashing lights contributed to or caused the collision and, if so, their source

7. Whose decision it was that the Princess of Wales and Dodi Al Fayed should leave from the rear entrance to the Ritz and that Henri Paul should drive the vehicle

8. Henri Paul's movements between 7 and 10 pm on 30 August 1997

9. The explanation for the money in Henri Paul's possession on 30 August 1997 and in his bank account

10. Whether Andanson was in Paris on the night of the collision

11. Whether the Princess of Wales' life would have been saved if she had reached hospital sooner or if her medical treatment had been different

12. Whether the Princess of Wales was pregnant

13. Whether the Princess of Wales and Dodi Al Fayed were about to announce their engagement

14. Whether and, if so in what circumstances, the Princess of Wales feared for her life

15. The circumstances relating to the purchase of the ring

16. The circumstances in which the Princess of Wales' body was embalmed

17. Whether the evidence of Tomlinson throws any light on the collision

18. Whether the British or any other security services had any involvement in the collision

19. Whether there was anything sinister about (i) the Cherruault burglary or (ii) the disturbance at the Big Pictures agency

20. Whether correspondence belonging to the Princess of Wales (including some from Prince Philip) has disappeared, and if so the circumstances

A particular concern is the witnesses who have been ignored, deliberately by the French and British 'investigations. The witness statement below was made by a French family who witnessed the events immediately prior to the car crash in the Alma Tunnel which killed Princess Diana, Dodi Al Fayed and Henri Paul. They were first interviewed at home by Captain Eric Crosnier of the Criminal Brigade on 16th September 1997. The Paget 'Investigation' conducted by Lord Stevens ignored the family's witness statement along with seventeen other witnesses.

"We made statements to the police on 16 September 1997. The police came to our house to take statements. One of them took notes by hand and the other typed them up on a machine. They printed up our statements and asked us to sign them. They spent about half an hour with each of us. We were not given a copy of our statements and today we are re-reading them for the first time. We have neither of us been interviewed by the police since September 1997.

We were walking along beside the dual carriageway just before the accident and were conscious that the cars entering the tunnel were driving rather fast, at a speed normal for Parisians; just a few moments before we had commented 'These Parisians are crazy'.

However, our attention was drawn by the arrival of two large cars coming towards us and heading for the tunnel. They were large, powerful and dark in colour. Although they were probably being driven at the same speed as the other cars we had seen passing earlier, we noticed them because they were very close to each other.

Just after they left our field of vision, we heard a series of loud noises, the sound of braking, the scrunching of metal (car bodywork), a third louder noise consisting of a bang, and lastly a very loud bang followed by the sound of a horn that had jammed.

Although we did not go into the tunnel we looked inside and saw a mass of metal that was undoubtedly the car that had crashed. We did not see the second car. We thought that this second car could have left the tunnel already. No one asked us for any information about this second car apart from the information we gave in the statement we made to the [French] police.

A taxi was following behind at a normal distance. It stopped just at the entrance to the tunnel, nobody got out of it and we thought they were telephoning for help. Apart from the statement we made [to the French police] nobody asked us any questions about the taxi or its occupants.

There was talk of a [white] Fiat Uno in the press. It was said to have collided with the Mercedes that crashed. We do not know if this car was in the tunnel beforehand, because our attention was focused on the two large cars. No one asked us about this car and in any case we could not have said anything because we did not see it.

Absolutely immediately after the crash we saw a man running towards us along the pavement in the Cours Albert, coming in the direction of the Place Concorde and going towards the tunnel. He was 30 metres from us when we saw him. He ran past and went straight into the tunnel. He was fairly young and appeared to be fairly athletic."

This disturbing testimony of a second large car shadowing the Princess's Mercedes S280, confirmed by other witnesses, prior to the crash was ignored by Lord Stevens. Even more importantly, British and French police made no attempt to locate or identify the "athletic man" seen running into the Alma Tunnel in synchrony just a second or so after the crash.   There   is   a calculated   cover-up   in   action   and   the   British   and   French authorities have directly colluded in their attempt to conceal the truth by ignoring the witness statements of eighteen witnesses to the events immediately prior to and after the crash.

The ignored witnesses include: Abdellatif Redjil, Jean-Pascal Peyret, Benoit Boura, Eric Petel, Olivier Partouche, Jean-Claude and   Annick   Catheline,   Georges   and   Sabine   Dauzonne,   Mr Gooroovadoo, James Huth, Christophe Lascuax, Gaelle Lhotsis, Mohamed Medjahdi, Souad Moufakkir, Severine Banjout, Mr Rassinier and Lionel Ronssin.

But true to form, Scott-Baker who replaced Baroness Butler-Sloss in June 2007 as the coroner to the Inquest, said that he had no power to summon any of these witnesses to the Inquest. For a matter of this nature, he should be able to move heaven and earth to summon relevant witnesses to the Inquest but maybe the fault line is lack of inclination on his part.

Many people hoped that at after Butler-Sloss resigned as coroner to the Inquest, Scott-Baker would come in with a more fair and level-headed attitude but this hope was soon quashed when he announced that the 'testimony' of MI5 and MI6 officers would be held *in camera*. Those of us who have experience of dealing with these matters were not surprised in the slightest.

But there has been progress of sorts in that Scott-Baker realised early on that the allegation Henri Paul was drunk at the wheel of the Mercedes S280 could not stand. He admitted that he has serious doubts about the French version of events. In reality, during June and July 2007, the great accident theory was simply blown out of the water.

A Channel 4 documentary in the UK, showed for the first time the photographer's version of events, backed up by witness testimony. The 'pursuing' paparazzi were in fact several minutes behind the crashed Mercedes S280 and therefore could not have caused the car to crash. The paparazzi had already been cleared by the French investigation.

One by one, the central tenets of the great accident theory started to fall like ninepins before a steady and unstoppable avalanche of hard evidence. The next to fall was the suicide theory that James Andanson killed himself, as fireman Christophe Pelat came forward to confirm that he saw bullet holes in the skull of James Andanson.

Fresh evidence also emerged from France where the pathologists are being sued for negligence over the 'faulty' or swapped tests on Henri Paul's blood samples. It is now clear that Henri Paul was not drunk at the wheel of the doomed Mercedes S280. All of the accident theories are now destroyed! What other verdict than death by misadventure could a jury reach in view of the damning evidence?

But true to form Scott-Baker would not consent to Queen Elizabeth II, Prince Philip or Prince Charles to be cross-examined at the Inquest. No one should be fooled that Scott-Baker is anything other than an Establishment old boy through and through. He has yielded on certain points simply to create the impression that he is a fair judge.

Scott-Baker can no longer ignore the facts and dismiss the reality that Henri Paul was not drunk and serious legal argument on this issue must be allowed at the Inquest. Equally, he also ruled that more questions should be asked to determine the role the paparazzi played in causing the crash. It all sounds and reads very well but one must ask where has he been for the last ten years?

Point five of his twenty points states: *Whether the road/tunnel layout and construction were inherently dangerous and if so whether this contributed to the collision.* This is a very interesting point indeed in that Scott-Baker, I dare say will blame a great deal of the so-called 'accident' on poor road construction and a hazardous tunnel, renowned for being an accident black spot. In which case why was Henri Paul instructed to take that route by his French and British Intelligence handlers? An escape clause of this nature, inevitably leads the escapologist into another trap.

Whichever way Scott-Baker twists and turns he will simply walk into another trap. There is no way out of this myriad Inquest and he will be lucky to escape with an ounce of his reputation intact. I will predict here that the moment he finds himself trapped, he will dismiss the jury, members of the public and press to reconvene *in camera* until he has wriggled free.

This Inquest is now no more than mere window dressing for the British Establishment because the original tenets of the great accident theory have already been destroyed outside the parameters of this loaded Inquest which will favour the Establishment from start to finish. But there will be great shocks in store for Scott-Baker and likely also Mohamed Al Fayed.

The Ritz Hotel CCTV footage extended to covering the ground at the front of the building where the crowd and paparazzi were gathered. Al Fayed has gone on record to say that his security chief John McNamara has identified several British and French spooks mingling with the crowd on 30/31 August 1997. So why has the world not seen the footage in which it is claimed several spooks are mingling with the crowd? Al Fayed, forever seeking media attention, has had no problem releasing the CCTV footage from inside the Ritz Hotel and did so almost immediately after the crash.

I have written to Al Fayed and his press officer Michael Cole offering to publish the photographic stills of the alleged spooks so that a worldwide appeal can be made to identify them. Cole was at first quite warm but when I pressed him again and again on this vitally important issues, he replied to the effect that the CCTV images of the alleged spooks would not be released.

If the images exist, then why not release them? Unless, of course, Al Fayed has concocted this tale to embellish his argument which would be foolish given the sheer weight of evidence against the great accident theory. Therefore, Al Fayed either does not have the images to release and never has had them, or he is saving them for a rainy day which is implausible given the fact that we are now ten years on from the crash.

I remain sceptical that these images exist and there has been no mention of them before the Inquest, which is another odd aberration considering the damage the release of the images can cause. Nor am I prepared to give Al Fayed the benefit of the doubt on this matter given the fact that he lied about having the princess's last words as related to him by a nurse on 31st August 1997. This was a pathetic outright lie. Princess Diana was unconscious when she was admitted to the hospital and spoke to no one.

I do not believe everything that Al Fayed says and nor should anyone else. He should be treated with professional distance until he can prove that the images exist. The same is also true of the details of the last telephone calls to and from Dodi's phone which he purchased from an 'anonymous source'. He has never made public the details of Dodi's last telephone calls. How can he claim that everyone else is covering up significant details when he does pretty much the same thing?

This Inquest does not only put the British Establishment on trial, which he tried to destroy long before the crash, but also Mohamed Al Fayed himself! An old Chinese proverb says, "May you live in interesting times".

Chapter 13

The Accident Theory Collapses

In the immediate aftermath of his son's violent death, Mohamed Al Fayed was roused from his state of shock by a letter from private investigator Joe Vialls, reprinted below: -

REGISTERED MAIL

STRICTLY PRIVATE AND CONFIDENTIAL

Tel: XXX XXXX XXXX (silent line)
45 Merlin Drive
Carine, Perth
Western Australia 6020

22nd September 1997

Mohammed Al Fayed,
Proprietor
Harrods Department Store
Brompton Road,
Knightsbridge
London, England

Dear Mr Mohamed,

REF: PARIS CAR CRASH - POSSIBLE DEPLOYMENT OF LTL WEAPONS

First may I offer my sincere condolences on the tragic death of your son, although as I write these words they seem woefully inadequate in acknowledging your overwhelming loss. My reason for writing to you is that I am a private investigator and analyst specializing in military matters, and my most notable achievement to date was destroying the long-standing media lie that WPC Yvonne Fletcher was killed by the Libyans outside their Embassy in St. James Square on 17 April 1984.

My investigation, which took four years starting in 1992, proved Fletcher was shot from the top floor of Enserch House, an American Multinational building located further to the west at 8 St James Square.

During August 1994, Channel 4 Television sent me a letter asking if I would be prepared to work with them on my investigation. Then finally on 10 April 1996, Channel 4's flagship current affairs programme

Dispatches ran a special on Fletcher's death called "Murder in St. James's", though ominously, more than half of the hard scientific evidence provided by me was inexplicably excluded from the programme.

In addition Channel 4 suddenly removed me from the film credits, although I have two files full of correspondence on Channel 4 and Fulcrum Productions letterheads, proving that the controversial investigation into Fletcher's death was instigated and conducted solely by me.

Experience gained during that extended investigation indicates strongly to me that that the root cause of the deaths of your son Dodi, and Princess Diana, is being distorted by the media using exactly the same techniques employed back in 1984 when Yvonne Fletcher was murdered in St. James Square.

Clearly the heavyweight establishment media, or perhaps government, must have compelling reasons for this deliberately deceptive behaviour. Because of the continually shifting and conflicting reports from the media, it is manifestly obvious that foul play is either known or suspected where the crash is concerned, and someone somewhere is determined to muddy the waters, thereby obscuring the reason for the Mercedes 600 SEL suddenly losing control as it approached the entrance to the Paris tunnel.

The "drunk driver" claims are in my view as impossible as a two-ton armoured Mercedes reaching a terminal speed of 121 mph on the short approach to the tunnel, so exactly what caused Henri Paul to lose control?

Many years ago a LTL (Less-Than-Lethal) weapon was designed at the Los Alamos National Laboratories for exactly this purpose, and what little evidence I have 10,000 miles away from the scene of the crime, indicates a high probability of its deployment near the Paris tunnel crash site.

The term Less-Than-Lethal is deliberately misleading, because these systems are frequently designed to augment lethal weapons. One example of this technique would be the use of LTL chemical or acoustic weapons to flush terrorists out of a secure building and into the open, thereby exposing them to lethal machine gun fire .

Just after the crash it was reported that one or two motorcycles or motor scooters had been seen motionless near the entrance to the tunnel by witnesses, waiting for the approaching Mercedes, and more recently a white Fiat was reported in the same position.

In addition there was a report of a brilliant white flash blinding driver Henri Paul at exactly the same point on the route. Media speculation (suppressed within one hour) was that Henri Paul was temporarily blinded by a powerful camera flash gun fired from one of the waiting motorcycles, and lost control as a direct result.

As with the impossible vehicle speed cited, it seems most unlikely that a Mercedes-trained driver like Henri Paul would be unable to cope with an entirely predictable camera flash gun. What Henri Paul would have been completely incapable of coping with would be a pulsed-strobe LTL weapon operating in the visible light band of the electromagnetic spectrum, designed from the outset to look identical to a powerful camera flash gun.

When this LTL weapon fires, it pulses high-intensity brilliant white light at brain frequencies, inducing complete neural confusion for between two and five seconds. Line-of-sight exposure is overwhelming and renders the target completely incapable of meaningful brain function. Exposure at oblique angles causes moderate to severe mental confusion.

If this LTL system was deployed at the tunnel entrance in order to trigger a lethal event, the two-ton mass of the Mercedes colliding with a solid concrete wall at sixty mph, would have ensured lethality due to the car's inertia, which could be accurately calculated in advance. Although pulsed-strobe LTL by its very nature leaves little hard evidence of its use, there are indicators which might be useful in determining whether or not it was deployed at the Paris tunnel.

If bodyguard Trevor Rees-Jones remembers nothing about leaving the Ritz hotel, then he is probably suffering from normal retrograde amnesia. If however he remembers part of the journey, after which he has no recall of events, or remembers only mental confusion, that in itself would be a positive indicator of pulsed-strobe LTL having been deployed against the occupants of the Mercedes.

Rather more obscure (and highly classified) are the effects of pulsed-strobe LTL on blood properties. One trusted forensic source advises that the sudden stress caused by the magnetic component of the weapon causes a sharp and measurable increase in blood serum triglycerides in the target, though the same increase can also be caused by other electromagnetic LTL systems including High Powered Microwave (HPM) and anti-personnel lasers.

Though there is no direct relationship between serum-triglycerides and blood alcohol levels, it is instructive that doctors frequently use enhanced serum-triglyceride levels as a positive indicator of long term alcohol abuse: An accusation that was swiftly directed at Henri Paul shortly after his death.

There are other more complicated points to consider but I will not bother you with them now, because determining which might be relevant would require access to all of the evidence existing in the case, which I do not have at my disposal.

If you find the use of LTL weapons impossible to believe, then I for one would not blame you. But it might be wise to remember that for twelve long years, 60 million Britons believed WPC Fletcher was killed by an impossible shot fired by the Libyans, when in reality she was the victim of a premeditated assassination carried out from the top floor of an American multinational building.

I also have documented proof that the British forensic pathologist who carried out Yvonne Fletcher's post-mortem, subsequently blatantly lied under oath at the Coronial Inquest into her death.

My credibility and credentials can be confirmed by a single phone call to Tripoli, if required. Four months after the Channel 4 film went to air in 1996 the Libyan Government discovered that it was me who had conducted the investigation into Fletcher's murder in London.

I was invited to visit Tripoli as the guest of the Libyan Foreign Minister, and stayed there for two weeks. I feel sure that senior diplomats xxxxx xxxx or xxxxx xxx xxxx of the Libyan Foreign Liaison Bureau in Tripoli, would be willing to provide you with confirmation of my professional expertise   .

Yours sincerely,

Signed

JOE VIALLS

A security back-up of this letter has been sent to the Ritz Hotel in Paris, also by registered mail.

Mohamed Al Fayed still grieving intensely for his beloved son must have been hit by a thunderbolt at the sight of this letter. His suspicions, quite rightly, that British Intelligence were responsible for his son's death grew deeper.

And further suspicions were aroused when he discovered that on the lead up to the Alma Tunnel off the Pont de l'Alma, eleven CCTV cameras failed simultaneously as the Mercedes S280 drove by at no more than 65 mph. French police state that the CCTV cameras were not switched on or simply developed a fault. Eleven CCTV cameras in a row leading all the way up to the Alma Tunnel, were switched off or failed at the time Diana passed by in the Mercedes driven by dupe Henri Paul.

And yet, surprisingly, the speed camera in the roof of the tunnel did not fail, and clocked the speed of the Mercedes limousine at 64 mph. The French refuse to release the photograph, most likely because the white Fiat Uno was captured in the same photographic still and the speed of the Mercedes completely contradicts the 112 mph spurious theory of the French police. Drunk, speeding driver, did not kill Diana is a story neither the British or French authorities want to listen to.

I first became suspicious of the British and French tales when I learned that eleven CCTV cameras had 'failed' at the same time. And as the Mercedes S280 approached the Alma Tunnel, every police radio in Paris failed; the police said it was a technical glitch. As an investigative journalist, I have come across countless examples of cameras failing to work or being switched off or the recording media was "lost" and one immediately smells a bloody large rat or nest of rats at work. **Too much of a coincidence means it's no coincidence** and the spooks work by this very same maxim.

There is clear evidence of intelligence agents involved in the events leading up to the crash and a mountain of evidence of their involvement in the days after the crash. Mohamed Al Fayed's director of security, John McNamara has identified several British and French intelligence agents in the crowds outside the Ritz Hotel from its CCTV footage. But to date, Al Fayed has not released the images of these 'suspects' and duty of care now falls on him to present the images to the world.

Perhaps Al Fayed was waiting to present the images to the Inquest at the High Court. He should also release the pertinent data from his son's mobile phone, if indeed there is anything of note. There is no doubt that Al Fayed has waged a war against the British Establishment in his quest for the truth to come out. In reality, the Establishmentarians will fight to the last breath and will never, never admit to any wrongdoing in any matter, let alone the murder of Princess Diana, Dodi Fayed and Henri Paul. But Al Fayed still refuses to comment on the CCTV images outside The Ritz on the fateful night. Why?

And on this note it should also be noted that Lord Stevens, has confirmed that Henri Paul was on the payroll of the French DST as a "low-level informer" but Stevens denies MI6 were running him as well. In fact, it is quite common for freelance informers, as Paul was, to offer their 'services' to other intelligence agencies, in his case MI6 and Mossad.

The Paget Report is completely loaded against Al Fayed and the witnesses of the crash, who know a damn sight more about what happened that dreadful night in Paris, immediately before and after the crash. And one must not forget the poor Eric Petel, who witnessed the crash, only to be threatened by the head of Paris police and told to "forget" what he had seen. All these desperate tactics are incontrovertible examples of an organised cover up.

And Lord Stevens Paget Inquiry was not left untouched by the spooks either. The offices where the inquiry was based in the north-east of England were also raided by silent burglars, who stole a laptop containing much of the Inquiry's findings. Within weeks, the Inquiry which was set to last for several more months, was wound up and the Inquest was thrown into the arena but Butler-Sloss at first attempted to hold the hearings in camera and then without a jury. If we are dealing with an 'accident', then why all of this secrecy and dirty tricks designed to prevent the truth from spilling out into the public domain?

The tales of the British Establishment and the Royal Household are laughable, the more so if we were not dealing with such a serious matter of inarguably historic proportions. No one should forget that we are dealing with history and that it is being written before our very eyes and we owe our grandchildren far more than passive contempt for the British Establishment.

We, the public must demand more of this historic Inquest to ensure that no evidence is kept from the jury by a loaded process. The jury must also be allowed to deliver one of three verdicts: accidental death, open verdict or death by misadventure – nothing less will be acceptable!

Diana's 'clairvoyant' Simone Simmons certainly doesn't either, she did not even possess the foresight to foresee her client's death, let alone concoct her stupid tales that Diana had contacted her from the 'afterlife' to say she had died in an accident – how sweet. Only MI6 could 'predict' her nonsensical paranormal or abnormal 'revelation' – a proper tale from the crypt.

Chapter 14

'A Living Saint'

(A detachment of the Welsh Guards escorts
Diana's coffin into Westminster Abbey)

The public would not allow the people's princess to go unmourned and turned out in their millions to pay their last respects to the fallen princess. Hundreds of millions of people across the world, tuned in to the TV coverage of the world's first international princess, 'a very British girl who transcended nationality'. The fervour swept the entire nation, entire cities across Britain seemed almost deserted.

There was no mistaking that something truly historic, probably even spiritual had happened that day. The energy of mourning was palpable everywhere and sadness was etched on the faces of the vast majority of people. It seemed as though a goddess had died and passed over to the heavens, safe at last from the evils of the world she had departed so tragically in a car accident made to look like an 'accident' in the world's most romantic city.

It was the stuff of legend, a living myth played out before our eyes and the whole nation, probably most of the world, was shocked. The British Establishment, as so often happens with their ill thought out schemes, was rocked to the very foundations. The royal courtiers could never have imagined the sheer depth of feeling of grief at the loss of the People's Princess. The Monarchy teetered on the brink of collapse and the possibility of a British Republic seemed to dangle ever closer. The Republicans rejoiced at the desperation of the House of Windsor to retain their inherited and unelected power.

The Queen refused to leave Balmoral for days after the crash. The British public were furious and perceived the Windsors as remote, cold and uncaring and there was serious danger of public disorder. The Royal Standard, as convention dictated, did not fly at half-mast over Buckingham Palace. Diana had been disowned by the royals and dismissed from the royal household just a year before, following her very public divorce from Prince Charles. The halcyon days were over and the British Establishment faced the very real threat of being overthrown.

At a meeting of senior police officers in London, palace courtiers were told that if the Queen or Prince Charles returned to London to mark the occasion, their safety could not be guaranteed. There was a strong likelihood that the royals would be pelted with rotten fruit or worse, rioting could break out. No one could have foreseen this mass action backlash and were it not for the fact that the nation wanted to grieve, rioting could easily have broken out, spread across the nation and collapsed the House of Windsor.

The analysts had got it completely wrong yet again. They did not understand the psychology of the masses was simply to mourn their fallen princess. No one really wanted to riot but the public was pushed closer to mass rebellion than at any time since the outbreak of the English Civil War. The royals were safe, in reality, because Tony Blair was no Oliver Cromwell and his New Labour machine had just swept to power and the public perceived that there had already been a socio-political revolution.

But the damage done to the House of Windsor in the eyes of the public, during that terrible and tense week, has not dissipated. Light had shone inside the magic and 'magic' was revealed as a complete sham. the mythology and mystery of monarchy was stripped bare and the public were far from impressed. The House of Windsor invited this disdain which endures to this day.

(Queen Elizabeth II addresses "a nation in mourning in a world in shock" after being heavily lambasted by her 'subjects')

Persuaded against her will, the Queen appeared on television to pay tribute to Diana, claiming she "admired and respected" her but few subjects believed their monarch; the tension between the Queen and Diana was well-documented. But the Queen's TV tribute was enough to allow the nation to begin to mourn. Hostility began to wane as the masses saw the Union Flag, not the Royal Standard, flutter at half-mast above Buckingham Palace.

The public thought, quite wrongly, that the royal attitude had softened towards Diana. In reality, a sigh of relief went up in the royal household the moment news of Diana's death was broken to them. The persistent thorn in their side had been pruned forever. The Greek tragedy, no pun intended on Prince Philip's heritage, was playing on the international stage but fortunately for the House of Windsor, attention was diverted from its many inadequacies onto the desire to mourn Diana's death. Recriminations, and there would be a great many, would come later.

Earl Spencer, was perhaps the first to begin the cavalcade of bitterness towards the House of Windsor. He had crafted and polished a speech, more than just a tribute to his fallen sister, it was an undisguised attack on the Royal Family and he would deliver it with great brio inside Westminster Abbey. The Royals were shocked, and sat biting their lips, knowing they could say nothing in their defence. Earl Spencer also realised that they were powerless to intervene and lauded the stage for all it was worth.

As tears flowed inside the Abbey and outside in the streets and across the world, the strangest thing happened. A huge round applause erupted outside the Abbey and soon swept inside. But the rapturous applause was not just for his fitting tribute to his hunted sister, but rather a recognition of the fact that he had the courage to stand up before the world and tell the world exactly what he thought of the Windsors and in that moment the world loved him for it.

Earl Spencer's tribute to Diana was eloquent and stunned the Royal Family, sitting just yards away, they fumed but could say nothing, completely outmanoeuvred. He began: " I stand before you today, the representative of a family in grief, in a country in morning before a world in shock. We are all united not only in our desire to pay our respects to Diana but rather in our need to do so. For such was her extraordinary appeal that the tens of millions of people taking part in this service all over the world via television and radio who never actually met her, feel that they, too, lost someone close to them.

"Diana was the very essence of compassion, of duty, of style, of beauty. All over the world she was a symbol of selfless humanity. All over the world, a standard bearer for the rights of the truly downtrodden, a very British girl who transcended nationality. Someone with a natural nobility who was classless and who proved in the last year that she needed no royal title to continue to generate her particular brand of magic.

"We have all despaired at our loss and only the strength of the message you gave us through your years of giving has afforded us the strength to move forward. There is a temptation to rush to canonise your memory; there is no need to do so. You stand tall enough as a human being of unique qualities not to be seen as a saint. Indeed, to sanctify your memory would be to miss out on the very core of your being, your wonderfully mischievous sense of humour with a laugh that bent you double.

"Your joy for life transmitted wherever you too your smile and the sparkle in those unforgettable eyes. Your boundless energy which you could barely contain.

"But your greatest gift was your intuition and it was a gift you used wisely. This is what underpinned all your wonderful attributes, and if we look to analyse, we find it in your distinctive feel for what was really important in all our lives.

"Without your Godgiven sensitivity we would be immersed in greater ignorance of AIDS and HIV sufferers, the plight of the homeless, the isolation of lepers, the random destruction of land mines. Diana explained to me once that it was her innermost feelings of suffering that made it possible for her to connect with her constituency of the rejected.

"And here we come to another truth about her. For all the status, the glamour, the applause, Diana remained throughout a very insecure person at heart, almost childlike in her desire to do good for others so she could release herself from deep feelings of unworthiness of which her eating disorders were merely a symptom. The world sensed this part of her character and cherished her for her vulnerability whilst admiring her for her honesty."

As the funeral cortège passed through the streets of London, bearing Diana to the Althorp Estate in Northamptonshire, millions bowed their heads in respect to the People's Princess who will be remembered not just as an icon of style and fashion even though she was, but also for her great humanitarian work.

Diana's anti-landmines campaign brought her considerable friends and enemies but she seemed oblivious to the fact that by campaigning to ban landmines she was herself walking through a virtual minefield of scheming politicians and arms manufacturers who desired her to be stopped.

Diana was an expert media manipulator, even if she complained of press intrusion on many occasions. Indeed, in her BBC TV Panorama interview with Martin Bashir in 1995, she said that Charles was not suitable for the "top job". Her private secretary Patrick Jephson said afterwards that she had just "committed suicide". Royal commentator Anthony Holden said he thought that this was the "end game".

Diana had crossed the Rubicon by stating that Charles was unfit to be King. The royal courtiers were outraged again as they had been so many times in the past. The Queen ordered Charles and Diana to divorce and in July 1996 their sham marriage was over and a year later, Diana was dead. It truly was the "end game".

In the 1990s, Prince Charles' friends and supporters had gone on the offensive against Diana in the press. Their most scurrilous allegation was that Diana was mentally ill, suffering 'borderline personality disorder'. Penny Junor, hired character assassin, picked up the attacks on Diana where Jonathan Dimbleby had begun them, egged on by royal courtiers. Their concerted campaign to reinvent Prince Charles and character assassinate Diana, met with moderate success but Diana was loved by the public and the press knew only too well that she sold newspapers, Prince Charles did not.

British newspapers were interested in using Diana's face and her revelations to sell newspapers and boost profits and Diana used the press to attack and counterattack the royals and their hangers-on. It was a very public war, and a vastly profitable one for the press. But even so, in the final count, Diana always seemed to thwart the royals and their hired character assassins and won the war of the media for the hearts and minds of the British people.

Ultimately, tributes aside, Diana was a human being. Of course, she could be manipulative, what human-being isn't manipulative!? But in real terms Diana was caught in a vortex of schemers and liars who were ruthless and she too had to be equally ruthless to survive. These are the hard, harsh realities of life, like it or not. Diana wounded as much as she was wounded, describing the Queen Mother as the "chief leper in the leper colony". Diana could be scathing and took the slightest rejection badly.

This stemmed in part from the divorce of her parents but primarily also from the rejection by Prince Charles and his parents, who treated the princess as little more than a baby making machine of 'good blood' to produce heirs to the throne. In the final count, 'good blood' counted for nothing and the British Establishment did not hesitate to shed her 'good blood'. And the subsequent campaign of royal courtiers to erase her memory has been a colossal failure.

With Mohamed Al Fayed refusing to give up the struggle for truth and justice, and with a vast fortune he has vowed to exhaust in his battle, the British Establishment have a great foe. Al Fayed has not allowed the royals and their servants off the hook. He has described them as "gangsters and murderers and Nazi bastards" and he means business. But then the British Establishment has always been in the business of meaning business against Al Fayed, his family and his assets.

If the British people were given a free and fair public vote, it is highly likely that, in the privacy of a polling booth, over 80 per cent of people would vote in favour of Diana being murdered by British Intelligence with varying degrees of commission and passive agreement from the Royal Family. The myth and legend of Diana lives on and the debate over whether she was killed in an accident or murdered by sinister forces will doubtless rage on through the centuries.

Yet, one thing is already clear: there has been an organised cover-up between the French and British authorities to suppress vital evidence and silence witnesses who do not conform to the accident theory. These same witnesses were actually there at the scene and know far better than those who were not there, what happened in the moment before and after the crash. The British Establishment's whitewash will not stand, and we the public who deserve far better, must not let it stand!

Ten long years after her premature death, millions of people across the world, from different cultures and faiths have proclaimed Princess Diana a saintly figure. The Princess meant so many things to so many people but I find the story of her completely remarkable life is best summed up by an exchange between Professor Magdi Yacoub and Piers Morgan on 27th June 1996.

Diana had gone to visit young patients at the Royal Brompton Hospital in London, to bring them hope and cheer, for which she was renowned. During the photo call, Professor Yacoub whispered to Morgan: **"Look at Diana, she's like a living saint, isn't she?"** And to those children that day she was.

Chapter 15

Unlawful Killing

Having been granted a silver press pass to attend the quasi-inquest but only from the atrium that was annexed to the main court for journalists to report on proceedings, I was not surprised when my press pass was revoked. Within twenty-four hours of the press pass being granted, Richard Bailey, Private Secretary to Lord 'Justice' Scott-Baker, telephoned me at home to say that my pass had been revoked with "immediate effect.". He was delighted, dripping venom at the mouth like the spectre at the feast but I found him to be very amusing.

Bailey suggested that I had published material on a website that was "factually incorrect" but when challenged to cite specific examples he could not. I asked him to highlight the material he disliked and supply me with hard evidence to contradict what I had written but again he could not and would not. His line of attack had fallen apart within five minutes and so he switched to the rearguard 'attack', a last desperate attempt to save face. *"Well, you've published material that we don't like and don't agree with and we don't believe you can be <u>trusted </u>to report on the inquest with impartiality."*

I retorted, *"What you really mean Mr Bailey is that I cannot be trusted to repeat the Establishment line, like a tame scribbler from the mainstream puppet media and that is why you're revoking my pass because you're afraid. Just 'following orders' sunshine is not a line I'm prepared to accept from you or anyone else for that matter."*

He had no answer for my swift, cutting riposte. He paused a moment to collect his slow thought processes and said: *"Well, <u>we</u> don't believe you're a journalist and your press pass is revoked and we've not seen any evidence to prove you're a journalist either."* I laughed at him, typical Establishment little-Hitler with a serious attitude problem. I conducted a cursory search of the internet and found Richard Bailey Associates listed at offices on Buckingham Palace Road, five minutes' walk from Buckingham Palace....

Bailey had the temerity to lecture me about 'impartiality' and here he was representing Lord 'Justice' Scott-Baker from his offices on Buckingham Palace Road; a nest of typical

Establishment incest discovered within two minutes of searching on Google. The Establishment have so little respect for the public they claim to serve that they arrogantly and contemptuously make no attempt to hide their professional incest. Impartiality? If that was the case, why was Scott-Baker – apparently an 'impartial' judge – represented by a royalist flunkie with direct links to Buckingham Palace?

There was also another perfectly good reason why I had to be banned from attending the quasi-inquest and it had nothing to do with impartiality, it was to do with playing 'them' at their own game. I had already arranged for the testimony of Paul Burrell to be covertly recorded inside the court room. The plan was to use an infinity transmitter secreted inside a mobile phone that appeared to be switched off. The remote dialler could be called into from anywhere in the world and the audio within fifteen metres listened to and recorded for posterity. Our intention was to release the audio recording on the Internet through untraceable third parties.

But having made a well reasoned decision to abandon that plan because the GSM network might interfere with amplifiers inside the court room and cause audible back chatter and alert officials that someone was using a mobile phone in the courtroom, another plan had to be hatched. I then purchased an expensive stealth recording watch that appeared to be just that, a watch with no visible sign that it was anything but a timepiece. A press of a button on the side of the watch activated an MP3 or Wav recording and the audio quality was excellent. When the banning order came through I had little doubt that my financial transactions were being monitored and the decision to ban me from the quasi-inquest proved that I was being subjected to intrusive surveillance.

I then had to arrange for trusted contacts to attend some of hearings instead so that I could get a feel of the hearing from people who had attended. I decided not to attend in the public gallery as a matter of principle. If I was not allowed to attend as a journalist with an accredited press pass, then I would not give the Establishment the pleasure of seeing me sidelined to the public gallery. That was what they wanted and denying them their wish was paramount in my considerations. Nonetheless, I monitored the proceedings every day and was glued to the website created to carry transcripts of the hearings and host the 'evidence' they wanted to the public to see.

Day one kicked off with the 'impartial' judge Scott-Baker telling the jury that the engagement ring Dodi purchased for Diana was NOT an engagement ring at all. He offered no compelling evidence to support his statement and arrogantly believed that his paid-for opinion was 'hard evidence'. Likewise, Scott-Baker told the jury that the 'relationship' between Diana and Dodi was nothing of the sort and for 'evidence' he used his paid-for opinion. The dictator had spoken and had established the Rubicon; his word was 'law' and 'evidence' rolled into one and no one had better challenge him.

No wonder they did not want me at their precious quasi-inquest. I could not be relied on to spin their treacherous lies and would question, in print at least, every morsel of 'evidence' they released to the watching world. The hits on the website I edited escalated and the mainstream media realised they had a serious competitor and I had to be stopped. Nonetheless, mass media plotting aside, it was clear from the opening statements of Scott-Baker that this was going to be a one-sided hearing in which impartiality was akin to a loaded gun in a game of Russian roulette. Moreover, it was clear that the 'verdict' would never be one of 'murder'.

In many ways I gave serious thought to abandoning our coverage of the hearing because it was a foregone conclusion and a murder verdict was never on the table. But having come so far and invested time, energy and money in the whole business leading to this charade, it was imperative to carry on if only to nail one lie after the other, and expose one altered story after the other and they would come thick and fast until the public could no longer tolerate any more Diana mania.

In fact, most of the public had already switched off after the first week, realising the quasi-inquest was a sham and many people were sick of hearing about Diana. "Let her rest in peace," came the counter cry from exhausted members of the public. To which the most ardent supporters retorted by saying, "Would you rest in peace if someone you loved was killed in this way?" The show would go on and that is precisely what it was, a mass media circus.

With the predictable ruling that Prince Philip – actually a centrifugal witness – would not be allowed to testify at the hearing, it was clear that the real moments of tension and public excitement would come with the testimony of Paul Burrell and Mohamed Al Fayed. But the real issue with Al Fayed was whether he could restrain his emotions and not launch into an impassioned outburst that the press would dismiss as a furious rant. Burrell, of course, had long-since become an Establishment play thing and was busy raking-in thousands in America from flogging imitation royal furniture. Diana's death and the quasi-inquest had become a means to an end for many people whose only interest was making money out of misery; the very thing Diana had opposed with her campaign against landmines.

(Mohamed Al Fayed outside the 'Royal' Courts of 'Justice' at the start of the quasi-inquest is flanked by the mainstream puppet media)

Many Diana campaigners took to supporting the Daily Express – whose editor Peter Hill had close links with MI5, for evidence of which read my book *COUNTER SPY* – and our role was to steer them away from the Express. That 'newspaper' had not shown the slightest interest in Princess Diana and the many unanswered questions surrounding her murky death until Peter Hill needed to boost circulation or lose his job. Hill had doubled circulation at the sister newspaper the Daily Star but had run into big trouble at the Express from the outset. It was decided to back the campaign to uncover the 'truth' about Diana's death and almost every week-day in the years prior to the quasi-inquest, the Daily

Express ran a front page headline story about Diana.

The reasoning of the senior executives at Express Newspapers was lost on the public. Most people simply bought anything that had Diana's face printed on it and any toilet paper manufacturer could have boosted sales by putting Diana's face on their own brand of paper. The truth was becoming irrelevant in the circulation war and the Express stuck to its line that the accident theory was unsafe but at no time did the rag ever come out and state unequivocally that Diana was murdered.

But the fanatical Diana faction was not interested, they merely stuck to any rag that dared to question the accident theory. Their pockets provided the financial boost necessary for Richard Desmond's pornographic empire to flourish. Diana was opposed to pornography on the grounds it exploited women and here she was being touted on the open market by a porn baron. But her desperate supporters turned a blind eye to the moral principles of their heroine. Reason and logic had gone out of the window in both camps and it was fast becoming a grudge match and the best or worst was to come.

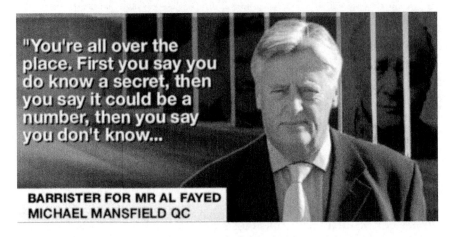

"You're all over the place. First you say you do know a secret, then you say it could be a number, then you say you don't know...

BARRISTER FOR MR AL FAYED
MICHAEL MANSFIELD QC

The 'testimony' of Paul Burrell was seen by many as the fulcrum of the case against the Establishment. Never put all of your eggs in one basket is a maxim everyone should remember. Why was Burrell so important to the outcome of the case? People actually believed he would stand up in court and repeat what he had published in *A Royal Duty* and do so to devastating effect. I hoped he would but experience and cold logic told me otherwise. Burrell was on to a good thing in the States, making sums of money trading on the name of the Royal Family. If he appeared in court to slate the Queen, there would have been a serious financial backlash and he knew it only too well. Not to mention what the Queen had told him about "dark forces" at work over which she had no control.

The truth of the matter is that Burrell lost his nerve, was too much of a coward to repeat his lines performed in *A Royal Duty* and put saving his own skin and growing wealth first. How could anyone be surprised by his eventual antics at the quasi-inquest on 14th January 2008. There is little point in reprinting the farce word-for-word, a transcript can be downloaded at the quasi-inquest website. But Scott-Baker described his 'evidence' as an "important insight" into the case. Michael Mansfield QC ridiculed Burrell, pinned him down on the issue of knowing a secret and then not knowing a secret. It was clear Burrell was lying through his back teeth to save his beloved Monarchy and his own skin. His evasive 'style' earn him widespread and immediate enmity from the masses, particularly the majority Diana faction.

Several days after Burrell returned to his Florida mansion, I contacted him through his Internet activities and struck up a rapport with him. We came from similar backgrounds and his father like mine had been a miner in the local area. I had also worked in his home town of Grasmere near Chesterfield in Derbyshire for several months and knew the area very well. In dozens of messages he seemed to be hitting the bottle, his prose was almost that of a drunken man overcome with self-pity for what he had done. He was full of remorse and having been caught out in a sting by *The Sun* newspaper in a New York hotel room , admitting that he had lied at the quasi-inquest, I had little sympathy for his actions.

But it was clear why he had lied: The big boot of the British Establishment and their long reach across the globe. Burrell was too scared to do anything other than lie for the Monarchy to save the rotten institution. Tony Blair had done precisely the same thing in 1997 after Diana's death but not out of fear but because he was an Establishment puppet to the bone. Burrell was scared of being recalled to the quasi-inquest to face a savaging from Michael Mansfield QC but there was no danger that was going to happen and I told him so in writing.

If Burrell had been recalled to the hearing to be cross-examined again it would have been a disaster that could have ensured entirely the 'wrong verdict' for the Establishment. There was no way on this earth that Burrell was going to be recalled but

Scott-Baker and the tame media kept the public hanging on a thread in the belief he could be recalled. It was all part of the appeasement game played by the Establishment criminal gang and their ersatz media. They had played the same game for ten years before the hearing began to ensure public anger had dissipated to the extent it represented no organised threat to the regime.

With Burrell in the clear but hated by the majority of people in Britain, he refused to return to the UK out of fear. Scott-Baker duly announced that Burrell would not be recalled to the anger of many but the situation was contained. Burrell had done his dirty deed for which he will never be forgotten and the Establishment gang were in the clear the moment they got round to announcing a murder verdict would not be allowed. For that they needed a performance from Mohamed Al Fayed and he was certain to give them what they wanted.

But the fundamental issue at the hearing was the Lord Mischon note, suppressed by the Metropolitan Police. Not to mention the fact that Stevens had changed his mind - under duress - about Henri Paul. First Stevens accepted Henri Paul was not drunk and then changed his mind to 'accept' the theory that Henri Paul was 'drunk as a pig' in a clear betrayal of what he had told the Paul family during the Paget 'Inquiry'. The Mischon note was more serious in that it put Prince Philip in the clear and ensured he would never have to testify at the quasi-inquest. Sir John Stevens is known as Baron Stevens of Kirkwhelpington - a title conferred on him by no other than Queen Elizabeth II....

No one therefore should be surprised at his antics to support the Monarchy because he is an Establishment puppet to the bone and his conduct at the hearing was mere payback for the gang that had made him a Lord for his 'loyal service' to the Crown. But his performance at the quasi-inquest was hilarious and was delivered in the style so typical of British police officers who would not know the truth if they tripped over it and if they did, it would have to be concealed. "The suggestion that I could lie after what I uncovered in Northern Ireland" was superlative theatre. Stevens was almost in tears to complement his lies with contrived 'emotion' to con the jury. I found his 'testimony' to constitute not such much contempt of court in *de facto* terms but rather contempt of the public.

In actual fact, his investigation into paramilitary killings in Ulster was condemned on both sides of the sectarian divide for not going far enough. John Stalker had tried to do the job properly before Stevens and had been set up by MI5 and the RUC Special Branch. The Establishment, particularly MI5, did not want Stalker to succeed in uncovering the multitude of dirty tricks waged against the Republican movement and the IRA, including dozens of State-sanctioned murders. Stalker was forced to step down with his career in tatters because he had tried to do the job as a real policeman. When he was crushed, John Stevens came into the fray as the tame Establishment man who would only take the investigation so far and he did just that in Ulster and again with the Paget 'Inquiry.

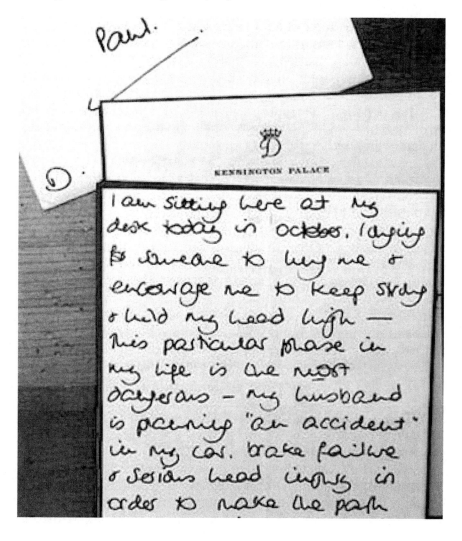

The suppressed Mischon note is damning evidence and future historians will refer to it repeatedly to build the case against the Monarchy that will no longer exist by then. Princess Diana had confided that she feared a plot to murder her involving Prince Charles and his father in a car 'accident'. Diana 'died' in the manner she predicted but the evidence was kept from the French pseudo-investigation and the public for several years. Why? It is self-explanatory but the real issue was to defend and protect the Crown at all costs.

One should remember that all police officers and judges swear an oath of allegiance to the Crown and it means just that. As a young soldier in 1986/87, I had also taken the oath of allegiance to the Crown. In later years I regretted it immensely and joined the Republic organisation campaigning for a democratic Britain free of the Constitutional Monarchy. Only when the police, judiciary, armed forces and civil servants are compelled to swear an oath of allegiance to Parliament and the people will this tidal of wave nepotistic corruption be ended. Currently there is no accountability and the Crown and its flunkies view public accountability with horror and contempt.

I viewed the 'testimony' of Sir Richard Dearlove, former Controller of the MI6/Oxbridge criminal gang, with similar horror and contempt. He claimed that MI6 of course did have a licence to kill but it had not been used for years and dissident MI6 officer Richard Tomlinson was a liar to boot. One has only to study the role and history of British Intelligence in Northern Ireland to understand that Dearlove was lying through his well-trained back teeth. Furthermore, the quixotic Dearlove had overlooked the sordid confessions of former Special Forces soldiers who had admitted that the SAS – particularly the Increment – had been deployed on shoot-to-kill black operations, not just in the Ulster context, but on deniable operations around the globe for MI6 and MI5. Only a retard was going to believe Dearlove's 'not me guv' routine and of course Scott-Baker fitted the description perfectly.

All the Establishment's puppets had strolled into court, lied through their rotten back-teeth in the knowledge that contempt of court and perjury did not apply to them. In Parliament – for years a cesspit of corruption – New Labour MPs started a campaign to prevent anymore 'damaging' testimony be senior intelligence officers. The whole Establishment pack had joined the fray but some MPs would not back such a motion. With the threat of even more damaging publicity for the New Labour regime – if that was remotely possible - the matter was dropped but the grandstanding proved that New Labour was just another Establishment tool.

Shortly before the predetermined verdict was announced and a murder verdict had been ruled out, just as I predicted from the outset, I was contacted by the BBC. The Beeb wanted me to cooperate with their 'Conspiracy Files' show that would coincide with the verdict being delivered at the 'Royal' Courts of 'Justice'. Katherine Bancroft wanted to ask me piece to camera why I had been banned from the quasi-inquest. I was willing to cooperate until Bancroft kept changing the location for the interview in London and practically asked me not to tell anyone where I was going. Why?

After repeated questioning on the matter of why I could not give the interview at BBC White City, she said *"we are not allowed to do these things from a BBC TV centre. We only have a certain budget and have to stay within the budget."* Which begged the question why the BBC was prepared to hire a smart hotel room at considerable cost to conduct an interview that should have been recorded at White City, a much cheaper alternative. Bancroft would not budge on the issue and after days of wrangling she finally admitted that the BBC had hired the Sloane Club for the interviews and I was to be one of the 'experts' interviewed there. But having been messed around for days and fed one evasive line after the other, the trust issue was entirely destroyed.

I refused to cooperate and when Bancroft asked if I was prepared to speak on camera about my uncle's Government Service across eighteen years I was almost gobsmacked. John Francis Smith had been sacked from the Home Office, Homeland Security Department, for leaking documents to the press that proved impropriety on the part of public servants. What did this have to do with the quasi-inquest and the death of Princess Diana? My uncle was out of Government Service before February 1976 and Diana was still a young girl. I recorded all of my conversations with Bancroft and have released some of the material on the Internet.

Quite apart from which fact, I had no intention of cooperating with the BBC's hatchet job on Diana and painting everyone who supported the evidence she was murdered as conspiracy nuts. But Bancroft did agree with me that the Mischon note was the fulcrum of the entire hearing and that it would decide the outcome. With Mohamed Al Fayed having performed true to form, slinging wild accusations at everyone in creation, the Establishment had got precisely what they wanted and Al Fayed had walked straight into the trap set for him just as his son had in 1997. No amount of spin could paint a brighter picture of Al Fayed after his outburst at the quasi-inquest and he turned to the public for sympathy and got it.

The verdict was announced and 'unlawful killing' was returned by the jury that had been vetted more than any jury in British history. It was astonishing given the fact that it had been established before and again at the hearing that the press photographers were minutes behind the Mercedes when it crashed in the Alma underpass. How could anyone arrive at such a 'verdict' when the evidence contradicted it but the Establishment of course were very happy and swung into full 'it was an accident' mode but that was not what 'unlawful killing' meant at all. On the contrary, contributing factors from the press and other unknown vehicles in the Alma underpass was the closet it could get to death by misadventure.

And the unknown or unidentified vehicles in the Alma Tunnel? Read the foregoing chapters. The Establishment had escaped the murder verdict and they were never going to allow that anyway because they have total control of the corrupt legal system. But 'unlawful killing' was not death by accident, it was more akin to open verdict and left the matter hanging in the air. In many ways, it simply fuelled the conspiracy theories pushed by obsessive cranks across the world. But the Monarchy had been saved and that was priority number one for the Establishment. The New Labour criminal gang had cooperated as usual to the hilt and a devastating defeat for the Royal Establishment at the hearing would have meant the end for a New Labour regime hell-bent on propping up the Monarchy at all costs. It was rather neat because the verdict also appeased Diana fanatics.

Michael Mansfield QC applauded the verdict as a triumph of his interrogative skills in the courts but privately he knew the truth that his client Mohamed Al Fayed had made himself look stupid and had been shafted by the System at the same time. All factions were trying to save face and claim some form of victory but in the midst of the furore, the only losers were Princess Diana, Dodi Al Fayed and Henri Paul. They had been 'unlawfully killed' but not by the press snappers who were minutes behind.

They had been slaughtered by the British Establishment and the real cause of their deaths had been covered up within minutes of the crash.

(Memorial to Diana at Kensington Palace on 31 August 2007)

Irrespective of the findings of the quasi-inquest and the quest by the British and French Establishment to conceal a mountain of evidence from the public; it should be noted that 90% of Britons polled believe that Princess Diana was murdered by the British Establishment. The loaded process of a 'hearing' in London and the French 'investigation' have done nothing to dissuade the majority from their damning murder verdict. The Establishment gang, with all their dirty tricks have failed to win the battle for hearts and minds.

At the Cannes Film Festival in May 2011, actor Keith Allen premiered his documentary *Unlawful Killing* but censors in Britain announced immediately that they would NOT allow the title to be screened in the UK until 38 pieces of the documentary had been chopped and left gathering dust on the cutting room floor. The reason? Fear of the truth and the indisputable FACT that Britain is not a democracy and freedom of expression is NOT tolerated by the criminal regime. But the truth will out.

Piers Morgan gave an interview to Keith Allen in which the

former Daily Mirror editor said "If MI5 and MI6 don't have people killed, what's the point of them then?" Morgan went on to elucidate his view that Princess Diana was murdered. In complete contrast to his exclamation "there is a God" when the police announced Henri Paul was 'drunk as a pig' at the wheel of the doomed Mercedes.

Of course all of the evidence proves that Henri Paul was not drunk or drugged up at the wheel and the press minutes behind the limousine when it crashed. The usual suspects have been eliminated in the death or murder of Princess Diana. It is therefore entirely proper that a verdict of 'unlawful killing' was reached at the 'inquest'. But if the jury had been given the opportunity to reach a murder verdict - precluded by Establishment puppet Scott-Baker - what would the jurors have decided?

(Mohamed Al Fayed meets the crowd at Harrods on
the Tenth Anniversary of Diana and Dodi's deaths)

And in the wake of the Hackgate scandal in Britain, it is certain Princess Diana's mobile telephone was targeted but no one wants to discuss the matter, least of the all the guilty press. Apparently, it should remain dead and buried with the Princess. A string of witnesses at the Leveson 'Inquiry' testified to the fact that phone hacking started around 1996 and there is little doubt Diana was hacked. Indeed, the Princess would have been target number one for the press hackers. But the real hacking that should concern everyone, was the hacking and slicing in the ambulance that delayed her all the way to the grave.

Whilst Diana cannot sue the press for hacking her mobile phone, her former butler Paul Burrell has employed internationally renowned 'hacking lawyer' Mark Lewis to represent him against News Corp in the USA. I went for dinner with Lewis in London on 3 May 2012 and told him precisely what I knew about *The Sun* and *News of the World* targeting his client during and after the inquest. I am sure the press wanted to glean information on the precise nature of the 'deal' Burrell struck with the Monarchy to lie at the inquest? By his own admission, he admits to lying at the inquest and dismissed his tricks with a simple, "well, she's the Queen."

I gave Mark Lewis all the relevant information I had, not so much to help Burrell, but because I do not condone phone hacking and do not accept that Burrell was a "legitimate target" for invasion of privacy. I have little doubt that Burrell has a conscience and the bitter sting of his betrayal will haunt him for the rest of his life. In many ways, he was also an innocent victim, a working class boy unprepared for the ruthless machinations of the snakepit he found himself in. He had to learn a *modus operandi* for survival and did just that and I do not condemn him for it. The alternative is destruction and one should ever surrender to the Establishment without a fight.

And despite Farrer & Co Solicitors becoming embroiled in the Hackgate corruption scandal, both Prince Charles and the Queen will retain the services of the legal firm that lied and cheated for News International and Rupert Murdoch. I am not in the least surprised by their decision and having dealt with Farrer & Co over the disputed Hampden Estate, I know only too well what they are capable of. In fact, I called James Furber's bluff and challenged him to sue me over my book *Sons of Soldiers*. He backed down but it was clear the Establishment will attempt to bully anyone who dares to oppose them into submission.

There is also little doubt that the Establishment has resorted to dirty tricks behind the scenes to suffocate the dissemination of Keith Allen's film 'Unlawful Killing'. Having failed to stop Allen with censorship, insurance certificates were refused him and the film was shelved indefinitely. The objective was always to 'ban' the film by any means necessary and if it was the case that targets felt they had been libelled, they would have sought remedial action in the courts. Instead, censorship was used, coupled with refusing insurance, an old trick used against anti-Establishment political parties and their publications.

What does this prove? Without doubt it shows that the Establishment - rotten to the core as many recent corruption scandals have proved - will resort to any desperate method to stop the truth from gaining widespread attention. If Diana's death was a mere 'accident', then why resort to an innumerable litany of lies, threats and dirty tricks? You are the jury, and I shall leave you to pass judgement on the 'British' Establishment.

Printed in Great Britain
by Amazon

82860558R00132